1/01

19.95

RUSSIA

Revised Edition

MICHAEL KORT

☑ Facts On File, Inc.

*F*or Marty

---

The author wishes to thank Rodion Romanov for his invaluable help with the transliterations.

Russia—Revised Edition

Copyright © 1995 by Michael Kort, Revised Edition © 1998 by Michael Kort
Maps © 1998, 1995 Facts On File

Facts On File, Inc.
11 Penn Plaza
New York NY 10001

Library of Congress Cataloging-in-Publication Data

Kort, Michael, 1944–
    Russia / Michael Kort. — Rev. ed.
        p.   cm. — (Nations in transition)
    Includes bibliographical references and index.
    Summary: Examines the people, religion, daily life, politics,
culture, history, and geography of Russia, emphasizing its
transition, since 1991, from a communist to a free nation.
    ISBN 0-8160-3776-0
    1. Russia (Federation)—History—Juvenile literature. [1. Russia
(Federation)] I. Title. II. Series.
DK510.56.K67   1998
947.085'4—dc20   98-10751

Facts On File books are available at special discounts when purchased in bulk quantities for businesses, associations, institutions or sales promotions. Please call our Special Sales Department in New York at 212/967-8800 or 800/322-8755.

You can find Facts On File on the World Wide Web at http://www.factsonfile.com

Cover design by Nora Wertz
All photos in this book are from Wide World Photos.

Printed in the United States of America

MP FOF 10 9 8 7 6 5 4 3 2

This book is printed on acid-free paper.

Contents

Introduction   v

1   The Evolution of Old Russia   1

2   Imperial Russia   13

3   Soviet Russia   28

4   Russian Culture   53

5   Russia: A Country Map   63

6   Politics and Government   80

7   Building a New Economy   118

8   Daily Life   139

9   Problems and Prospects   164

Chronology of Russian History   186

Further Reading   193

Index   195

Russia

Russia

Pacific Ocean

Bering Sea

Chukchi Sea

Providetiya

Anadyr'

Evensk

Cherskiy

Petropavlovsk-Kamchatskiy

Sea of Okhotsk

Magadan

Amur R.

Khabarovsk

Vladivostok

JAPAN

Sea of Japan

NORTH KOREA

East Siberian Sea

Kolyma R.

Verkhoyansk

Yana R.

Aldan R.

Blagoveshchensk

Amur R.

Laptev Sea

Tiksi

Lena R.

Yakutsk

Lensk

Lena R.

Chita

CHINA

Arctic Ocean

Dikson

Noril'sk

Yenisey R.

Tura

R U S S I A

Bratsk

Irkutsk

MONGOLIA

Kara Sea

Novyy Urengoy

Krasnoyarsk

Tomsk

Kemerovo

Ob' R.

Novosibirsk

Svalbard (NORWAY)

Barents Sea

Vorkuta

Irtysh R.

Omsk

KAZAKHSTAN

Murmansk

Arkhangel'sk

Yekaterinburg

Kurgan

Perm'

Orenburg

UZBEKISTAN

NORWAY

SWEDEN

FINLAND

Vologda

Kirov

Ivanovo

Yaroslavl'

Ul'yanovsk

Samara

Chelyabinsk

Volga R.

TURKMENISTAN

St. Petersburg

Novgorod

Tver'

Nizhniy Novgorod

RUSSIA

EST.

LAT.

LITH.

BELARUS

Smolensk

Moscow

Kursk

Voronezh

Don R.

Rostov

Volgograd

Astrakhan'

Caspian Sea

POLAND

UKRAINE

Black Sea

GEORGIA

ARM.

AZER.

TURKEY

IRAN

Introduction

The history of Russia is the history of a people's struggle against the elements and the odds. It is a struggle first of all against nature, for the Russian people live in a harsh land that demands an extraordinary effort just to survive. It is also a struggle against other nations, for circumstance and ambition often have brought the Russians into long and bitter conflict with many rivals. And it is a struggle against themselves, for to overcome both natural and human challenges the Russians have endured rulers who in return for protection and power have demanded the people's wealth, freedom, and lives.

The Russian Federation, as Russia is officially called today, is an immense territory, over 6.5 million square miles (17 million sq. km), or about one-ninth of the world's total land area. Canada, the world's second largest nation, would fit almost twice inside Russia's vast borders. Russia extends over 6,000 (9,660 km) miles from west to east and about 2,000 miles (3,220 km) from north to south. In the west, its territory begins in the center of Europe, on the coast of the Baltic Sea. From there, Russia stretches eastward to Europe's border with Asia at the Ural Mountains, and from the Urals across Asia until the world's largest continent finally ends at the barren shores of the Bering Sea. The ice-choked Arctic Ocean and a few windswept islands above the Arctic Circle mark Russia's northern border. Its southern limits are the lush slopes and majestic peaks of the Caucasus Mountains.

A colossus standing astride most of Eurasia, Russia is unique among the nations of the world. Only two other countries, Turkey and Kazakhstan (kah-ZAKH-stahn)*, have territory in both Europe and Asia. But both are predominantly Asian nations with a sliver of territory in Europe, while Russia is culturally a European country that includes a huge swath of northern Asia. Russia is, in fact, not only the world's largest nation, but at once the largest nation in both Europe and Asia. The European part of Russia would easily swallow the next five largest European nations, while Asiatic Russia could neatly hold both China and India, the second and third largest nations on that continent.

Unmatched in size and unique as the world's only truly Eurasian country, it is not surprising that Russia also borders on more countries—a total of 12—than any other nation. Its immediate European neighbors are Norway, Finland, Estonia, Latvia, Belarus, and Ukraine. Where Europe meets Asia at the Caucasus Mountains, Russia borders on Georgia and Azerbaijan (ahz-uhr-by-JAHN). In Asia, Russia borders Kazakhstan (whose European territory also borders on Russia), as well as Mongolia, China, and North Korea. In addition, Russia is separated from Japan at two different points only by narrow straits, while further east in the Bering Strait only six miles of frigid water lie between Russian and American territory.

It is somewhat ironic that Russia borders on so many countries, since for centuries it was known as a country that feared and mistrusted foreigners. Another irony is that today Russia no longer even shares a border with countries that until 1991 were part of the former Soviet Union. The former Soviet republics of Moldova, Armenia, Uzbekistan (ooz-BEK-ih-stahn), Turkmenistan (terk-MEN-ih-stahn), Tajikistan (tah-JIK-ih-stahn), and Kyrgyzstan (kir-GEEZ-tahn) are all cut off from Russia by other former Soviet republics. Approximately 147 million people live in Russia today, about 82 percent of whom are ethnic Russians. Between the 16th and 19th centuries, the Russians built an empire that annexed lands occupied by other peoples; barely half the empire's population was Russian. Over 100

---

*Note: Pronunciation keys have not been provided for some Russian names and terms with common English pronunciations. In places where pronunciation is given, it is the Russian pronunciation.

distinct nationalities and ethnic groups lived within the Russian Empire, so that some people referred to it as the "prison house of nations." When that empire collapsed in 1917, a few nationalities succeeded in establishing their independence. However, most could not break free. They were absorbed into the newly formed Soviet Union, which like the old Russian Empire was about half Russian and dominated by Russians. The Soviet regime created a fiction of national autonomy by dividing the Soviet Union into 15 "Soviet Socialist Republics (SSRs)," one each for 15 of the country's most numerous national groups. The reality was that each SSR—such as the Ukrainian or Armenian SSR—was tightly controlled by the Russian-dominated Communist Party that governed from Moscow.

With the collapse of the Soviet Union in 1991, the 14 non-Russian republics broke away to form independent states. However, dozens of smaller groups remain within Russia's shrunken, but still enormous, territory. Together they account for about 18 percent of the country's population. They include some Ukrainians and Belarusians, as well as Jews, Tatars, Finns, Germans, Chuvash, Ossetians, Tuvinians, Chechens, Yakuts, Buryats, Altais, and other groups scattered across the land.

When the old Russian Empire collapsed in 1917, Russia was still primarily an agricultural and rural society. Most of its people lived in small farming villages and scratched out a meager living from small pieces of land. Moscow and St. Petersburg, the country's two largest cities, were major cultural and industrial centers, but they were only islands of modern life in a poor and backward peasant ocean. By 1991, the country had changed. As a result of Soviet economic development policies, today most Russians live in cities and large towns, mainly in the European part of the country. Moscow, with 9 million people, is one of the largest cities in the world. Formerly the capital of the Soviet Union, it is now Russia's capital city. St. Petersburg, with over 5 million people, remains not only a modern cultural and industrial center, but one of the most beautiful cities in Europe. Novosibirsk, a city of 1.5 million people, is the largest city in Siberia, a great swath of Russian land that spans northern Asia.

Whereas in 1917 most Russians worked in agriculture, today the overwhelming majority work in industry or in white-collar office or professional jobs. Russia has a large and varied industrial sector. It is a major producer of oil, coal, and natural gas, as well as steel, machine tools, and tractors. However, under the Soviet regime far too many of these resources, including the talents of its best scientists and engineers, went to the military. As a result, while the Soviet Union produced some of the most advanced weapons in the world, both nuclear and nonnuclear, it never produced enough consumer goods.

Today, with the fall of the Soviet Union and the end of the long Cold War with the United States, the Russian government has cut military spending. As a result, many of the Soviet Union's best and most modern factories have no customers for their products. In addition, under communism the government owned all industry and controlled all the farms. Almost everyone worked for the state. Now Russian industries and farms are being told they must make it on their own in the marketplace, rather than relying on government orders and funds. Declining military spending and the difficulties in changing over to a market economy have driven many factories and farms to the verge of bankruptcy and cost many workers their jobs.

Russia's current government must deal with these and many other urgent problems. Since 1992, its most important goals have been to establish and stabilize a democratic regime and manage the transition from a planned economy to one based on the free market. At the same time, it is trying to restore Russia's standing in the international arena as a great power. Any one of these goals, given Russia's history and current problems, would be daunting. Together they present a monumental challenge. Why that challenge is so enormous and how Russia is coping with it are the subjects of this book.

1

The Evolution of Old Russia

*T*oday's Russians, along with the current Ukrainians and Belarusians, are descended from a people known as the East Slavs, who themselves were part of a larger group known as the Slavs. The Slavs probably originated in central Europe, and the group that became the East Slavs migrated eastward over the course of several centuries. Gradually, the East Slavs sank roots in the forests and steppe of eastern Europe. Although the East Slavs spoke a common language that is the ancestor of modern Russian, Ukrainian, and Belarusian, for generations they were divided into at least a dozen feuding tribes that lived in scattered communities over a wide area.

The land the East Slavs chose to settle in has been fought over many times. Beginning in about 1000 B.C., the Cimmerians, Scythians, Samaritans, Goths, Huns, and other nomadic tribes successively swept into eastern Europe as conquerors, only to succumb to new invaders and be driven from the Eurasian Plain and disappear from history. It is likely that some of those conquered by these various invaders were East Slav farmers, who remained on the land as each conquering wave came and washed away. By the 9th century A.D., they occupied territory ranging northward from the Black Sea to well past where Moscow stands today and eastward from the Danube River to beyond the Don River.

While most East Slavs were farmers, many worked at cattle raising, hunting and fishing, and a variety of crafts. By the 8th century, they also were involved in widespread commerce. Commerce thrived because of the so-called river road, a latticework of rivers including the Dvina (dvee-NAH), Dneiper (DNEE-per), Don, and Volga. The river road linked the Baltic Sea and Europe to ports on the Black Sea and to the Caspian Sea, which in turn led to the wealthy and exotic Middle Eastern and Asian lands to the east.

Kievian Russia

In the middle of the 9th century, the feuding East Slavic tribes finally were brought together in a loosely organized state centered at Kiev, a city on the Dneiper River. The founders of this new state actually were not East Slavs at all, but powerful merchant warriors from Scandinavia called Varangians. However, the Varangians were a small minority in the country, and within about a century had become Slavicized. They and their subjects were called Rus; today historians refer to their state as Kievian Russia, the first organized state of the Russian people.

Kievian Russia actually was a federation of city-states. It prospered primarily because of its control over trade that traversed the river road. Members of the ruling dynasty governed as princes in their individual cities, although they often shared power with nobles known as *boyars* and sometimes with town assemblies called *veches* (Russian singular: VYAY-chuh). In 988, Kievian Russia received some unifying glue when

Vladimir, the prince of Kiev, converted to Christianity and commanded his subjects to do the same. According to *The Primary Russian Chronicle,* a record of events, legends, and myths compiled by monks in the 11th and 12th centuries, Vladimir sent emissaries to the Muslim Bulgars, Catholic Germans, and Greek Orthodox Byzantines to find a suitable religion for his realm. The monks recorded that this is what Vladimir's emissaries said they found:

> When we journied to the Bulgarians, we beheld how they worship in their temple, called a Mosque, while they stand ungirt. The Bulgarian bows, sits down, looks hither like one possessed, and there is no happiness among them, but instead only sorrow and a dreadful stench. Their religion is not good. Then we went among the Germans, and saw them performing many ceremonies in their temples, but we beheld no glory there. Then we went on to Greece, and the Greeks led us to the edifices where they worship their God, and we knew not whether we were on heaven or on earth. For we know that God dwells there among men, and their service is fairer than the ceremonies of other nations. For we cannot forget that beauty.[1]

In fact, Vladimir's choice of Greek Orthodoxy—which later evolved into the Russian Orthodox Church—rather than Roman Catholicism or Islam had nothing to do with the comparative beauty or spirituality of the three religions. It reflected instead the enormous influence on Kievian Russia of the Byzantine Empire, Kiev's southern neighbor and main trading partner and the most culturally advanced Christian state in the world.

Russia's conversion to Orthodoxy was a fateful choice. In 1054, the Christian world split in half when the Greek Orthodox Church centered in the Byzantine capital of Constantinople broke from the Catholic Church based in Rome. That split divided Russia from most of Europe, which followed Roman Catholicism. At the same time, allegiance to Orthodoxy became a fundamental part of the Russian national identity. The Russian Orthodox Church played a central role in the development of Russian art, literature, and education. At first, the Russians followed Byzantine models. In architecture, for example, the steeples of early Russian churches, such as the beautiful St. Sofia Cathedral in Kiev, were topped by flat Byzantine-style domes. But by the 11th century, Russian churches were crowned by the distinctive Russian "onion" dome, possibly because the steeper onion shape shed the heavy Russian snows better than the flatter one imported from the south. Russian religious art followed a similar pattern. Local artists developed a tradition of painting icons, which are religious pictures painted on panels of wood, that became a source of deep national pride.

By the 11th century, Kiev was an impressive city graced by many beautiful churches. It was the largest city in Eastern Europe and probably equal in size to Paris. Other towns also prospered during the Kievian era. In the north, Novgorod grew into a major trading center with extensive ties to Europe. Its *veche* held considerable power in the city. Meetings were announced by the ringing of the city's famous bell that came to symbolize Novgorod and its form of government. Several other Russian towns also grew into busy urban centers. In terms of literature, architecture, and other cultural achievements, Kievian Russia compared favorably with the states of central and Western Europe. Although slavery did exist, the bulk of its population were free peasants.

However, Kievian Russia faced several formidable, and in the end, fatal problems. Its economic base began to erode in the 12th century when Western European nations were able to break the Muslim grip on the Mediterranean Sea and open up a direct sea route to the east. Feuding and warfare between jealous princes from competing Russian cities further weakened the realm. Worst of all, Kievan Russia was constantly under pressure from nomadic tribes moving relentlessly westward out of inner Asia. *The Tale of the Host of Igor*, one of the Kievian Russia's great epic poems, tells of a disaster that befell Russian forces fighting an invading nomadic horde called the Polovtsians:

> And on the third day around noon
> Igor's banners fell!
> Here the brothers parted on the banks of the swift Kaiala
> Here too the bloody wine ran out. . . .
> The grass wilts because of the sorrow
> And the tree bends because of grief!
> Brothers, a sad time has descended!
> A wilderness has covered our strength. . . .
> Igor's brave troops cannot be resurrected!
> The mourners began to weep
> And sorrow spread throughout the Russian land.[2]

The Mongol Invasion and Its Aftermath

In the early 13th century, a terrible new enemy burst from inner Asia whose savage power dwarfed anything the Kievian Russia had yet faced. They were the Mongols, or Tatars (TAHT-ers), as the Russians called them, who were about to become the builders of the largest empire the world had yet seen. The Mongols overwhelmed the Kievian princes and put the land and its people through a gruesome reign of terror. A witness recorded what he saw at Riazan, the first Russian town to fall to the Mongols:

> And not one man remained alive in the city. All were dead. All had drunk the same bitter cup. . . . And there was not even anyone to mourn the dead. Neither father nor mother could mourn their dead children, nor the children their fathers or mothers. Nor could a brother mourn the death of his brother, nor relatives their relatives. All were dead. And this happened for our sins.[3]

Kiev's turn came shortly thereafter. The "mother of Russian cities" was burned to the ground. So total was the destruction that six years later a foreign visitor found only 200 houses standing in what had once been a bustling city.

For the next two centuries, the Russian people endured what they called the "Mongol yoke." Their country was subject to a Mongol state called the Golden Horde that occupied much of the southern steppe region stretching eastward from the Black Sea. Although the Golden Horde governed Russia indirectly through local princes, each of whom managed his small principality, its rule was harsh. High taxes impoverished the people. Russia's cities shrank as trade ties with the West and the Byzantine Empire withered. In addition, Russia was cut off from the European Reformation and Renaissance. Any opposition to Mongol rule was smashed swiftly and brutally. Most important, the Mongol system of rule in which their khan held absolute power over his subjects was passed on to Russia. Most of the town councils of Kievian days disappeared, and the power of the nobles waned. In their place grew the power of the princes, each of whom ruled increasingly like a mini khan within his small domain.

A final consequence of Mongol rule was that the East Slavs split into three different nationalities. Today's Russians evolved in the eastern and northern territories most directly subject to Mongol control. Further west, where Russia's western neighbors Poland and Lithuania were expanding into former Kievian territory, the Ukrainians and Belarusians emerged.

The Rise of Moscow

Deep in Russia's northeastern forests far away from the plains around Kiev, close to the sources of the Volga and Oka Rivers, stood the town of Moscow. It was the center of a tiny principality called Muscovy. A remote backwater during Kiev's heyday, Moscow began to grow after the Mongol conquest as Russians fled the exposed steppe near Kiev for the greater safety of the forest regions. It developed economically because it was well located to trade its timber, tar, and other natural resources along Russia's river system. Muscovy also gained political strength because its line of able princes were able to win the support of the Mongol khan against their rivals. In particular, in the 14th century the prince of Muscovy became the tax collector for all of the khan's Russian territories. At about the same time, the Russian Orthodox Church moved its headquarters to Moscow. This made the city a symbol of Russian identity and added to its prestige. Meanwhile, bit by bit, Moscow annexed neighboring territories, a process that its princes called the "gathering of the Russian lands."

Moscow's prestige soared in 1380, when its Prince Dmitri became the first Russian to defeat the Mongols in battle. Although after his victory Dmitri became a great hero to the Russian people and Muscovy, the leading principality in northeastern Russia, two years later the Mongols again defeated the Russians. It fell to a later prince, Ivan III, known as Ivan the Great (1462–1505), to establish Russia's independence from the Mongols once and for all. Ivan's achievements were enormous. He annexed the other Russian principalities and, in effect, reunified Russia. In 1480, after what amounted to a standoff with a Golden Horde army rather than a decisive battle, Ivan proclaimed Russia's independence from the hated Mongols. Thirteen years later, he officially proclaimed himself the sovereign of all Russia.

Rise of the Principality of Moscow

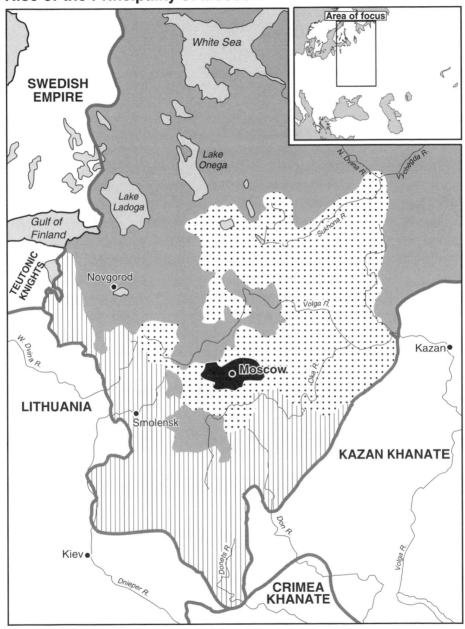

Area of focus

White Sea

SWEDISH
EMPIRE

Lake
Onega

N. Dvina R.

Vychegda R.

Lake
Ladoga

Gulf of
Finland

Sukhona R.

TEUTONIC
KNIGHTS

Novgorod

Volga R.

Kazan

W. Dvina R.

Moscow

Oka R.

LITHUANIA

Smolensk

KAZAN KHANATE

Don R.

Kiev

Donets R.

Volga R.

Dnieper R.

CRIMEA
KHANATE

Principality of Moscow

1300

Lands gained under Ivan III the
Great (1462–155)

Lands gained by 1462

Lands gained under Vasiliy III
(1505–1533)

At the same time, Ivan ruthlessly crushed opposition to his royal power among his subjects. He undermined the remaining political power of Russia's nobles, often by seizing their land. After annexing Novgorod, he deported and executed many of that city's nobles and destroyed its *veche*. As he put it:

> The veche bell in my patrimony, in Novgorod, there shall not be . . . and I will rule the entire state.[4]

To emphasize his point, Ivan the Great carried off Novgorod's famous bell.

Ivan's work of building Russia's absolute monarchy was finished by his grandson, Ivan IV (1533–84), who well deserved his unofficial title: "Ivan the Terrible." Ivan was determined to eliminate all possible opposition to his will and power in Russia. He left no doubt about his ambitions when in 1547 he had himself crowned "czar (the Russian word for caesar) of all the Russias." To break all opposition to his rule, Czar Ivan created a special political police, the *oprichnina* (ah-PREECH-nee-nuh), which he used to unleash a reign of terror that lasted years and took thousands of lives, including that of his most capable son. Some of Ivan's worst excesses took place in Novgorod, whose inhabitants made the mistake of trying to preserve some of their former liberties. A contemporary chronicle described the carnage that took place in 1570:

> The Tsar commanded that the powerful *boyars*, the important merchants, the administrative officials, and the citizens of every rank be brought before him, together with their wives and children. The Tsar ordered that they be tortured in his presence in various spiteful, horrible, and inhuman ways. After many various unspeakable and bitter tortures, the Tsar ordered that their bodies be tormented and roasted with fire in refined ways. . . . He ordered that each man . . . be dragged to the Volkhov bridge behind . . . fast moving sleds, and be thrown into the Volkhov River from the bridge. The Tsar ordered that their wives and children be brought to the Volkhov bridge . . . and then be thrown . . . into the waters of the Volkhov River.
>
> . . . In a horrible manner they were submerged without mercy in the depths of the river, and abandoned to a terrible and bitter death.[5]

Traditional Moscow: The mighty Kremlin, the seat of Russia's government before the reign of Peter the Great and since 1918, has long stood as a symbol of Russia and of the power of its rulers. Its massive walls, spiked by 21 towers, extend for a mile and a quarter and enclose an area of 69 acres that contains historic churches, such as those shown here, as well as museums, government buildings, and theaters.

Together the two Ivans were crucial in building a new form of absolute monarchy: the Russian autocracy. The Russian ruler's power was far greater than that of any European monarch, as visitors from Europe consistently pointed out. In contrast to European monarchs, the Russian czar made no distinction between his property and his political power. He ruled Russia as if he personally owned it. Also unlike Europe, there were no laws that limited the czar's power. Thus a 16th-century visitor noted that "in the sway which he holds over his subjects, he surpasses all the monarchs of the whole world," while 150 years later a European diplomat offered the opinion that "no master hath more power over his slaves." Even when the royal line of the two Ivans died out in the 1590s and Russia was plunged into 15 years of turmoil known as the "Time of Troubles," the autocratic idea was so firmly entrenched that it emerged unscathed when a new dynasty finally was established in 1613.

Russia in the 17th Century

By the 17th century, Russia was a powerful state and an increasingly important player in European affairs. Russia, in fact, had pushed eastward beyond Europe into Asia, occupying most of Siberia and reaching the Pacific shore by 1649. That expansion made Russia the largest country in the world. Its autocratic form of government, while cruel and oppressive by European standards, enabled Moscow to control its vast domains. However, along with its immense size and great strength, Russia had two equally enormous problems that even the powers of the strongest czar could not solve.

The more visible was serfdom, a system of unfree labor one Russian intellectual called a "monster, gross, savage, hundred-mouthed, and bellowing."[6] Russian serfdom developed gradually over a period of about 150 years, beginning in the late 15th century. It grew in part out of Russia's successful expansion eastward, which opened up new lands to which peasants could flee to escape demanding landlords or heavy czarist taxes and military service. Peasant flight to open lands in the east left landlords in the central parts of the country without a reliable supply of labor and the government with a shortage of taxpayers and army recruits. A series of czarist decrees therefore began to tie the peasants to the estates on which they lived.

By the middle of the 17th century, Russian serfdom had developed into a harsh system that combined elements of American slavery and European serfdom. Russian serfs were bound to the land and forced to provide labor in their landlords' fields. Landlords could punish serfs harshly, deny them the right to marry, and remove them from the land. Serfs also paid heavy taxes to the state, and male serfs were subject to military conscription. Since the term of service in the army was 25 years, conscription amounted to a life sentence.

Serfdom proved to be an effective way of controlling the Russian peasants. But it left them ignorant and browbeaten, was responsible for low productivity, and therefore led to poverty in the countryside. It also led to uncounted small peasant rebellions and several huge ones, including the 1606–07 uprising led by Ivan Bolotnikov (boh-LOT-nih-koff) and the 1670–71 rebellion of the legendary Stenka Razin, the Robin Hood of Russia.

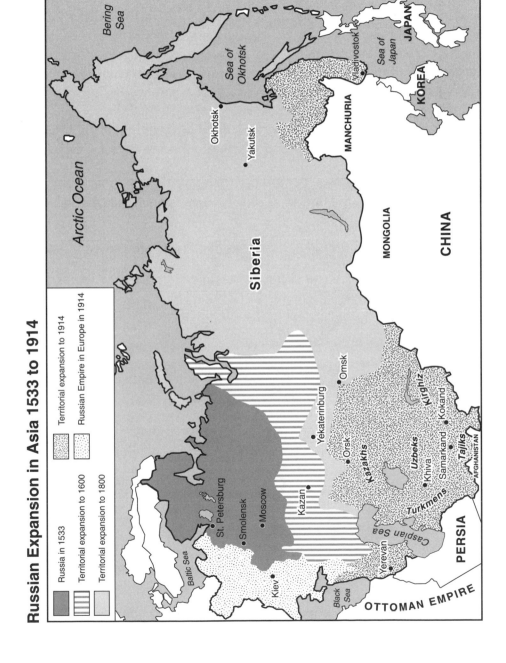

Russian Expansion in Asia 1533 to 1914

Russia's other major problem was that since the Mongol conquest, it lagged behind its European neighbors to the West in both economic development and technological progress. Ivan the Terrible learned about the price of technological backwardness the hard way, during unsuccessful wars against some of Russia's western neighbors. Experts in artillery and other military arts that Ivan hired in the West helped his troops conquer more backward peoples in the East, but not even an army of experts could make up the gap against the technologically advanced countries of Europe. And the gap that loomed before Ivan only grew after his death, as Europe underwent its scientific revolution which set the stage for unprecedented technological leaps.

Ivan's successful wars of expansion eastward actually laid the basis for yet another problem that grew over time. When Ivan's troops overwhelmed two Muslim states in the lower Volga region, their victory brought large numbers of non-Russians into his realm. That process continued for several centuries as Ivan's successors expanded Russia's borders to the south and west as well as to the east. Russia soon became a multinational empire with many unhappy non-Russian subjects.

All these problems became the burden of the new dynasty of the Romanov family that came to the Russian throne in 1613. How the Romanovs dealt with them helped determine the fate of Russia for the next 300 years.

NOTES

1. "The Russian Primary Chronicle," trans. Samuel Cross, in *Medieval Russia: A Source Book, 900–1700,* 2nd ed., ed. Basil Dmytryshyn (Hinsdale, Illinois: The Dryden Press, 1973), p. 40.
2. "The Tale of the Host of Igor," trans. Basil Dymtryshyn, in *Medieval Russia: A Source Book,* p. 87.
3. Serge A. Zenkovsky, ed., and trans., *Medieval Russia's Epics, Chronicles, and Tales* (New York: E. P. Dutton, 1963), p. 57.
4. Quoted in Nicholas V. Riasanovsky, *A History of Russia,* 4th ed. (New York: Oxford University Press, 1984), p. 105.
5. From *Polnoe Sobranie Resskikh Letopisei* (Complete Collection of Russian Chronicles), trans. Basil Dmytryshyn, in *Medieval Russia: A Source Book,* p. 238.
6. Quoted in Jerome Blum, *Lord and Peasant in Russia from the Ninth to the Nineteenth Century* (New York: Antheneum, 1965), p. 562.

2

Imperial Russia

---

*R*ussia's early Romanov czars were rulers who usually managed to cope with crises as they arose, whether a peasant rebellion, a war with Poland, or a religious dispute between competing Russian Orthodox factions. What they lacked was vision, a sense of Russia's long-term challenges and problems. In particular, they neither understood nor responded to the growing technological and economic gap between their country and the major Western European countries, such as France and Britain. This changed after 1694 when 22-year-old Peter I, who had been a figurehead czar under the control of regents since the age of 10, finally took the reins of power into his huge, powerful, and capable hands.

The Era of Peter the Great

It was Peter himself who decided that he should be known as "Peter the Great." Yet rarely has a historical figure better deserved the title of "great" than this extraordinary man. Peter stood nearly seven feet tall. He was also enormously capable and phenomenally energetic. Despite a limited formal education, Peter's unquenchable curiosity and impressive abilities enabled him to master a wide range of subjects, from geometry to shipbuilding to military science. His great capabilities were matched by equally great faults, including pitiless cruelty and ruthlessness. He led his country into costly wars and mercilessly crushed those who opposed his policies. Peter's personal life was filled with drinking bouts, episodes of crude and vicious humor, and scandalous sexual escapades. During his lifetime, he was either hated or loved; it was impossible to be neutral about Peter Romanov. At the same time, the passage of almost 300 years has not produced a czar or ruler who better symbolizes Russia in the minds of its people.

Peter recognized that Russia had to modernize in order to compete successfully as a European power, a fact driven home by military defeats suffered against Sweden early in his reign. He also knew that Russia would have to do much more than employ foreign experts and advisers. It had to change the way it worked and learn to produce modern machines and weapons on its own. Otherwise, Russia never would achieve equal status with the great powers. At the same time, Peter was determined to preserve the Russian autocratic institutions, from czardom to serfdom. His reforms were intended to make Russia equal in power to the West, not to turn czarist Russia into a Western-style society. He wanted power for his country, not freedom for its people.

Peter's reforms were dramatic and far-reaching. He founded technical schools to produce the specialists Russia needed for a modern army, as well as a national Academy of Sciences to promote higher learning. He encouraged the establishment of modern industries, including mines and metallurgy factories needed to build modern weapons. Russia's government was modernized based on techniques used in Europe. Peter also introduced a civil service system that allowed men to advance on the basis of ability until they achieved noble rank. And he poured immense resources into Russia's military, modernizing the army and creating a navy from scratch. After several embarrassing and frustrating defeats, Peter achieved the military results he wanted when Russia defeated Sweden in a long war and seized most of the Baltic coast from its defeated rival.

These reforms and victories came at a very high price. Peter not only demanded that Russia learn from the West, he required that his noblemen dress and act like Westerners. Those who resisted his orders were punished. Sometimes the punishments were more insulting than severe, such as when Peter personally cut off the beards of nobles who refused his order to shave and look like Westerners. Other punishments were far worse; among the many tortured to death for opposing the czar's policies was his own son. To further root out opposition, Peter founded a political police known as the *Preobrazhensky Prikaz* (pray-oh-brah-ZHEN-skee PREE-kahz).

As usual in Russian history, those who suffered most from the czar's policies were its ordinary people, especially the peasants. Peter paid for his expensive projects by raising their taxes drastically and fastening the straitjacket of serfdom even more tightly around them. He also conscripted tens of thousands of unlucky peasants for his army, his various construction projects, and for Russia's new factories, where they endured horrible conditions.

The great symbol of Peter's reforms, both in terms of what it achieved and what it cost, was Peter's new capital city, St. Petersburg. Peter founded the city in 1703 on territory conquered from Sweden, where the Neva River runs into the Baltic Sea. The site was an unlikely place to build anything, much less a city: a desolate, uninhabited swamp with a damp, unhealthy climate and subject to constant flooding. But it was also the westernmost part of Russia and therefore the place where Peter decided to build what he called his "window on Europe." From that window, Peter and Russia could look out on Europe, master its scientific and technological skills, and begin to modernize.

Peter spent a great deal of time in St. Petersburg when it was being built and was well aware of the problems involved. But he did not let them bother him. After one of the city's innumerable floods, he wrote cheerfully to a close adviser:

> The day before yesterday, the wind from the southwest blew up such waters as, they say, have never been seen before. In my house, the water rose twenty-one inches above the floor; and in the garden and on the other side along the streets people went about freely in boats.

However, the waters did not remain long—less than three hours. Here it was entertaining to watch how the people, not only the peasants but their women, too, sat on the roofs and trees during the flood. Although the waters rose to a great height, they did not cause bad damage.[1]

Others were less cheerful about the city Peter called his "paradise," "Eden," and "darling." Of the tens of thousands of forced laborers who toiled in the soggy Neva swampland to build St. Petersburg, at least 30,000 died. To them, and to many other ordinary Russians, St. Petersburg, far from being a paradise, was the "city built on bones." Nor did much of the tradition-bound nobility share Peter's enthusiasm for the city. One member of the royal family said she hoped the city would "remain a desert."[2]

None of this deterred the czar, and in the end he triumphed. Peter brought many of Europe's finest craftsmen to create elegant and graceful stone buildings, and his successors continued his work. By the late 18th century, St. Petersburg was a large and impressive city that admirers called the "Venice of the north." In the 19th century, the great poet Aleksandr Pushkin spoke for many educated and forward-looking Russians when he wrote in "The Bronze Horseman":

And before the younger capital
Ancient Moscow has paled
Like a purple-clad widow
Before a new empress.[3]

St. Petersburg remained Russia's capital until 1918, when the new Bolshevik government moved its seat to Moscow. Despite that loss, by the late 20th century there were few inhabitants of Peter's city, by then a metropolis of 6 million, who did not consider it the most beautiful and sophisticated city in Russia. Even when it was called Leningrad, from 1924 to 1991, those who lived there continued affectionately to call the city "Peter."

Russia Fails to Catch Up

After Peter's death in 1725, Russia again failed to match the progress taking place in Western Europe. The problem was that while Peter's reforms strengthened the czarist government and increased its ability to control Russia, they did not strengthen Russian society. In fact, in many ways they weakened it. Peter's wars had drained resources from civilian needs into the military. Serfdom actually was strengthened and made even more oppressive. During 1707–08, the suffering caused by Peter's wars, high taxes, and conscription for building St. Petersburg ignited one of the four major serf rebellions in Russian history. At the same time, Russia's unfree society simply could not generate the economic and technological progress taking place in countries such as England and France, where individuals had far greater opportunities.

Peter was succeeded by a string of undistinguished and sometimes incompetent rulers. Then in 1762, the young German-born wife of Czar Peter III overthrew and murdered her husband and seized the throne. She would rule Russia until 1796 and eventually be known as "Catherine the Great." The pattern of increasing Russia's glory at the expense of its people marked Catherine's reign, just as it had Peter's. Catherine led Russia to military victories, expanded its borders to the south and west, and talked a great deal about reforming the government. Her reputation rests largely on her support for cultural and intellectual life in Russia. Catherine corresponded with many of Western Europe's leading intellectuals, including the famous French Enlightenment *philosophes* (phee-lo-SOF) Voltaire and Diderot. She also bought the paintings, sculptures, and other works of art that became the core of the collection of the world-famous Hermitage Museum and constructed some of St. Petersburg's most magnificent buildings.

But Catherine, like Peter, did nothing to make Russia a freer society. Instead of limiting serfdom, she extended it into Russia's new territories and increased the nobles' power over their serfs. These and other harsh policies, including heavy taxation, triggered a peasant explosion led by a former soldier named Yemelyan Pugachev (puh-gah-CHOFF). The most massive peasant rebellion in Russia's history, the Pugachev Revolt blazed across the vastness of the steppe for two years before it was finally extinguished. While Catherine was shaken by the Pugachev revolt at home, she was genuinely terrified by the French Revolution in Europe, which broke out in 1789, 15 years after Pugachev's defeat. The last years of her reign were increasingly repressive. Among the victims of that repression were the two leading intellectuals of that era—Aleksandr Radischev (rah-DEESH-chef) and Nikolai Novikov—both of whom were imprisoned. Russia remained a country of dangerous extremes: magnificent palaces filled with art treasures and wretched peasant hovels lacking the most basic comforts; a few educated and sophisticated nobles and millions of ignorant peasants; impressive military power and corrosive economic weakness; an all-powerful autocracy and a general population without any rights.

Russia's failure to deal with its fundamental problems continued into the 19th century, although for a time its size and military forces masked its weaknesses. In 1812, Russia's power in Europe reached its pre-Soviet peak when Alexander I, Catherine's grandson, played a major role in the European coalition that defeated the French emperor Napoleon. Russian soldiers reached Paris, where they encountered the ideas of the French Revolution. When they returned home, some Russian officers brought with them Western European ideas about freedom and equality. Against the background of what these young noblemen had seen in the West, Russia seemed backward, poor, and cruel. When Alexander I died in December 1825, a group of these officers tried to overthrow czarism. They were, however, poorly organized and not even in agreement about how they intended to govern Russia if their revolt succeeded. The revolt was crushed. Despite their failure, the "Decembrists," as rebellious officers were called, did achieve a sort of victory in defeat by serving as a heroic if tragic inspiration to later generations of Russian revolutionaries.

For more than 20 years after the Decembrist Revolt, Czar Nicholas I tried to hold the line against change. His new secret police, the Third Section, tracked down those who opposed the czar's absolute powers. Serfdom continued to hold Russia's peasants in bondage. A revolt in Russia's Polish provinces, which Catherine had added to the empire, was put down with great severity. But change came to Russia despite Nicholas's efforts. Russia's first railroad was built during his reign. As education and literacy spread, so did knowledge about other countries and ideas about freedom. The "Golden Age" of Russian literature began with the works of Aleksandr Pushkin, Mikhail Lermontov (LAYR-mon-tof), and Nikolai Gogol. Nicholas meanwhile led Russia into the disastrous Crimean War (1853–56) in which Russia's huge army, fighting on its own soil, was defeated by the smaller but more modern forces of Britian, France, and other Western European powers. Leo Tolstoy, one of Russia's greatest novelists, fought at the 11-month-long siege of the port city of Sevastopol, whose fall signaled Russia's defeat in the war. He provided a grim and shocking picture of how Russian army's was unable to care for its casualties in a battle that cost it 100,000 dead and wounded:

> Prince Galtzine . . . directed his steps toward the field hospital. Making his way to the entrance with difficulty through soldiers, litters, stretcher-bearers who came in with the wounded and went out with the dead, Galtzine entered as far as the first room, took one look around him, recoiled involuntarily, and precipitately fled into the street. What he saw there was far too horrible!
>
> The great, high, somber hall, lighted only by four or five candles, where the surgeons moved about examining the wounded, was literally crammed with people. Stretcher-bearers continually brought new wounded and placed them side by side in rows on the ground. The crowd was so great that the wretches pushed against one another and bathed in their neighbors' blood. . . . A confused murmur of groans, sighs, death-rattles, was interrupted by piercing cries. . . . Surgeons with their sleeves turned up, on their knees before the wounded, examined and probed the wounds by the flare of torches held by their assistants, despite the terrible cries and supplications of the patients. . . .
>
> Forty or fifty stretcher-bearers awaited their burdens at the door. The living were sent to the hospital, the dead to the chapel. They waited in silence, and sometimes a sigh escaped them as they contemplated this picture.[4]

The Abolition of Serfdom and the Great Reforms

The Crimean War showed just how backward Russia was relative to Europe, while smoldering unrest in the countryside demonstrated the danger czarism faced if it did nothing about serfdom. These realizations led to the Great Reforms, which were undertaken by Alexander II, who had become czar upon the death of Nicholas in 1855.

The Great Reforms began with the abolition of serfdom in 1861, but did not end there. Additional reforms created new elected rural governments called *zemstvos*, (Russian singular: ZEMST-voh), revamped city government, overhauled military service, and set up a new judicial system.

They enjoyed varying degrees of success, with the zemstvo and judicial reforms probably being the most successful. But the linchpin of the Great Reforms was the abolition of serfdom. In a single stroke, it freed 20 million serfs, five times the number of slaves Abraham Lincoln liberated with his Emancipation Proclamation two years later. The problem was that nothing was done to lift the ex-serfs out of their grinding poverty. They were forced to buy land at prices they could not afford. Most had to remain members of communal organizations called *mirs*, which controlled their land and discouraged individual initiative. Several other laws further restricted the freedom of the ex-serfs. Russia's "state peasants," whose pre-1861 status resembled that of the serfs but who lived on state owned rather than on privately owned land, were freed in 1866 under similar conditions.

As a result of these failures and restrictions, 30 years after their emancipation most Russian peasants, and therefore most of Russia's population, remained miserably poor. An occasional exceptional peasant managed to prosper, and others moved to the cities and towns to work in newly built factories. Overall, however, the Russian countryside remained a troubled place. Anton Chekhov (1860–1904), Russia's outstanding dramatist and master of the short story, sadly described what he witnessed during the 1890s:

> During the summer and winter there had been hours and days when these people seemed to live worse than beasts. They were frightful people to live with—rough, dishonest, filthy, drunken. Holding each other in mutual disrespect, fear, and suspicion, they were always at loggerheads, always squabbling.
>
> Who . . . makes the peasant drunk? The peasant. Who squanders his village, school, and church funds on drink? The peasant. Who steals from his neighbors, sets fire to their property and purjures himself in court for a bottle of vodka? The peasant. Who is the first to run down the peasant at a council or town meeting? The peasant.
>
> Yes, they were frightful people to live with. Still, they were men and women, and they suffered and wept like men and women, and there was nothing in their lives for which an excuse could not be found—back-breaking work that makes you ache all over at night, cruel winters, poor harvests and overcrowding, with no help and nowhere to turn for it. The richer and stronger are no help, for they are rough, dishonest, and drunken themselves and use the same filthy

language. The pettiest official or clerk treats the peasants like tramps, even talking down to elders and churchwardens as if by right.[5]

The era of the Great Reforms lasted into the 1870s, by which time Alexander II had become increasingly conservative and fearful of change. After he was assassinated by revolutionaries in 1881, his son Alexander III relied on repression rather than reform to keep Russia under control. However, after a terrible famine in 1891–92, even Alexander was forced to look for new solutions to Russia's problems. Taking a page from Peter the Great and the advice of his able new finance minister, Sergei Witte, Alexander III began a program of industrialization to modernize the economy. It lasted until 1903 (nine years after Alexander's death) and was extremely successful. Existing industries were modernized and new factories and mines built, often with money and skills provided by foreign investors. Among the new industries was oil production, which was based on rich oil deposits near and under the Caspian Sea. But it took high taxes to finance this program, and those taxes fell, as usual, on the peasantry. In the new factories, mines, and oil fields, workers unprotected by labor laws toiled in dreadful conditions. In 1902, a wave of peasant uprisings swept across several provinces. The next year, workers across southern Russia went out on strike in unprecedented numbers. Russia had entered a new century, but without leaving behind its old problems.

The Revolutionaries

The goal of every czarist reformer was to strengthen Russia's social, political, and economic system in order to preserve it. Some Russians, however, wanted an entirely different type of change. They were revolutionaries who wanted to overthrow czarism and replace it with a new type of society. The revolutionaries did not emerge out of the peasantry or factory workers, the people in Russia who had the least to lose and therefore might be expected to turn to revolution. The peasants, illiterate and in awe of the czar, directed most of their hatred and frustration at the nobility and local authorities when they rioted or revolted. The factory workers, few in number even in the early 20th century, cared primarily about their immediate need to improve their working and living conditions. The revolutionaries, instead, emerged out of Russia's tiny educated elite. At first they were nobles, like the men who led the Decembrist Revolt in 1825. By the 1840s, as education spread, revolutionaries increasingly came from Russia's growing middle class and even from poorer people who managed to obtain an education, such as the children of lower level government workers or clergy.

While there were many different types of revolutionaries and while their views often changed from decade to decade, they shared some common ideas. Until the 1880s, all of them believed that any revolution would have to be based on a peasant uprising. This belief in a peasant-based revolution was called populism. Another key point of agreement was that much like the czars they hated and wanted to destroy, the revolutionaries did not want Russia to become like the West. Specifically, they rejected the capitalist free-enterprise economic system and its system of political democracy. The revolutionaries' main goal was socialism, an economic system that would be based on cooperation and planning, not on competition and free enterprise. Under socialism, there would be no rich and no poor; instead, all would receive an equal share of society's wealth.

To ensure the triumph and maintainance of socialism, many, though not all, Russian revolutionaries were ready to set up a dictatorship. They argued that their socialist dictatorship would be different from the czar's, because as socialists they would be serving the interests of the people. As for democracy, these revolutionaries rejected it outright. They were convinced that the situation in the West proved that democracy was nothing more than a tool the capitalist class used to fool and oppress the poor.

The lack of faith in democracy was part of a deeper belief that had nothing to do with the West but was rooted in Russian history. Although in theory the revolution depended on the peasantry, from the start, Russia's revolutionaries were unable to get their message across to those peasants. Either revolutionary activists were arrested by the czar's ever-present police, or, even worse, the peasants refused to listed to them. Instead of accepting the truth as the revolutionaries saw it, the peasants remained loyal to their czar—whom they called their "Little Father." Or they simply were too busy trying to survive to bother with the revolutionaries. Many populists, therefore, drew the conclusion that an educated elite had to take charge, organize, and control the revolution. Nikolai Chernyshevsky (cher-nih-SHEF-skee), who became a hero to several generations of revolutionaries, wrote that the revolution would be made by "New Men," people who were "superior beings" and were "high above the common run of men." As for the majority of the population that was supposed to benefit from the revolution, according to Chernyshevsky:

> The mass of the population knows nothing and cares about nothing except its material advantages. . . . The mass is simply the raw material for . . . political experiments. Whoever rules it tells it what to do and it obeys.[6]

Nor would matters change *after* the revolution. Then, according to an admirer of Chernyshevksy named Peter Tkachev (t'kah-CHOFF), the revolutionaries would have to set up a dictatorship to make sure socialism was established and properly run. Why? Because, as Tkachev bluntly put it:

> The people are incapable of building, upon the ruins of the old, a new world that would be able to move and develop towards the communist ideal; therefore they cannot play any significant or leading part in building this new world. Such a part belongs solely to the revolutionary minority.[7]

Not all revolutionaries agreed with this point of view. They opposed the idea of a revolutionary dictatorship and argued that change had to come from the people themselves. But the reliance on the peasantry was a fatal flaw in the populists' strategy. Whether they tried to get the peasants to act on their own, or to control their actions by organizing a secret revolutionary party, nothing the populists did worked. The secret plots failed, the peasants did not rise up on their own, and two generations of revolutionaries were bitterly disappointed.

Against this background of defeat, beginning in the 1880s, a new revolutionary doctrine called Marxism began to win converts in Russian revolutionary circles. Marxism grew out of the ideas of a German philosopher and revolutionary named Karl Marx, whose theories were based primarily on his study of capitalism in Western Europe. According to Marxism, no country could have a socialist revolution until it went through a capitalist stage of development and became a modern industrial society. In that society, the factory working class would be the overwhelming majority of the people. Marxists called this class, which was just starting to be formed in Russia, the proletariat. It was the proletariat, not the peasantry, that would make the socialist revolutions, the Marxists insisted.

The first Marxist groups, who called themselves Social Democrats, began organizing in Russia in the 1890s. In 1898, they failed in an attempt to set up a national party when their meeting was broken up by the czarist police. They finally succeeded in organizing their party in 1903, when they were clever enough to meet in Western Europe, far away from the czar's police, rather than in Russia. However, at the very start the Social Democrats split into two groups. One group, called the Mensheviks, believed that they should model their party on the Social Democratic parties in Western Europe. This included running the party according to democratic rules. The second group was called Bolsheviks. Led by Vladimir Lenin, a superb organizer and ruthless infighter, the Bolsheviks drew on the ideas of people like Chernyshevksy and Tkachev. They were a tightly organized and dictatorial group, driven by Lenin's belief that only their party, not the factory workers themselves, could lead and control the revolution. At first it made little difference whether one agreed with the Mensheviks or the Bolsheviks, since the Marxists proved to be no better than the populists in getting their revolution off the ground. But then czarism began to crack, opening up a window of opportunity that changed the course of Russian history.

The End of the Old Order

In 1904, a confident, arrogant Russia blundered into a war with Japan, with whom it was competing for influence in China and Korea. The Russo-Japanese War brought Russia humiliating defeat and enormous casualties at the front and economic hardships at home. In January 1905, after almost a year of war, a peaceful demonstration in St. Petersburg turned into a massacre, when troops fired on a huge crowd of factory workers and their families. "Bloody Sunday," as the day became known, was the spark that set off Russia's 1905 Revolution. The country was swept by riots and protests. Not only workers and peasants were involved;

among those demanding change were members of Russia's middle and upper classes. As one participant later recalled:

> Thus there was organized in the year 1905 a common front, from the revolutionary to the conservative strata of our society. There could be no common view in this camp. But on one point they all agreed: *that to continue as before was impossible.*[8]

The upheaval reached its peak in October, when a wave of strikes threatened to cripple the country. In St. Petersburg, the center of the action, a general strike shut down the city. The workers formed a council, or "soviet" in Russian, called the St. Petersburg Soviet of Workers' Deputies to run their strike. They were led by revolutionaries who had returned home from exile, including both Mensheviks and Bolsheviks. Nicholas II, who had become czar in 1894, was on the verge of being overthrown. He therefore was forced to compromise with the Russian people, something he did only with great reluctance and bitterness. He issued the October Manifesto, which promised the Russian people a parliament and basic civil rights. In that way, he broke up the united front against him, since moderates and liberals who feared what revolution might bring were satisfied. Having won some breathing space, Nicholas was able to save his throne. After the war ended, he used troops returning from the front to crush the revolutionaries, workers, and peasants who still opposed him. While victory came quickly in the cities, resistance in some parts of the country continued for as long as two years.

Nicholas II was a reactionary who always regretted what he called his "terrible decision" of October 1905 and spent much of his time trying to undermine Russia's new parliament. Nonetheless, Russia made considerable progress after 1906. Although the parliament, called the Duma, enjoyed only limited powers, its existence represented the first limits on the czar's autocratic power. And the Duma used its authority to pass progressive laws, including a program to establish universal primary education in Russia by 1922. Meanwhile, Nicholas appointed a new prime minister named Piotr Stolypin who launched an amibitious program to overhaul Russia's agriculture and improve the lives of the peasantry. Stolypin's program removed the restrictions on the peasants that remained from 1861. It permitted them to leave their mirs and encouraged them to become independent farmers. Stolypin claimed he needed 20 years to transform Russia's countryside into a land of prosperous and conservative peasants who would support their czar.

Neither Stolypin nor Russia got the 20 years. Stolypin was assassinated in 1911 while attending a concert, as the horrified czar watched from his royal box. Three years later, Russia was dragged into World War I along with the rest of Europe. Caught in the midst of reforms and the long, painful transition from an agricultural to an industrial society, Russia was unprepared for war. The men Nicholas chose to lead the country were as incompetent as he was. Facing the ultramodern and well-led German army, Russia suffered defeats and disruptions that dwarfed what had occurred in the war with Japan. Yet somehow Russia continued to fight on for two and one-half years.

By early 1917, however, Russia reached the brink of collapse. Its army had suffered more than 8 million casualties and was crumbling. Its civilians, especially in the large cities like St. Petersburg and Moscow, were starving. It took only a small demonstration and strike to begin the revolution that brought czarism down. The trouble began early in March in St. Petersburg. Nicholas could find no reliable troops to restore order; some of them even joined the demonstrators. On March 12, the workers in the capital, whose name had been changed from St. Petersburg to Petrograd, organized a new soviet: the Petrograd Soviet of Workers' and Soldiers' Deputies. That same day, meeting in the same building as the Soviet, the Duma, ignoring the czar's orders, set up a committee to run the country. On March 14 that committee became Russia's new Provisional Government. The next day the czar abdicated.

The old order in Russia had collapsed. Russia stood on the start of a new era, one full of hope but also filled with danger. The country was still in the middle of a disastrous war, and its people were divided against themselves. As they looked forward for a sign of what was to come, at once hopeful, battered, and terrified, the Russian people might well have been asking the same question as the Irish poet William Butler Yeats:

> Surely some revelation is at hand;
> Surely the Second Coming is at hand; . . .
> And what rough beast, its hour come at last,
> Slouches towards Bethlehem to be born?[9]

NOTES

1. Quoted in Robert K. Massie, *Peter the Great: His Life and World* (New York: Ballantine Books, 1980), p. 363.
2. Quoted in ibid., p. 365.
3. Quoted in Yevgeny Yevtushenko, "The City With Three Faces," in *St. Petersburg: Insight City Guides* (Hong Kong: APA Publications, 1992), p. 24.
4. Leo Tolstoy, *Sebastopol* (Ann Arbor: University of Michigan Press, 1961), pp. 68–71.
5. Anton Chekhov, "Peasants," in *Chekhov: Eleven Stories,* trans. Ronald Hingley (London, Oxford, New York: Oxford University Press, 1975), p. 170.
6. Quoted in Tibor Szamuely, *The Russian Tradition* (New York: McGraw Hill, 1974), pp. 217, 219.
7. Ibid.
8. Quoted in Sidney Harcave, *First Blood: The Russian Revolution of 1905* (New York: Macmillan, 1964), pp. 116–117.
9. William Butler Yeats, "The Second Coming," in *The Premier Book of Major Poets,* ed. Anita Dore (New York: Fawcett, 1970), p. 257.

3

Soviet Russia

*T*he Provisional Government that came to power in March 1917 was led by moderates and liberals who had served in the Duma. These men belonged to Russia's middle and upper classes. They believed in parliamentary democracy and the free enterprise system that existed in Western Europe. While they recognized that Russia needed further reforms, they opposed radical change and, in particular, did not want Russia to have a socialist revolution. Even when socialist politicians were added to the Provisional Government over the next few months, they agreed that Russia was too unstable to go beyond a program of moderate reform. In short, with the czar gone, the Provisional Government wanted to hold the line on major change while Russia got back on its feet.

These goals proved to be unreachable. Russia was locked in a losing war with Germany and its allies. The constant pounding by the German war machine caused conditions in Russia to worsen during the summer and fall of 1917. Yet the Provisional Government kept Russia in World War I. Russia was allied with Britain, France, the United States, and other

Western democracies against Germany, and Russia's new leaders considered their country obligated to stand by its allies. The Provisional Government also hoped to gain territory and prestige for Russia if it stuck it out and was on the winning side when the war ended. But as conditions deteriorated by the fall of 1917, Russia's workers and peasants, who were suffering terribly, lost confidence in the Provisional Government. By November, the Provisional Government was losing its grip on the country. It therefore was easily overthrown on November 7 in an armed coup by the Bolshevik Party led by Vladimir Lenin. Russia's first experiment with democracy came to an end after only eight months.

Lenin and the Bolshevik Dictatorship

When the Bolsheviks seized power on November 7, most people expected them to join with other socialist parties and form a coalition government to run Russia. They were wrong. Lenin, the party's founder and leader, was a dedicated Marxist who hated capitalism. He also was an idealist who believed it was possible to build a perfect socialist society in which all people would live well and be treated equally. At the same time, Lenin was a devoted admirer of authoritarian non-Marxist Russian socialists like Nikolai Chernyshevsky and Peter Tkachev. Like them, he was convinced that only a strict dictatorship of a tightly controlled revolutionary party could build socialism in Russia. That party, of course, would have to be the Bolshevik Party under his leadership. That in turn meant that all other political parties in Russia, including even the Mensheviks, who like the Bolsheviks were Marxian socialists, had to be denied any power.

Lenin's attitude obviously left no room for democracy, since democratic elections might very well put a political party in power other than the Bolsheviks. This was one reason he urged his followers, most of whom actually doubted they could succeed, to seize power. Having taken over the government, Lenin was deeply worried about plans the Provisional Government had made for national elections for an assembly to write a new constitution for Russia. The Bolsheviks dared not stop the scheduled elections, which took place a few weeks after the Bolshevik coup. And

Vladimir Lenin, the founder of the Communist Party and the Soviet state.

as Lenin feared, the people of Russia did not support the Bolsheviks. Lenin's party finished second with about a quarter of the vote, far behind the Socialist Revolutionary Party. When faced with the people's clear non-Bolshevik choice, the Bolshevik government did not hesitate. It allowed the assembly to meet exactly once, in January 1918, and then dispersed it by force. Lenin did not hide what he was doing. His government's action, he said bluntly, was "a complete and frank liquidation of the idea of democracy by the idea of dictatorship."[1]

Meanwhile, even before the assembly met, the Bolsheviks set up a secret police called the Cheka to crush all opposition to their rule. They also strengthened themselves in March 1918 when they signed a peace treaty with Germany, thereby finally getting Russia out of World War I. The treaty was a humiliating one. It cost Russia a great deal of territory and valuable resources in what had been the western part of the former czarist empire. But at least it brought Russia peace, although not for long. Millions of Russians were unwilling to exchange the czarist dictatorship for a Bolshevik one, and by the middle of 1918 the country was locked in a destructive civil war. The civil war caused great suffering, even worse than what the country endured during World War I. Russia was torn apart and its people, who had stood together to defend their country against the Germans, were reduced to fighting each other to survive:

> The law of survival of the fittest found its cruelest, most naked applications in the continual struggle for food. The weaker failed to get on the trains to the country districts, or fell from the roofs, or were pushed off the platform, or caught typhus and died, or had the precious fruits of the foraging taken away by the . . . hated guards who boarded the trains as they approached the cities and confiscated the surplus food from the passengers.[2]

The Bolsheviks, who renamed themselves the Communist Party in 1918, won the civil war, despite support from the western powers for anti-Bolshevik forces. A key reason for their victory was excellent leadership, especially from Lenin, but also from other party leaders such as Leon Trotsky and Joseph Stalin. Ruthlessness and a willingness to go to any lengths to win also were crucial factors. The Bolsheviks unleashed the Cheka to hunt down and execute their enemies. They established concentration camps and used forced labor to support the war effort.

Under a series of policies that came to be called "War Communism," they took over factories, railroads, mines, and other businesses, seized food from the peasants, and forcibly mobilized all resources in the regions they controlled to supply their army.

By early 1921, the civil war was over and the Bolsheviks were still in power. But Russia, far from moving toward the socialist utopia promised by Marxism, was gripped by famine and lay in ruins. Once again, as during the seizure of power in 1917 and the civil war, Lenin's leadership was decisive in keeping the party in power. To restore the economy, the Bolsheviks ended War Communism, which was very unpopular with the majority of the people, and introduced their "New Economic Policy," or NEP. The NEP ended food seizures and allowed the peasants to grow and sell their crops with minimal government interference. Most businesses were returned to private owners. Only major enterprises, such as railroads and large factories, remained under state control.

The NEP enabled the country's economy to recover by the mid-1920s. Although hardship remained at all levels of society, the peasants, still the overwhelming majority of the population, were prospering as never before. The NEP, however, was not popular with many Communist Party members. They argued that by allowing the peasants and small business-men to operate freely, the party was permitting capitalism to continue, and even to expand. This violated the party's goal of building socialism and its commitment to guarantee equality to all people. Also, under the NEP heavy industries like steel, coal, and machine building, which were the basis of a modern industrial economy, were not doing well. This was a serious problem for the Bolsheviks because according to Marxism, socialism required a modern industrial economy that could produce enough for everybody to live well. The NEP, despite its success, therefore became a divisive issue within the party.

While the Bolsheviks loosened their grip on Russia's economy in 1921, they tightened their grip on political power. All other parties were banned, the secret police continued its activities, independent trade unions were suppressed, and other areas of life, such as the arts, increasingly were put under party control. Even within the party, rules were tightened to make it more difficult for the rank-and-file membership to oppose the leader-ship. Those who violated the rules were threatened with expulsion from the party.

As long as Lenin, the party's undisputed leader, was at the helm, disputes over policy and differences between various party leaders under Lenin remained under control. However, he became ill in 1922 and died in January 1924. By then a fierce struggle to succeed him had begun. The two leading contenders were Leon Trotsky and Joseph Stalin. The brilliant and charismatic Trotsky had joined the Bolshevik Party in 1917. His extraordinary talents—he had played a leading role as a non-Bolshevik in the 1905 Revolution—quickly made him Lenin's right-hand man. Stalin, a master at back room maneuvering and intrigue whose ruthlessness knew no limits, was a longtime Bolshevik who had moved into the party's inner leadership circle during the grim days of the civil war.

In 1922, with Lenin's support, Stalin was appointed to the newly created post of general secretary, which gave him enormous behind-the-scenes power. As Stalin's power grew, his unlimited ambition and viciousness became more obvious, so much so that Lenin turned against him and wanted to demote him. But Lenin's illness and death blocked his plans. Stalin then triumphed over Trotsky and several other party leaders in a bitter, topsy-turvy struggle that lasted until 1929. With Stalin in charge, the NEP was immediately scrapped. The fate of Russia, which had been renamed the Union of Soviet Socialist Republics (or Soviet Union for short) in 1922, took a drastic and horrific new turn.

The Stalin Era

Two words basically sum up the Stalin era: industrialization and terror. As soon as he was firmly in power in 1929, Stalin launched his industrialization drive. All available resources were diverted to building the modern industries that would make the Soviet Union the military equal of the Western powers. The industrialization drive was backed by brute force that by the mid-1930s swelled into a nationwide campaign of arrests, imprisonment, and murder that engulfed millions of people and terrorized the entire nation. These twin campaigns were interrupted in 1941 by World War II, when Nazi Germany invaded the Soviet Union. After 1945, the Soviet Union endured eight more years of suffering until Stalin finally died in 1953.

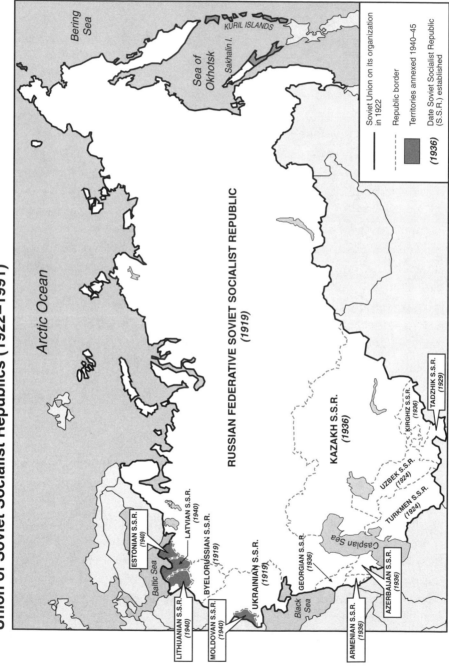

Union of Soviet Socialist Republics (1922–1991)

Joseph Stalin, the brutal dictator of the Soviet Union, whose policies caused the death of millions of people.

Stalin's goal was to industrialize Russia fully and catch up with the West in 10 years. This supposedly was possible because, according to Marxist principles, the new Soviet economy would operate according to carefully worked out five-year plans. In theory, these plans would be far more efficient than the unplanned and often illogical capitalist economy. In practice, however, Soviet planning had problems of its own. Stalin's plans included goals that were impossible to achieve, given the conditions in the Soviet Union. When all resources were diverted to meet these goals, they resulted in waste and hardship on a massive scale.

The industrialization drive actually began with agriculture. The problem from Stalin's point of view was that the Soviet Union's millions of small peasant farms not only were inefficient, but were free of government control. The Communist Party also viewed independent peasants as potential capitalists and therefore as enemies, especially the more prosperous farmers known in Russian as *kulaks* (Russian singular: KOO-lahk). Stalin's plan was to end private farming in the Soviet Union by forcing the peasants to give up their land and move onto "collective" farms. These farms, in theory, would be large cooperative organizations in which dozens or hundreds of peasant families pooled their land and tools and worked together. They were to make use of modern machinery that could not be used efficiently on small private farms.

The reality was much different. The collectives were tightly controlled by the Communist Party. Many peasants understandably wanted to keep their own farms and bitterly resisted collectivization. When faced with opposition, the Soviet government did not hesitate to use brutal armed force to compel collectivization. The following eyewitness account of what took place in one region of the country could have come from many other places as well:

> In 1930 . . . thousands of peasants armed with hunting rifles, axes, and pitchforks revolted against the regime. . . . NKVD [secret police] units and militia were sent. . . . For three days . . . a bloody battle was waged between the . . . people and the authorities. . . . This revolt was cruelly punished. Thousands of peasants, workers, soldiers, and officers paid for this attempt with their lives, while the survivors were deported to concentration camps. In the villages of Ternovka and Baganovka . . . mass executions were carried out. . . . The soil of this region was soaked in blood. After these executions, these villages were set on fire.[3]

The government won its collectivization war against the peasants, at the cost of millions of lives. But collectivization ultimately succeeded in one sense only: It gave the Soviet government control of the crops it needed to feed the growing number of factory workers in the cities and for export to buy necessary machinery. In every other sense it failed. Millions of kulaks and their families were sent to labor camps or deported to remote regions of the country to live under miserable conditions. At least 5 million peasants died during 1932–33 when large parts of the country were swept by famine after the regime seized all available food. One collective farm resident described the results:

And no matter what they did, they went on dying, dying, dying. They died everywhere—in yards or streetcars and on trains. There was no one to bury these victims of the Stalinist famine.[4]

Despite the famine, the government did nothing to provide the starving peasants with food, and, in fact, used the famine to break resistance to collectivization. Once the collective farm system was established, it proved to be extremely inefficient. Officially there were two types of farms. Collective farms in theory were owned by those who worked on them, and their workers were paid according to the farm's earnings. "State" farms were officially owned by the state and their workers were simply wage earners. In reality, there was little difference between the two types of farms, since both were tightly controlled by the Communist dictatorship. The peasants who worked the farms were badly paid and responded by working poorly. A huge government bureaucracy, based in Moscow, handed down piles of orders and instructions that made everything worse. Roads and storage facilities, essential for getting food from the fields to market, were never built. The peasants, whom many compared to the serfs of the czarist period, only managed to survive by raising fruits, vegetables, and small farm animals on tiny private plots of land they were allowed to keep for their own use. Food production actually decreased in the years immediately after collectivization and remained pitifully low during the Stalin years. The Soviet Union became and remained a country unable to provide its people with an adequate diet, until it collapsed in 1991.

The Soviet state was more successful in building modern industries, at least in terms of Stalin's primary goal of making Russia militarily equal to the advanced nations of the West. The cities and countryside were transformed by new iron and coal mines, steel mills and machine tool factories, and electric power plants and hydroelectric dams. Important new industries were built from scratch, such as the automobile, aviation, and chemical industries. By the end of the 1930s, heavy industry had increased by over 400 percent, and the Soviet Union was building some of the world's best modern weapons.

The price of this growth, however, was dreadfully high. With all resources being poured into heavy industry that could build weapons, little was left over for consumer products. Everything from housing to clothing was neglected as the Soviet Union's standard of living was allowed to plunge. Ordinary workers in factories and on farms were deprived of the most basic needs. And they were the lucky ones. Many of the new canals, factories, mines, and other projects of the 1930s were built by millions of prisoners from the largest network of forced labor camps in history. The forced laborers toiled in inhuman conditions and often literally were worked to death. The following description of conditions in a forestry camp indicate why millions of Soviet citizens did not survive Stalin's industrialization drive:

> We were forced to work in temperatures of −40 degrees [F]. Rain and snow storms were disregarded. We had to cut trees in forests even when the snow was waist deep. Falling trees hit the workers, who were unable to escape in the snow. In the summer . . . men had to stand knee deep in water or mud for 10 to 12 hours. . . . Influenza, bronchitis, pneumonia, tuberculosis . . . malaria, and other diseases decimated our ranks. . . . The men were compelled to work by force . . . camp authorities would force the prisoners to work by beating, kicking, dragging them by their feet through mud and snow, setting dogs on them, hitting them with rifle butts, and by threatening them with revolvers and bayonets.[5]

These policies did not dim the enthusiasm of party members and even many ordinary people who were convinced by the Soviet propaganda machine that they were building a new and better world. They fervently and blindly believed that the Communist Party and its leader, Joseph Stalin, knew what was best and were dedicated to the country's welfare. That helps explain why they never understood the nature of the murderous storm that crashed down upon them between 1934 and 1938 known as the Great Purge. The Great Purge was a firestorm of arrests that swept through both the party and the nation as a whole. At least 1 million people were shot outright and millions more shipped to labor camps, where death often came after months or years of brutal treatment. Those arrested, who ranged from virtually the entire Bolshevik leadership that had served with Lenin to loyal and hardworking nonparty citizens, were accused of fictitious crimes they had never committed. "Confessions" were beaten out of many of them, including a series of top former party leaders who were judged and condemned to death in three highly publicized show trials between 1936 and 1938. Stalin's great bloodletting decimated the ranks of the Communist Party, set back the country's economic development, and terrorized the entire nation.

Not since the time of Ivan the Terrible had Russia seen anything remotely similar to Stalin's Great Purge. The best explanation for Stalin's motives is that he used the purge to secure absolute power over the Communist Party and Soviet Union, which he lacked prior to 1934. By 1938, Stalin's status in the Soviet Union had been inflated by endless propaganda to little short of a living Communist god. At the same time, the Great Purge completed a process that had been under way since Lenin's time: building a totalitarian state. In a totalitarian state, a one-party dictatorship makes use of modern technology to exercise an unprecedented control over society. People's lives are regulated far more than in traditional dictatorships by a huge government bureaucracy backed by the power of a secret police. During the 1930s, totalitarianism developed most completely in Nazi Germany and Soviet Russia, the former representing the Fascist variety and the latter the Communist variety.

World War II, which began in Europe when Germany invaded Poland in September 1939, eventually brought those two totalitarian powers face to face on the battlefield. For the first two years, from 1939 until 1941, the Soviet Union managed to stay out of the war, thanks to Stalin's policy of cooperating with Hitler. In August 1939, Stalin agreed to a nonaggression pact with Hitler in which the two powers in effect agreed to divide eastern Europe between them. The Nazi-Soviet Pact allowed Hitler to wage war against the nations of western and central Europe without having to worry about a Soviet response from the east. That pact, meanwhile, allowed the Soviets to seize the eastern part of Poland in 1939 and to annex the Baltic states of Lithuania, Latvia, and Estonia in 1940.

In June 1941, however, Hitler double-crossed Stalin and invaded the Soviet Union. The Soviet armed forces, weakened by the Stalin's purges, were caught off guard and routed. German forces advanced deep into Soviet territory, reaching the outskirts of both Leningrad and Moscow. Despite Stalin's blunders that had cost the country so dearly, the people rallied behind him against the German enemy. In four years of desperate fighting, at least 20 million Soviet citizens died in a struggle for national survival. From the suburbs of Moscow, the approaches to Leningrad, and rubble-strewn Stalingrad, Soviet forces at first stood their ground and then fought their way westward to Berlin, where the last vicious battle of the savage Nazi/Soviet struggle was fought in the spring of 1945. Stalin took most of the credit for the victory, although his personal military incompetence and the continued oppressiveness of his regime cost the Soviet Union millions of lives. Victory, instead, belongs to the Soviet people, who between 1941 and 1945 endured both Nazism and Soviet communism and somehow managed to survive. The heroism of the people, whether soldiers or civilians, in the face of seemingly impossible odds and unspeakable suffering, lent new truth to the old saying, "Only the Russians can conquer Russia."

Victory in World War II added to the Soviet Union's international power. Soviet armies occupied most of eastern Europe after they drove the Germans out, and Stalin used that opportunity to set up puppet Communist regimes in most of the region. The process began in Poland even before the war was over, and within a few years extended to Hungary, Romania, Bulgaria, Czechoslovakia, and East Germany. Meanwhile, Communist forces seized power in Yugoslavia and Albania, although the former broke with the Soviet Union in 1948 and the latter in 1961. Never before had Moscow's power extended so far into Europe. This expansion of Soviet power in the wake of World War II quickly exacted its price. It alarmed the United States and its Western European allies and set the stage for the Cold War, which for 45 years drained the strength and resources of both the Soviets and the Americans. Europe was divided into two military camps, the American-led North Atlantic Treaty Organization (NATO) and the Soviet-dominated Warsaw Pact.

At home, the postwar Stalin years brought only more hardship for the Soviet people. Several waves of terror, although smaller than the Great Purge, again swept the country, including one in which Stalin singled out the Soviet Union's Jewish community for special persecution. Stalin's slave labor camps, known as the Gulag, remained filled to the brim. Once again, all resources were poured into heavy industry and to the budding nuclear arms race with the United States. When Stalin finally died in 1953, he left behind a country with enormous military power and a people exhausted and drained by 25 years of turmoil and terror. The death toll from collectivization, the 1932–33 famine, various purges, and other policies stood at no less than 20 million. To Stalin's successors fell the job of restoring a battered society to health and fulfilling some of the unkept promises of a better life continually made since 1917.

Khrushchev and Reform

The struggle to succeed Stalin was won by Nikita Khrushchev (krooh-SHOFF), a peasant-born, barrel-shaped, semieducated lieutenant of the dead dictator. Khrushchev had been a candidate who at first was not taken seriously by several seemingly more powerful and better-placed rivals. Once in power, little originality was expected of this rather crude, homespun former mechanic. And once again, as during the post-Stalin struggle for power, those who dismissed Khrushchev as a nonentity badly underestimated him.

Khrushchev faced enormous problems as he grasped the reins of power. There was a general but vague recognition among the party leadership that reforms were needed in Soviet life. Stalin's successors were determined that never again could one man become as powerful as the dictator they had all served and feared. They knew that Stalin's terroristic policies, which had left them as vulnerable to sudden arrest as any Soviet citizen, had to be ended. The party leaders also realized that it was vital to raise the miserably low Soviet standard of living, which made a mockery out of Marxist promises of a life of abundance under socialism and potentially threatened their rule.

Beyond those general principles, however, there was little consensus and often bitter disagreement. As a result, only one significant reform was achieved during the first three years after Stalin's death. In 1953, as the struggle for power was taking shape, the secret police, which had served Stalin's will, was brought under the control of the party leadership as a whole. This was a crucial step in assuring that no man would become an all-powerful dictator and that whoever emerged as number one would require the support of other top party leaders to stay in power. Khrushchev realized that this was not nearly enough. He also knew that in order to undertake major reforms, Stalin's reputation, which justified the status quo, had to be challenged. Khrushchev's place in history stems from his willingness to face those issues directly and to act on them, often in the face of strong resistence from his colleagues.

Khrushchev's challenge to the Stalin myth came in 1956. On the night of February 24–25, Khrushchev delivered a four and one-half hour speech to a closed session of the Communist Party's 20th Congress. His supposedly "Secret Speech," whose contents soon were known in the West, came as a shock to the several thousand party loyalists who heard it. They heard Khrushchev denounce Stalin as a cruel dictator who had murdered innocent party members, blundered in World War II, and glorified himself at the expense of others. Of course, Khrushchev left out as much as he put in. He said nothing about collectivization, Stalin's millions of nonparty purge victims, or about the henchmen, like himself, who had done Stalin's bidding. Still, what he said was enough to shatter the myth of Stalin and leave his audience stunned. As Khrushchev put it, "It was so quiet in the huge hall you could hear a fly buzzing."[6]

After his speech, Khrushchev launched a series of reforms that together are called "destalinization." They ranged from freeing over 8 million people from the Gulag during 1956 and 1957, to permitting greater cultural freedom than in the past and diverting resources to raise the country's standard of living. Khrushchev also tried to improve relations with the West, which had reached a postwar low point during the Korean War when American, South Korean, and other allied soldiers battled North Korean and Communist Chinese forces between 1950 and 1953.

Khrushchev had his successes and undeniably made life much better for the average Soviet citizen. Nothing he did was more important than ending Stalin's terror, which gave Soviet citizens security as long as they stayed within the strict limits set by the Communist Party. He also dramatically increased housing construction in order to lessen the country's housing crisis, which he considered scandalous:

> Young couples . . . couldn't even find a place . . . in a dormitory. Isn't that awful? . . . How could we expect Soviet man, who'd given his all for the future of socialism and the ultimate victory of Communism, to live in a beehive.[7]

At the same time, Khrushchev increased investments in agriculture and launched a massive project to grow grain in the previously uncultivated grasslands of Central Asia. These programs increased food production considerably, although they did little to make collectivized agriculture more productive. Other Khrushchev programs reduced taxes for low-income workers, provided some social services for peasants, and abolished tuitions for secondary and higher education to open opportunities for poorer children. To help pay for these programs, Khrushchev tried to hold down military spending.

Khrushchev's support for science helped the Soviet Union score several spectacular firsts in space, including launching the first artificial satellite in 1957 and putting the first man in orbit in 1961. Increased cultural freedom lifted the pall of darkness that had covered the country in gloom and conformity during the Stalin era. Among the important works Khrushchev permitted to be published were Aleksandr Solzhenitsyn's (sohl-zhen-NEET-sihn) *One Day in the Life of Ivan Denisovich,* a stunning exposé of conditions in Stalin's labor camps.

However, Khrushchev's reform program was plagued with trouble from the start. The most important obstacle he faced was opposition from other party leaders, who feared that reform could run out of control and threaten their power. In 1957, Khrushchev barely defeated an attempt by several of his rivals to remove him from power. Thereafter, continued opposition frequently forced him to retreat from his reform policies, which not only damaged his programs but undermined his power. Khrushchev had a bad habit of rushing ahead with poorly thought-out projects. For example, plowing up millions of acres in semiarid Central Asia eventually produced disappointing harvests and later massive and destructive dust storms when the rains did not arrive. In foreign policy, Khrushchev undermined his effort to improve relations with the West with rash attempts to make gains at the expense of the United States. His worst error, the placing of nuclear missiles in Cuba, led to the Cuban missile crisis of 1962. When the United States placed a blockade around Cuba and demanded the Soviets remove their missiles, Khrushchev was forced into a humiliating retreat that undermined his power at home. All of these problems finally brought Khrushchev down. Not only his rivals, but many of his supporters secretly plotted against him and removed him from office in October 1964. Ironically, even his removal from office was a reform, as Khrushchev, himself, pointed out when he arrived home the day of his final defeat:

> Well, that's it. I'm retired now. Perhaps the most important thing I did was just this—that they were able to get rid of me simply by voting, whereas Stalin would have had them all arrested.[8]

Brezhnev and the Status Quo

The coup against Khrushchev was led by Leonid Brezhnev (BREZH-nehv), one of the party leaders who turned against their former boss. Brezhnev reached and remained in power because he served the interests of the top party leadership whose main concern was stability and security. This meant ending all policies that threatened their power and privilege, including allowing intellectuals and artists too much freedom, tampering with far-reaching economic reforms, or restricting military spending. It also meant continuing to raise the Soviet standard of living, because only by using Stalin's methods could Soviet citizens be made to give up the expectations of a better life. Finally, the Brezhnev government was determined to make the Soviet Union immune from any foreign threats, particularly the threat of a nuclear attack by the United States. This led to two contradictory policies: an attempt to improve relations with the United States and a military buildup that raised the nuclear arms race to dangerous new levels.

On the surface, the Brezhnev regime had a long list of successes. Increased investments in agriculture and factories producing consumer goods noticably improved the lives of millions of citizens during the 1960s and early 1970s. For example, food production during the 1970s was double that of the 1950s, and appliances, such as televisions and refrigerators, became common fixtures in Soviet homes. Constant pressure on intellectuals did not silence all protest, but it kept dissent at manageable levels. Dissatisfaction on the part of non-Russian minorities required some strategic concessions, such as allowing several hundred thousand Jews and ethnic Germans to emigrate from the Soviet Union. But, overall, the lid was kept on ethnic protest. A massive military buildup made the Soviet Union approximately equal to the United States as a nuclear power by the late 1960s. Until the late 1970s, this buildup did not get in the way of improved relations with the United States and the signing of the world's first nuclear arms control agreement in 1972. The United States and its allies also officially accepted the boundaries in Eastern Europe that Stalin had drawn after World War II, a concession the Soviet Union had long sought. Nor did the United States react forcefully when the Soviet Union invaded its neighbor Afghanistan in 1979, a move that at the time seemed to represent a new and dangerous extension of Soviet power.

But this veneer of power overlay a deepening rot that was eating away at the Soviet Union. The need to reform the highly centralized Soviet economy already was clear in the early 1950s. As the Soviet economy grew and became more complex, central planners in Moscow could not efficiently distribute resources, decide what to produce, insure high quality, or introduce modern technology. Any increases in production came from increased investments, not from increased efficiency based on new methods and technology, as continually occurred in the West. By the early 1970s, Soviet economic growth was slowing noticeably. At the same time, the Soviet standard of living fell further behind that of the industrialized capitalist countries.

Another major untreated problem plaguing the country was runaway corruption at all levels of Soviet life. Endless shortages created an enormous black market that undermined both the official economy and respect for law. Officials, not responsible to the people they ruled, used their offices for personal benefit. High Communist Party officials lived far better than the rest of the population in clear violation of official socialist principles that stressed equality. This gave rise to resentment and cynicism, as expressed in the popular saying, "We have Communism, but not for everybody." Meanwhile, frustration and despair gave rise to rampant alcohol abuse and other severe social problems. In foreign affairs, the continued Soviet military buildup of nonnuclear arms frightened many countries, including China and the United States. This, combined with the Soviet invasion of Afghanistan and aggressive Soviet policies elsewhere in the world, soured Soviet-American relations, which reached a post-Stalin era low in the early 1980s. At the same time, the military buildup drained resources from civilian needs, while the war in Afghanistan went badly and led to demoralization and drug abuse in the Soviet army.

Brezhnev did not respond to these urgent problems. As he aged and became noticeably infirm in the late 1970s, his government, largely staffed by elderly bureaucrats, became increasingly incompetent and corrupt. Failure to reform had led to paralysis. Brezhnev finally died in 1982 after 18 years in office. He was succeeded by two equally sick and elderly men: Yuri Andropov (ahn-DROH-pof), who survived for 15 months, and Konstantin Chernenko (chuhr-NEN-koh), who died after only 13 months at the helm. The new Soviet leader selected in March of 1985 was, at last, a younger and energetic man: Mikhail Gorbachev (gohr-bah-CHOFF). His rise to power began the last phase in the history of Soviet Russia. For six exciting years, hope, drama, success, and failure swirled together in a whirlwind that at first seemed to lift the country out of its doldrums but, instead, eventually tore it apart.

Gorbachev: Restructuring and Collapse

Mikhail Gorbachev knew he had an enormous task facing him when he became the leader of the Soviet Union in March 1985. As he said several years later, after the Soviet Union had collapsed:

> When I found myself at the helm of this state it was clear that something was wrong in this country. . . . We were living much worse than people in the industrialized countries were living and we were increasingly lagging behind them. The reason was obvious even then. This country was suffocating in the shackles of the bureaucratic command system. Doomed to cater to ideology, and suffer and carry out the onerous burden of the arms race, it found itself at the breaking point.[9]

Gorbachev did not come into office with a comprehensive, carefully thought-out plan. His general goal was to make major reforms in the Soviet system. In particular, he was convinced that the Soviet Union's economy had to be overhauled in order to match the living standards and the military power of the West.

In part, because he had no specific program, Gorbachev had to improvise as he went along. He and his supporters had to make adjustments as they discovered that the Soviet Union's problems, which had been covered up for years, were far worse than they had expected. Gorbachev also found out that in order to make economic reforms he had to make political and social reforms as well. Another problem he faced was opposition to his reforms from powerful forces within the Communist Party. At times the conservative opposition forced Gorbachev to retreat, while sometimes he responded to his critics by taking bold steps to outflank or outmaneuver them.

Mikhail Gorbachev, the last Soviet leader, whose reform policies led to the end of the Cold War but nonetheless ultimately failed to rebuild the Soviet Union and contributed to its collapse.

Gorbachev also had to change and adjust his objectives as reforms he initiated began to run out of control. This happened in part because once the Soviet people received a small measure of freedom, they quickly demanded more. The pace of change also accelerated when certain reforms, such as those that weakened the grip of the Communist Party on the economy, undermined the very socialist system Gorbachev was trying to strengthen. Eventually, the forces of change grew so strong that Gorbachev was powerless to stop them. In 1991, six years after Gorbachev came to power to save the Soviet system, those forces ended up driving him from office and destroying the system he had intended to save.

Gorbachev's overall program for reform was called *perestroika* (peh-ruh-STROY-kuh), which means "restructuring." The term originally referred to the economy, but soon perestroika extended to most areas of Soviet life. Over time, three other policies became intertwined with perestroika and became essential to carrying it out. One was *glasnost,* or "openness." It began when reduced censorship allowed the Soviet people more truthful information about their country and the rest of the world. Books, plays, and films that had been banned for years became available. The news became more accurate. The official Communist Party version of history began to be challenged by Soviet intellectuals. However, a little glimpse of glasnost quickly led to demands to have the door to information fully opened, something Gorbachev had not intended but found himself unable to prevent.

A second policy was called *demokratizatsia* (day-moh-KRAH-tee-zah-tsee-ah). The term meant "democratization," rather than democracy. In other words, Gorbachev wanted to involve most common the Soviet people in *some* decisions, but leave the Communist Party in overall control of society. Demokratizatsia was designed to help Gorbachev overcome opposition to his reforms within the Communist Party. But as with glasnost, demokratizatsia soon took on a life of its own and grew too strong for Gorbachev to control.

Finally, Gorbachev applied what he called *novoye myshlenie* (NOH-voh-yeh mish-LEN-nee-yeh), or "new thinking" to foreign affairs. Since its founding in 1917, Soviet foreign policy had been based on the idea of inevitable conflict with the capitalist West. Under Lenin and Stalin, the assumption was that this would lead to war. Khrushchev, who lived in a nuclear world, rejected the idea of an inevitable war with the West; instead there would be "peaceful coexistence" and the competition would be economic and political. Under Gorbachev's new thinking, the idea of competition was rejected entirely. Traditional Soviet policies had contributed to a nuclear arms race with the United States and its allies. That arms race not only threatened the Soviet Union with destruction, it had become unaffordable and was denying Gorbachev the resources he needed for perestroika to rebuild the Soviet economy. Of course, Gorbachev's new thinking did not just benefit the Soviet Union. By 1990, it had helped end the Cold War, which for over four decades had held the entire world under the threat of nuclear destruction.

Gorbachev gradually began his reforms during 1985 and 1986. There was a glimmer of glasnost, such as the performances of several plays that openly discussed corruption in Soviet life. There also was a steady campaign to remove Brezhnev supporters from top party positions. Supporters of reform were promoted, including Eduard Shevardnadze (sheh-vahrd-NAHD-zuh), who became the Soviet Union's new foreign minister. Then, on April 26, 1986, disaster struck. The Chernobyl (cher-NOH-bihl) nuclear power plant in the Ukraine exploded. Tons of radioactive poisons spewed into the air and were carried by the wind across Ukraine and Belarus and westward into Europe. After at first trying to minimize the disaster, Gorbachev responded to international pressure and told the Soviet Union and the world what had really happened. The Chernobyl disaster then spurred the Soviet leader to increase the pace of reform. As Shevardnadze put it, "Chernobyl Day tore the blindfold from our eyes and persuaded us that politics and morals could not diverge."[10]

By 1987, Gorbachev had broken the power of the Brezhnev-era leadership. During the middle of the year, the government announced far-reaching economic reforms designed to reduce Communist Party control of the economy. But Gorbachev's reforms had created a new opposition: party leaders who originally had stood for change but now feared that Gorbachev was going too far. They were led by Yegor Ligachev, one of the most powerful party leaders. On the other hand, Gorbachev was under pressure to go farther and faster. Much of that pressure came from the Soviet Union's intelligentsia: its scientists, scholars, and cultural figures. One party leader urging a faster pace of reform was Boris Yeltsin, the head of the Communist Party's Moscow organization. In October 1987, Yeltsin publicly criticized Gorbachev for going too slowly; for doing so, Yeltsin lost his job as Moscow party leader.

Despite Yeltsin's demotion, the pace of change accelerated during 1988. Gorbachev pushed the last of the Brezhnev-era conservatives aside. Glasnost expanded to include the publication of 6,000 formerly banned books and the showing of over 100 formerly banned films. In 1989, for the first time since 1917, the Soviet Union held an election in which there was a choice of candidates. Under a complicated system that was not entirely free, but still radically different from anything permitted before, Soviet citizens elected a new 2,250-member parliament called the Congress of People's Deputies. Among those elected to the Congress was Boris Yeltsin, who began what would become a stunning political comeback.

Nowhere were Gorbachev's policies more important than in foreign affairs. In December 1987, Gorbachev and U.S. President Ronald Reagan signed an arms control agreement. The agreement eliminated all U.S. and Soviet intermediate-range nuclear missiles based in Europe. For the first time since the Cold War began in 1945, the number of nuclear weapons in the world actually was reduced. In 1989, Gorbachev refused to intervene when communism collapsed in Eastern Europe. The end of communism in Eastern Europe set the stage for the end of the Cold War, which officially was declared over in November 1990.

However, despite his triumphs abroad, it turned out that Gorbachev and his fellow reformers were unable to restructure the Soviet Union. The Soviet system turned out to be too deeply flawed to be saved. Two problems that proved impossible to solve were overhauling the economy—the central goal of perestroika—and managing the non-Russian nationalities of the Soviet Union. The basic economic problem was that the old Soviet economy disintegrated faster than a new economy could be built to replace it. The result was falling production and widespread economic hardship. Meanwhile, several minority nationalities began agitating for greater freedom from Moscow. Those demands gradually escalated until some of them grew into calls for complete independence. By 1991, the Soviet Union was staggering under the weight of economic crisis, political chaos, and ethnic turmoil.

The final blow to the Soviet Union came from an unexpected place in August 1991: opponents of Gorbachev's reforms who attempted to overthrow him. The plotters succeeding in placing Gorbachev under house arrest, but in little else. Their coup was poorly planned. They failed to arrest Boris Yeltsin, who by then was president of the Russian republic within the Soviet Union, and other reformers. Yeltsin was eating breakfast at his country residence near Moscow when he heard what was happening. After meeting with supporters, Yeltsin left for Moscow. As he got into his car, his daughter gave him a short but amazingly cogent summary of what he had to do and the situation he faced: "Papa, keep calm. Everything depends on you."[11]

Once in Moscow, Yeltsin became the focal point of resistance to the coup, as hundreds of thousands of Soviet citizens took to the streets to oppose the coup. He made his headquarters at the "White House," the building that housed the Russian parliament. At noon on the first day of the coup, Yeltsin emerged from the White House and climbed on top of a T-72 tank. In a clear, booming voice he spoke to the country:

> Citizens of Russia. . . . The legally elected president of the country has been removed from power. . . . We are dealing with a right-wing, reactionary, anti-constitutional coup d'etat. . . . Accordingly, we proclaim all decisions of this committee to be illegal. . . . We appeal to the citizens of Russia to give an appropriate rebuff to the putschists and demand a return of the country to normal constitutional development.[12]

The coup collapsed after three days and Gorbachev was restored to office. But the chaos of the last several years and the coup itself had destroyed Gorbachev's hold on the Soviet people. One by one, the non-Russian Soviet republics declared their independence. Gorbachev was powerless to stop them. On December 8, 1991, Boris Yeltsin, representing Russia, and leaders from Ukraine and Belarus announced the formation of an organization they called the Commonwealth of Independent States (CIS). The CIS was to replace the Soviet Union and be a loose organization of independent nations. On December 21, eight other republics joined the CIS.

All that remained was to declare the Soviet Union dead. That job fell to Gorbachev. On December 25, 1991, he resigned as president of the USSR. The country's official end came on December 31. As of January 1, 1992, in its place were 15 independent states—the former Soviet republics that had made up the USSR—including Russia. A new era in Russian history, the post-Soviet period brimming with hope but filled with danger, had begun.

NOTES

1. Quoted in Michael Kort, *The Soviet Colossus: A History of the USSR* (New York: Charles Scribner's Sons, 1985), p. 110.
2. William Henry Chamberlin, *The Russian Revolution,* vol. II (New York: Grosset & Dunlap, 1965), p. 345.
3. Victor Kravchenko, *I Chose Justice* (New York: Scribners, 1950), pp. 99–100.
4. Fedor Belov, *The History of a Collective Farm* (New York: Praeger, 1955), pp. 13–14.
5. David J. Dallin and Boris I. Nicolaevsky, *Forced Labor in Soviet Russia* (New Haven: Yale University Press, 1947), pp. 42–43.
6. Nikita Khrushchev, *Khrushchev Remembers,* Introduction, Commentary, and Notes by Edward Crankshaw, ed., and trans. Strobe Talbott (New York: Bantam Books, 1971), p. 382.
7. Nikita Khrushchev, *Khrushchev Remembers: The Last Testament,* Foreword by Edward Crankshaw, Introduction by Jerrold L. Schecter, trans. Strobe Talbott (Boston and Toronto: Little Brown, 1974), p. 87.
8. Quoted in Roy Medvedev, *Khrushchev: A Biography,* trans. Brian Pearce (Garden City, N.Y.: Anchor Books, 1984), p. 245.
9. Quoted in the *New York Times,* December 26, 1991.
10. Eduard Shevardnadze, *The Future Belongs to Freedom* (New York: The Free Press, 1991), pp. 175–176.
11. Quoted in David Remnick, *Lenin's Tomb: The Last Days of the Soviet Empire* (New York: Random House, 1993), p. 463.
12. Quoted in ibid., p. 466.

4

Russian Culture

*R*ussia has a rich cultural heritage that dates back over 1,000 years. In the course of their turbulent history, the Russian people have demonstrated enormous creativity in literature, music, dance, art, theater, and film. Today the poems of Aleksandr Pushkin, the novels of Leo Tolstoy and Fyodor Dostoyevsky (duh-stuh-YEV-skee), the music of Peter Tchaikovsky (chai-KOFF-skee), the plays of Anton Chekhov, and artistic works by dozens of other Russians inspire and thrill people all over the world.

Literature

The roots of Russian literature reach back to an oral folklore tradition of songs, poems, and tales dating from before the Kievian era (ninth to 13th centuries), prior to the division of the East Slavs into its Russian, Ukrainian, and Belarusian branches. The most important songs and poems were epics called *byliny* (bee-LEE-nee) that were recited by traveling bards. They generally told of heroes, battling the enemies of Russian on the vast and dangerous steppe, and have been compared to the epics of ancient Greece.

The first works of Russia's written literary tradition date from Kiev's conversion to Christianity in the 10th century. The bulk of this early literature reflects this religious link. It is made up of sermons, hymns, and other works that tell of the lives of church saints. However, churchmen also wrote a number of chronicles, which focused more on secular history than on religion. The most important of these, *The Primary Russian Chronicle*, was composed in the early 12th century. A blend of songs, biographies, and historical and legendary events, it is the best available source of Russian history between 800 and the early 1100s.

The most dramatic and most beautiful work of the Kievian era is *The Tale of the Host of Igor*, written late in the 12th century. Using both verse and poetry, this magnificent epic tells of a disastrous defeat suffered by Russian forces in 1185 at the hands of steppe nomads:

> The grass wilts because of the sorrow
> And the tree bends down because of grief!
> Brothers, a sad time has descended!
> A wilderness has covered our strength.[1]

During the centuries after the Mongol conquest, Russian literature was less creative than during the Kievian era. Not until the 18th century were seeds planted that led to the great flowering of modern Russian literature in the 19th century. It was during the 18th century that Mikhail Lomonosov (lah-mah-NOHS-of) (1711–65) produced the first Russian grammar, while Nikolai Karamzin (kah-rahm-ZIHN) (1766–1826) wrote the first Russian language novel.

The appearance of the major works of Aleksandr Pushkin (1799–1837) marked the beginning of what is called the golden age of Russian literature. Pushkin wrote brilliant plays and prose, but he is most revered as Russia's greatest poet. His poems *The Bronze Horseman* and *Eugene Onegin* are among the classics of world literature. In *The Bronze Horseman* Pushkin captured one of the most enduring tragic themes in Russian history: the conflict between Russia's rulers and the ordinary people who so often have become their victims. Pushkin's own life was a symbol of the tragedy and violence that have scarred his country's history. He was killed in a duel when only 37 years old. Ironically and eerily, Pushkin seemed to predict his own death in *Eugene Onegin:*

> The poet in the very dawn
> Of life has perished like a flower
> That by a sudden storm was drenched:
> Alas! the altar-fire is quenched.[2]

The two other outstanding writers of the first half of the 19th century were Mikhail Lermontov (1814–41) and Nikolai Gogol (1809–52). Lermontov was both a poet and novelist. It was a reflection of the oppressiveness

Fyodor Dostoyevsky, one of the two giants of 19th-century Russian literature.

of Russian life that Lermontov's greatest poem, "A Demon," was not published during his lifetime because of government censorship. Gogol, who was of Ukrainian birth but wrote in Russian, is best known for his novel *Dead Souls* and his play *The Inspector General*.

The giants of the Russian novel who brought the golden age of Russian literature to its glorious apex were Fyodor Dostoyevsky (1821–81) and Leo Tolstoy (1828–1910). Both of these literary geniuses wrote several novels that rank with the greatest in the world. Dostoyevsky was the master of the psychological novel. In *Crime and Punishment* he created one of literature's classic tormented criminals in the poverty-stricken student Raskolnikov. In *The Brothers Karamazov*, he brilliantly explored the themes of sin and redemption, power and principle, and faith and immorality. Tolstoy's major novels were *Anna Karenina* and *War and Peace*. *Anna Karenina* is one of literature's classic examinations of hypocrisy in society and the issue of human suffering. *War and Peace*, set during Napoleon's invasion of Russia, is Russia's greatest historical novel and one of the most acclaimed novels in any language. One of its many themes is that ordinary people, rather than would-be heroes like Napoleon, are decisive in history.

Russia's outstanding playwright and short story writer was Anton Chekhov (1860–1904). Chekhov was a pessimist and unflinching realist with a deep sympathy for the people he wrote about. His plays *The Seagull, Uncle Vanya,* and *The Cherry Orchard* still are performed to the acclaim of audiences around the world. Nor has he been surpassed as a craftsman of the short story.

The golden age of Russian literature ended with the last of Tolstoy's major works. However, in the late 19th and early 20th centuries, Russian culture enjoyed a remarkable "silver age." During the early 20th century, Russia produced outstanding writers such as Andrei Bely (BEH-lee) (1880–1934), Aleksandr Blok (1880–1921), and Maxim Gorky (1868–1936). Two outstanding poets whose lives spanned both the czarist and Soviet eras were Osip Mandelstam (MAHN-duhl-shtahm) (1891–1938) and Anna Akhmatova (akh-MAH-tuh-vuh) (1889–1966). Like so many other Soviet writers and intellectuals, both of them suffered terribly during the Soviet era. Mandelstam died in a Soviet labor camp.

Akhmatova saw both her husband and son imprisoned under Stalin and was herself brutally denounced in public. However, she survived

Alexandr Solzhenitsyn, shortly after he was forcibly deported from the Soviet Union in 1974.

Stalin, and one of her most famous poems, *Requiem,* deals with the suffering of the Russian people under Stalin and during World War II.

The giant of 20th century Russian novelists remains Aleksandr Solzhenitsyn (1918–), the 1970 winner of the Nobel Prize for literature. His short first book, *One Day in the Life of Ivan Denisovich,* portrayed the horrors of Stalin's labor camps. Solzhenitsyn was allowed to publish the book in the Soviet Union during the reformist Khrushchev years. However, his masterpieces—*The First Circle* and *Cancer Ward*—had to be smuggled to the West for publication during the Brezhnev era. Solzhenitsyn, who did not flinch from openly defying the Soviet regime, also secretly wrote and published in the West *The Gulag Archipelago,* a massive multivolume chronicle of the Soviet labor and concentration camp system. In 1974, the Soviet government forcibly deported Solzhenitsyn. After a long exile in the United States, Solzhenitsyn returned to Russia in 1994, three years after the collapse of the Soviet regime he so steadfastly resisted.

Music

Early Russian music was either folk music or church music. Modern Russian classical music began with Mikhail Glinka (GLING-kah) (1804–57), who often based his compositions on old folk themes and melodies. Peter Tchaikovsky (1840–93) was the towering giant of 19th-century Russian music. He earned an international reputation unmatched by other Russian composers. Tchaikovsky's lush and romantic operas, ballets, and symphonies are still admired worldwide, and he remains his country's most famous composer. Another legend of the era was Feodor Chaliapin (sha-LYAH-pihn) (1873–1938), whose magnificent bass voice and dramatic genius made him one of the world's most celebrated opera performers.

Sergei Rachmaninoff (rakh-MAHN-uh-noff) (1873–1943) and Igor Stravinsky (struh-VINH-skee) (1882–1971) were among many distinguished composers whose careers extended from the late 19th into the 20th centuries. However, after the fall of czarism, both men left their native land and settled in the West.

The best-known Russian composers of the Soviet era were Sergei Prokofiev (pruh-KOFF-yef) (1891–1953) and Dmitri Shostakovich (shahs-tuh-KOH-vich) (1906–75). Both endured harassment from Soviet authorities during their careers when they wrote music that did not meet with Communist Party approval. Cellist and conductor Mstislav Rostropovich (rahs-truh-POH-vich) (1927–) was one of many Soviet-era musicians who gained international fame. He also came into conflict with Brezhnev-era Communist authorities for supporting people in the Soviet Union who demanded democratic reforms during the Brezhnev years, including his friend Aleksandr Solzhenitsyn. In 1978, Rostropovich was stripped of his Soviet citizenship and became a resident of the United States. In 1993, he returned in triumph to his native land, where a crowd of 100,000 gathered in Moscow's Red Square to hear him conduct a free concert. As he toured Russia, Rostropovich introduced the Russian people to a talented young pianist: Ignat Solzhenitsyn, the son of the great writer. Rostropovich's message was not simply cultural; it was one of hope for a troubled country. In making that point, the great musician highlighted the importance of Russia's musical tradition to its people:

> Why is there a concert in Red Square? I want people to feel proud that they are Russian. People need to be given a chance to be proud of themselves.
>
> Russians need to be reminded at times like these that they're a great people. Events disrupt things a little sometimes, but listening to this music is a reminder that there's a great nation here.[3]

Dance

Among the many varieties of dancing in the world, it is ballet that the Russians have made their own. Ballet has a 270-year history in Russia. By the late 19th century, Russian ballet equaled any in the world. Tchaikovsky wrote the musical scores for three famous ballets—*Swan Lake, The Sleeping Beauty,* and *The Nutcracker*—whose popularity remain undiminished after more than a century. Vaslav Nijinsky (nuh-ZHIHN-skee) (1890–1950) and Anna Pavlova (PAV-luh-vuh) (1881–1931) were among the most brilliant ballet dancers of their day. During the Soviet era, the Bolshoi and Kirov ballet companies, respectively based in Moscow and Leningrad, were among the world's elite companies. However, because they were denied artistic freedom, several of Russia's most distinguished ballet dancers defected to the West. Among them were Rudolf Nureyev (nuh-RAY-yef), Natalia Makarova (mah-KAH-roh-vuh), and Mikhail Baryshnikov (bah-RISH-nih-kawf).

Theater and Film

As with literature, the 19th century marked the grand flowering of Russian theater. Works by Chekhov, Gogol, and other playwrights drew large and enthusiastic audiences. During the 1890s, the Moscow Art Theater under the director Constantin Stanislavsky (1863–1938) became a major force in Russian theater. In 1902, it staged Maxim Gorky's play *The Lower Depths,* a scathing exposé of life among Russia's poor. Stanislavsky believed in realism in the theater and developed a system of acting that had great influence both in Russia and the West. After the Bolshevik Revolution, many talented artists left the Soviet Union. One of those who stayed behind to serve the revolution with his art was Vsevolod Meyerhold (MY-er-hold) (1874–1940). During the 1920s, he pioneered experimental techniques, including reducing the barriers between actors and their audience. However, in the end, Meyerhold, like so many other artists, fell victim to Stalin's murderous repression. His theater was closed down in 1938, and he disappeared after his arrest in 1939.

The outstanding theatrical director of the post-Stalin period of the Soviet era was Yuri Lyubimov (lee-OO-bihm-off) (1917–), whose base was the Taganka Theater in Moscow. In 1977, Lyubimov dramatized a book called *The Master and Margarita* by Mikhail Bulgakov (buhl-GAH-koff) (1891–1940). The book, which was banned in the Soviet Union for three decades, poked fun at Soviet life. Lyubimov continued to innovate and shock Soviet audiences and officials until he was denied the right to return home while on a foreign trip in 1984.

The greatest Russian film director, an artist who ranks among the most creative directors during the early years of film making, was Sergei Eisenstein (EYE-zuhn-stine) (1898–1948). Two films he made in the 1920s—*Potemkin* and *Ten Days That Shook the World*—brilliantly portray the idealism that inspired the Bolshevik Revolution. Later Eisenstein ran afoul of Stalin and was forced to denounce one of his most creative achievements, *Ivan the Terrible,* as "worthless and vicious." Eisenstein endured brutal public criticism and died a broken man.

Painting and Sculpture

Russia's earliest painters created frescoes and mosaics to decorate the country's Orthodox churches, using techniques they learned from the Byzantine Empire. Another technique learned from the Byzantines was the painting of icons. Icons are pictures with religious themes that are painted on wood. The Russians developed their own styles for painting icons, relying on deep, natural-looking colors. Andrei Rublev (ROO-blef) (c. 1360–1420), Russia's outstanding icon painter, is credited with establishing an authentic Russian icon style in the late 14th and early 15th centuries.

Russian painters began turning to secular subjects in the 17th century. As time went on, especially after the reign of Peter the Great, they were influenced by Western styles. During the second half of the 19th century, the realist school of painting dominated Russian art. Its most famous practitioner was Ilya Repin (RYAY-pihn) (1844–1930). Repin tried to portray the suffering of ordinary people. His painting *Volga Boatmen* was typical of his work; it showed the brutal backbreaking conditions of the men who dragged barges upriver against the current of the mighty Volga. A younger painter who emerged from the realist school was Isaac Levitan (1860–1900), Russia's greatest landscape painter.

By the 1890s, Russians were well represented among the various schools of modern art popular in the West. Among the best known innovative Russian modern artists were Wassily Kandinsky (kan-DIHN-skee) (1866–1944), Constantin Korovin (koh-ROH-vihn) (1861–1939), and Casimir Malevich (mah-LAY-vich) (1878–1935).

Russian painting, like all Russian art, suffered dreadfully during the Stalin era. Painters were expected to conform to a doctrine called socialist realism, which in practice meant glorifying Stalin and soviet-style social-ism. Socialist realist paintings were dull and lifeless, much like the "art" used to glorify Nazi Germany. Not until the 1980s was Russian painting able to free itself completely from the straitjacket of Soviet political control.

Architecture

Architecture has been a medium of expressing Russia's cultural heritage since Kievian times. Among the first things people picture when they think of Russian architecture are the distinctive onion-shaped domes of Russian churches. These domes are the Russian variation of rounder domes built by the Byzantines, from whom the Russians first learned their architecture. Over time, however, architects during the Kievian era adapted Byzantine designs to Russian conditions. Russians built their churches with steeper roofs and smaller windows, to stand up to their harsh northern climate. Russian domes became more pointed in order to shed snow more efficiently; in other words, they became onion-shaped. The Church of St.

George, built during the 12th century in the city of Novgorod, is one of the first examples of the evolution of the Russian onion dome.

Russian building and architecture, like so many other aspects of Russian culture, declined during the Mongol era. For over 200 years, few buildings outside of Novgorod were built of stone. Churches were built of wood, but none from that era survive today. After independence was restored in the 15th century, Ivan III and Ivan IV had to import architects from western Europe in order to build new stone churches. Still, the basic design of Russian churches remained native. For example, Ivan III told his Italian architects, who were designing churches inside the Kremlin, to follow Russian building styles.

Ivan IV built Russia's most famous church, St. Basil's, in the center of Moscow. Ivan's legendary cruelty found expression in a report that the czar had the two architects who built the church blinded when it was finished "so they should never produce anything better."

By the 16th century, Russia's new stone churches had inherited additional features from the wooden churches built in earlier centuries. One of the most distinctive of these was the steep tent-shaped roof, which wooden churches had needed to shed Russia's heavy winter snow and avoid collapse. Another feature that helped shed snow was a curved gable called a *kokoshnik* (kuh-KOSH-nick), which is named after a curved headdress worn by Russian peasant women.

After the 17th century, Russian churches and other public buildings increasingly reflected Italian and French influences. This was particularly true after Peter the Great became czar. Two of Russia's most important architectural treasures are the Winter Palace and the Smolny Convent, both designed by Italian architect Bartolomeo Rastrelli.

The Bolshevik Revolution had a depressing effect on Russian architecture. The Soviet regime built huge, dreary blocks of buildings marked by massiveness, poor quality, and lack of character.

NOTES

1. From "The Tale of the Host of Igor," ed. Basil Dmytryshyn, in *Medieval Russia: A Source Book* (Hinsdale, Illinois: Dryden Press, 1973), p. 87.
2. Quoted in *The Poems, Prose, and Plays of Alexander Pushkin,* ed. Alexander Yarmolinsky, trans. B. Deutsch (New York: Random House, 1936), p. 240.
3. The *New York Times,* September 27, 1993.

5

Russia:
A Country Map

*D*uring the first half of the 19th century, a Russian historian named Mikhail Pogodin wrote in awe about the size, geographical variety, and natural richness of his native land:

> Russia! what a marvelous phenomenon on the world scene! Russia—a distance of about ten thousand versts [a verst is about a kilometer] in length on a straight line from the virtually central European river, across all of Asia and the Eastern Ocean, down to the remote American lands! A distance of five thousand versts in width from Persia, one of the southern Asiatic states, to the end of the inhabited world—to the North Pole. What state can equal it? Its half? How many states can match its twentieth, its fiftieth part? . . . Russia—a state which contains all types of soil, from the warmest to the coldest. . . . which abounds

in all the products required for the needs, comforts, and pleasures of life. . . . a whole world, self-sufficient, independent, absolute.[1]

Pogodin's Russia, to be sure, was less impressive than he pictured it. Most of Russia's people were unfree and wretchedly poor agricultural laborers. Despite its many natural resources, Russia lagged behind the countries of Western Europe in agricultural development. And its political system was oppressive and inefficient. Yet Russia was, as Pogodin claimed, uniquely endowed among the nations of the world. It may not have been "a whole world" that needed no one else, but it had a potential that few other nations could dream of matching.

Today's Russia is smaller than in Pogodin's day. It no longer possesses its "remote American lands," sold to the United States in 1867. Poland and Finland broke away after czarism's collapse in 1917. Many other non-Russian parts of what was Pogodin's Russia became independent when the Soviet Union collapsed in 1991. Yet Russia still possesses many of the qualities of which Pogodin boasted. Even today's downsized Russia of about 6.5 million square miles (17 million sq km)—about three-quarters as large as the former Russian Empire and Soviet Union—dwarfs any other nation in the world. It still has an immense treasure trove of natural resources: oil, natural gas, steel, rare metals, forests, and a great deal more. Like a gangling, awkward, but powerful youth, Russia still has great potential, if it can only learn to manage its vast but misdirected natural strength.

Geography, Climate, Natural Resources

Russia is a land of seemingly endless plains. Most of it is situated on the enormous Eurasian Plain that was once the bed of an ancient sea. Together with hill lands and low plateaus that rise less than 3,300 feet (1,000 m) above sea level, plains cover most of the country. Western, or European, Russia, the part of the country west of the Ural Mountains, lies within the North European Plain. The North European Plain extends from the Pyrenees Mountains in Western Europe to the Ural Mountains in Russia, the boundary between Europe and Asia.

East of the Urals is the West Siberian Lowland. Most of this area is less than 660 feet (200 m) above sea level, and about half is below 330 feet (100 m). After 932 miles (1,500 km), the West Siberian Lowland rises to the Central Siberian Plateau. Farther east in Siberia, as well as to the south, are a series of mountain ranges, a few of whose peaks rise above 2,500 feet (763 m).

Russia is also a land of great rivers. The Dnieper, along which the first Russian civilization evolved over 1,000 years ago, rises near Moscow before flowing through Belarus and Ukraine to the Black Sea. The Don rises south of Moscow and meanders for almost 1,242 miles (2,000 km) to the Sea of Azov, an inlet of the Black Sea. The greatest of European Russia's rivers is the mighty Volga, the longest river in Europe, whose 2,278 miles (3,669 km) journey to the subsea level Caspian Sea begins in the forests north of Moscow. The rivers of European Russia for centuries have been an important transportation network linking a widespread area.

The Volga, which Russians call their "Dear Little Mother," is Europe's longest river. Here it flows past onion-domed churches in the city of Yaroslavl, about 160 miles (257 km) northeast of Moscow.

Russia's longest rivers are in Siberia. The Ob and its tributary the Irtysh (eer-TISH), together comprising the world's fifth longest river, flow for most of their combined 3,353 mile (5,400-km) length through the West Siberian Plain to their icy terminus at the Arctic Sea. Farther east is the Yenisey, whose 2,484-mile (4,000-km) course to the Arctic Ocean marks the eastern edge of the West Siberian Plain. Along the Yenisey (yeh-nih-SAY) and its tributary, the Angara, the Soviet regime built two of the world's largest hydroelectric power stations. Farther east, the Lena River cuts through the Central Siberian Plateau for 2,653 miles (4,268 km) on its journey to the Arctic Sea. The Amur (ah-MUHR), about 2,732 miles (4,400 km) in length, flows eastward along the Chinese border before turning northward and reaching the sea near the northern tip of Sakhalin Island.

Russia is blessed with about 200,000 lakes, including some of the largest in the world. Among them are Lake Ladoga (LAH-duh-guh) and Lake Onega (oh-NAY-gah) in the northwest, the two largest lakes in Europe. However, neither these nor any other lake in the world can match Lake Baikal, the sickle-shaped sliver known as the "Pearl of Siberia." The oldest and deepest lake in the world—it is over about 25 million years old and more than one mile deep—Baikal (by-KAHL) holds one fifth of the world's fresh water, as much as all America's Great Lakes combined. Lake Baikal is fed by 336 rivers and is home to 1,200 species of plants and animals found nowhere else, including the world's only freshwater seal and a fish that gives birth to living young. During the winter, a layer of ice three feet thick, and in some places several times that, covers the lake, but in summer its waters are warm enough for swimming. The purity and clarity of Baikal's waters are legendary; a white sheet can be seen clearly over 100 feet beneath the water's surface. However, during the past 30 years, parts of the lake have been polluted by factories built during the Soviet era. Today, environmentalists from both Russia and other countries are campaigning to protect Russia's "Sacred Sea" and preserve its unique and magnificent ecological heritage.

Two mountain ranges have played a significant role in Russia's history: the Urals and the Caucasus. Each separates Europe from Asia, the Urals along an east/west divide and the Caucasus along a north/south divide. The Urals are an ancient range. They have been worn down over 250 million years to little more than rolling hills that stretch across Russia for 1,242 miles (2,000 km). Most of the Ural hills are only about 2,953–3,937 feet (900–1,200 m) above sea level, and the highest peaks only reach 4,922–6,234 feet (1,500–1,900 m). The Urals, therefore, provide no barrier to either icy winds blowing westward from Siberia or invaders from Asia who, over the centuries, have stormed into Russia. Nor, beginning in the 16th century, did they present a barrier to restless Russian adventurers, pioneers, and conquerers surging eastward into Siberia.

Russia's highest mountains are in the Caucasus range between the Black and the Caspian Seas. Although both the Russian Empire and the Soviet Union controlled territory south of the Caucasus, today Russia holds only the northern slopes of those majestic snow-peaked mountains. During the 19th century, the Russian Empire waged a long and bitter struggle to win control of the this region. That struggle, as well as the resistance to it, have been immortalized in works such as Pushkin's poem *Captive of the Caucasus*, Lermontov's novel *A Hero of Our Time*, and Tolstoy's short story "Hadji Murat." Among the Caucasus peaks still inside Russia's borders is Mount Elbrus, at 18,511 feet (5,642 m), the highest point in Europe.

Russia is famous, actually notorious, for its climate. Despite its great size, the country is not exposed to ocean breezes that tend to moderate climate. Russia, therefore, has what is called an extreme continental climate, which is characterized by long, cold winters and short summers. The main exception to this rule is the Russian part of the Black Sea coast and the strip of territory north of the Caucasus Mountains called the North Caucasus, where milder conditions prevail.

When Russia's weather comes to mind, it is the brutally cold winters that stand out. For centuries, foreign visitors have shuddered at the thought of the Russian winter. Thus a 17th-century English ambassador reported that:

> Loe thus I make an ende: none other news to thee
> But that the country is too cold, the people beastly bee.[2]

A 20th-century American visitor provided a less poetic but more detailed description of his encounter with the Russian winter:

> In the worst weather it is so cold that it seems to burn. You launch yourself out of double doors into the street and you gasp. You narrow your shrinking nostrils to give your lungs a chance to get acclimatized, but you gasp again and go on gasping. Ears are well covered against

frostbite, but eyebrows and moustache grow icicles in bunches, a
sweat runs from under your fur cap and freezes on your temples.
Another moment, surely, and the whole nostril will freeze over; in a
panic you warm your nose with your glove, but the nostrils do not
freeze, and you go on warming your nose and stinging cheeks with
your glove, and you go on gasping. Half an hour's walk gives you
the exercise of an ordinary afternoon. . . . it is impossible, you think,
to bear it for long, but you do.[3]

On the positive side, at least from Russia's point of view, its "General
Winter" (along with its "General Mud" and "General Distance") several
times has played a critical role in the defeat of invaders. Bitterly cold
Russian winters helped defeat both Napoleon's Grand Army in 1812 and
Hitler's murderous Nazi legions during World War II.

The Russian part of Eurasia is divided into several major vegetation
zones. In the far north, along the coast of the Arctic Ocean, is the tundra,
a collection of mosses, lichens, and small shrubs. To the south is the *taiga*
(tai-GUH), which means "thick forest" in Russian. The taiga is an enormous
evergreen forest, the largest in the world. South of the taiga, in the western
part of Russia, is a smaller deciduous, or leafy, forest. Farther south, the
forests give way to a vast prairie known as the steppe. The windswept
steppe is Russia's main agricultural zone, although it gets less rainfall that
America's Great Plains, with rainfall decreasing as one moves eastward.
Most of the desert lands that lie south of the steppe have been lost to the
new states of Central Asia since the collapse of the Soviet Union. All that
remains to Russia is a small patch of semidesert where the Volga flows
into the Caspian Sea. Farthest south, along parts of Russia's Black Sea
coast, is a strip of subtropical vegetation.

No country in the world has more natural resources than Russia. Despite
wasteful management and losses to pollution, it has vast reserves of
timber. Russia has enormous oil and natural gas deposits, although most
of these are in western Siberia. The oil wells that made Russia the world's
largest producer of oil at the turn of the 20th century now lie in Azerbaijan,
while other large oil fields in Central Asia now belong to Kazakhstan.
Large deposits of coal, iron, diamonds, gold, aluminum, copper, and
nickel still lie buried in Russia's soil. There are also supplies of rare metals
with important industrial and military uses such as tungsten, manganese,
cobalt, platinum, chromium, and vanadium. Many of these resources are

locked in the frozen storehouse of Siberia, which remains, as it has been since the 16th century, Russia's last and greatest frontier.

With the breakup of the Soviet Union, much of northern Eurasia's most fertile soil—the so-called black earth, or chernozem soil—fell within the boundaries of Ukraine. Other important chernozem agricultural lands became part of Kazakhstan. However, Russia still has productive agricultural land and chernozem soil, especially in the North Caucasus region and near the Ural Mountains.

Geographic and Economic Regions

The Moscow Region

Moscow has been Russia's leading city since the Mongol era, which lasted from the 13th to the 15th centuries. From its beginning as a small village on the banks of the Moskva River, it has grown into Russia's largest city and one of the world's great metropolises, with a population of more than 9 million people. In the 15th century, Moscow became the capital of a reunified Russia state. After a 200-year interval beginning in 1712, when St. Petersburg was Russia's capital, Moscow again became the country's capital in 1918.

But Moscow is more than merely a great city and capital of a country. Russians from all corners of their vast territory view Moscow as their country's heart and soul. In 1380, a Russian army marched from Moscow and inflicted the first defeat by Russian forces on the previously invincible Mongols at the Battle of Kulikovo. The Kremlin, with its onion-domed churches, and St. Basil's Cathedral, with its nine chapels commemorating military victories of Ivan the Terrible, the two most familiar symbols of Russia, stand in the middle of Moscow next to Red Square. Even when St. Petersburg was Russia's official capital, Moscow remained the country's cultural and economic center. Most of old Moscow, with its wooden buildings, burned to the ground during Napoleon's invasion of Russia in 1812. Modern Moscow, with its elegant stone buildings, dates from the rebuilding of the city after the Napoleonic Wars.

Today Moscow remains Russia's spiritual center. It is also the center of a vital industrial region. Railroads, air routes, and roads radiate outward from Moscow in all directions. If a circle with a radius of 250 miles (403 km) were drawn around Moscow—which would cover an area of about 230,000 square miles (595,700 sq km)—it would include the homes of one third of Russia's people. The Moscow Region is a major producer of machine tools, scientific equipment, machinery for textiles and other industries, electrical equipment, and a variety of consumer goods. It is also a center of Russia's chemical industry, which expanded greatly during the latter years of the Soviet era. Among the important industrial cities in the Moscow Region are Nizhnii Novgorod (NIHZH-nee NOF-gah-rod), a city of 1.5 million that is a major automobile producer. Other industrial cities are Yaroslavl (a tire-producing center), Tula (a mining and metallurgical center), and Ivanovo (a textile center). However, the Moscow region has few fuel resources and coal, oil, and natural gas must be brought in from other parts of Russia.

The St. Petersburg Region

St. Petersburg, 420 miles (676 km) from Moscow, is the center of an important industrial region in Russia's northwest corner. Since its founding in 1703, it has been the Russian city that is most oriented to the West. Aside from its economic importance, St. Petersburg is a cultural center with a world-famous ballet, many theaters, and over 60 museums, including the magnificent Hermitage. As in the days of Peter the Great, the city's skyline is dominated by the spire rising 400 feet (122 m) from the Peter and Paul Fortress.

St. Petersburg is built on 101 islands where the Neva River empties into the Gulf of Finland. Lying 60 degrees north of the equator, the same latitude as southern Alaska and the middle of Hudson Bay, St. Petersburg is one of the northernmost major cities in the world. During World War II, it became a symbol of resistance to the Nazis when its citizens held out against a German siege that lasted 900 days and cost over 800,000 civilian lives. The fallen are remembered in many ways and places, including in a cemetery where uncounted thousands were buried in mass graves and where a simple poem is etched into a concrete slab:

Their names we cannot list,
so many they are
who lie under the enternal guard of granite
But know you who hear this:
no one is forgotten
nothing is forgotten.[4]

Today St. Petersburg is a metropolis of 6 million people and is Russia's second largest city and its largest seaport. It takes icebreakers to keep the port open in winter. Over 60 rivers, canals, and channels cut through St. Petersburg, whose various parts are linked by 365 bridges. Strong winds buffet the city in winter and snow falls from November to March. Each summer, for about three weeks when the sun never sets, the city is bathed in its famous "White Night," a twilight that lasts for about a half hour each day.

Among St. Petersburg's industries are engineering, electrical equipment, metals, chemicals, textiles, consumer goods, and food processing. Its port and naval station also have made it a shipbuilding center. Not far south of St. Petersburg is Novgorod, the old merchant city whose republican form of government was destroyed by Ivan the Great. Slightly farther to the southwest is Pskov (puh-SKOHV), which lies near the lake on which the Russian prince Aleksandr Nevsky defeated an invading German army in 1242 in the famous "battle on the ice." However, 80 percent of the region's population lives in and around St. Petersburg.

The North

The northern region is the largest of the economic regions of European Russia, and the one with the lowest population density. It includes Karelia—which borders on Finland—the Kola Peninsula, and a vast stretch of territory along the Barents Sea, an inlet of the Arctic Ocean. Two large rivers, the Northern Dvina and the Pechora, flow through the region into the Barents Sea. In addition to the tundra along the coast, there are large areas covered by forests and swamps. The native peoples of the region, who are Finno-Ugarian rather than Russians, still follow their traditional activities such as reindeer herding, fishing, and hunting. However, far more important is the development of the region's mineral resources, which include lumber, coal, oil, natural gas, bauxite, nickel, and iron.

One activity that has caused terrible pollution and damage to public health in the region is the smelting of nickel. Two ports in the region, Murmansk (muhr-MAHNSK) and Archangel have played an important role in Russia's foreign trade for several centuries. Because it is exposed to sea breezes from the Atlantic Ocean, Murmansk is an ice-free port all year long despite its northern location.

The Volga Region

The Volga is Russia's most important river, both in terms of the economic role it plays and its symbolic meaning to the Russian people. The Russians call the river "Dear Little Mother." A river captain once spoke for millions of his countrymen when he said that "the Volga flows through the heart of every Russian."

The Volga Region refers to the middle and lower reaches of the Volga river, from the city of Kazan (kah-ZAHN), where the Volga turns southward, to Astrakhan (AH-strah-kahn) at the river's mouth. Over 25 million people live in the Volga Region. The most important city on the Volga from the point of view of national sentiment is Volgograd, or, as it was called during World War II, Stalingrad. It was at this city situated where the Volga bends, in a bitter house-to-house, hand-to-hand battle that lasted 200 days, that the Soviet army stopped invading Germans and turned the tide on the eastern front in Europe during World War II. No battle in World War II was more important, and no Russian can do anything but weep with pride in remembering the suffering and heroism it took to turn the Germans back.

Today a series of dams between Kazan and Volgograd has turned the once free-flowing river into a series of lakes. There are several large hydroelectric plants along the river. Heavy industry is important in the region, including factories that produce trucks and chemicals. The Volga Region also has an agricultural sector that produces meat, vegetables, and dairy products. In addition, there are a series of major oil fields between the Volga and the Urals. The Caspian Sea, into which the Volga empties, is famous for its caviar, or sturgeons' eggs. However, increasing pollution of the Volga threatens the caviar-producing areas of the Caspian Sea. Tragically, during the Soviet era, the "Dear Little Mother" Volga became one of Russia's most polluted rivers.

The Urals Region

Industrial development in the Urals Region dates from the 18th century. However, the most rapid industrialization took place during the Soviet era. The great steel complex at Magnitogorsk (mug-nee-tuh-GORSK) was built at brutal, breakneck speed during the 1930s to take advantage of the region's iron deposits. The region has been an important steel and iron center ever since. Magnitogorsk became a symbol of the triumphs and horrors of Soviet-style industrialization. Today, with its outdated and polluting factories, it remains a symbol of the failure of the Soviet centrally planned economic system.

The Urals also have rich deposits of other metals, including copper, aluminum, nickel, chrome, and platinum. During World War II, the Stalin regime moved over 1,300 factories from the western parts of the Soviet Union to the Urals to protect them from the invading Germans. Industrialization continued in the decades after the war. One result of Soviet industrialization policies was to make the Urals one of the most polluted regions in the world, leaving its people with severe health problems.

The main city in the region is Yekaterinburg (yeh-kah-teh-reen-BURK). It is 40 miles (64 km) east of the Europe/Asia border, making it the first Russian city in Asia. Yekaterinburg, which was called Sverdlovsk during the Soviet era after a leading Bolshevik, was the scene of the murder of Czar Nicholas II and his family in 1918. Later it became the political base for Boris Yeltsin, who was born in a village about 90 miles (145 km) from the city.

Another important and symbolic city in the region is Chelyabinsk (cheh-lyah-BEENSK). In 1957, a nuclear accident took place in a storage tank near that city. Over 80 tons of nuclear waste was blasted into the atmosphere. Although the accident was covered up for decades, 11,000 people were evacuated from the region, and farming was banned for years on over 400 square miles (1,036 sq km) surrounding the accident site.

The North Caucasus Region

The North Caucasus Region is one of the most fertile, productive, and varied in Russia. It is also one of the most beautiful. The steppe region that stretches westward from the Sea of Azov is part of the fertile black earth belt that begins in Ukraine and extends into Kazakhstan. In the south are snowcapped peaks of the Caucasus, and in the east the semidesert shore of the Caspian Sea.

Agriculture remains the region's leading economic activity. Farmers in the region grow a variety of crops, including wheat, sugar beets, rice, tobacco, and sunflowers. Fruits and vegetables—apples, pears, plums, peaches, tangerines, cucumbers, eggplant, and more—flourish in the region's fertile soil and mild climate. The vineyards along the slopes of the Caucasus produce outstanding wines.

The climate of the North Caucasus also supports a vigorous tourist industry. The most popular resort is Sochi on the coast of the Black Sea, which is protected from the cold northerly winds by surrounding mountains. Another popular resort in Mineralnye Vody (mihn-ehr-AL-nih-yeh VOH-dee) (Mineral Waters), where, as the name suggests, visitors come to be cured by natural mineral water springs.

The region also contains oil and gas deposits, as well as deposits of lead and zinc. During the late Soviet era, a native of the North Caucasus made a name for himself on both the national and international stage. He is Mikhail Gorbachev, who comes from a village near the town of Stavropol.

Siberia

Siberia is much more than a region; it is a huge expanse of 4.8 million square miles (12.5 million sq km)—about one and one half times the size of the continental United States and one third of Asia. One visitor to Siberia pointed out that no map can convey the immensity of Siberia. Only a description of the endless taiga seemed adequate to do the job:

> The taiga is a universe without an end
> Those that live within it are the stars
> Bright stars are the eyes of the beasts
> And of the men who walk with the beasts.
> The space between the stars is infinite
> For the taiga is a universe without an end.[5]

Siberia begins at the Ural Mountains and ends at the Pacific Ocean. Its easternmost tip is Big Diomede Island in the Bering Sea, just a few frigid

Novosibirsk, Siberia's largest city. A separate district of the city called Akademgorodok was built during the Khrushchev era as a research and academic center that attracted some of the Soviet Union's most brilliant scientists and scholars.

miles of water away from Little Diomede Island, where Alaska and the United States begin. Siberia has a polar climate, with bitterly long and cold winters. Temperatures are below freezing eight months of the year, and in the far northeast can drop to minus 94 degrees F, as opposed to minus 45 in Moscow.

Siberia has vast stretches of tundra and deep forests, great plains and mountain ranges, fast-flowing rivers and glistening lakes. It is also immensely rich in natural resources. Its soil holds coal and iron, gold and silver, and diamonds. Siberia also has some of the richest oil and natural gas deposits in the world. At the same time, it is the home to many forms of wildlife, including the nerpa, or Baikal seal, and the rare Siberian tiger.

While large areas of Siberia officially are set aside as Autonomous Republics for their native peoples, Russian settlement has made these peoples minorities in these republics. For example, the Buryat people make up only 23 percent of the population of the Buryat Autonomous Republic, while Russians make up 72 percent. In the huge Yakut Autonomous Republic (over one million square miles), the Yakuts comprise just over a third of the population, while Russians are about half.

Kamchatka: Land of Fire and Ice

The Kamchatka (kahm-CHUHT-kah) Peninsula is a huge 182,000-square-mile tongue of land, protruding into the sea from eastern Siberia. It is Russia's piece of the Pacific Ring of Fire, a zone where the movement of gigantic plates of the earth's crust have produced one of our planet's two main concentrations of volcanoes. There are over 100 volcanoes on Kamchatka, many of which have erupted since 1900. It is also a frozen land where snow covers the ground eight months of the year. There can be no wonder, then, why Kamchatka is known as Russia's "land of fire and ice."

Kamchatka's 450,000 people share their wilderness peninsula with between 10,000 and 20,000 bears, as well as sea otters, sables, eagles, falcons, salmon, deer, fox, and other wildlife. Life has never been easy there; there are no roads or railroads connecting the peninsula to the mainland, and all supplies must arrive by sea or air. But since 1991, conditions have grown even more difficult. There is less money from Moscow to keep the economy moving and people are leaving. In Milkovo, in the center of the peninsula, apartment construction has been at a standstill for two years. There are few activities for the youth of Kamchatka's sterile towns. In the dreary port town of Petropavlovsk (peh-troh-PAF-lofsk), a Russian naval base that is home to 250,000 people, a navy officer must moonlight as a taxi driver to make ends meet.

It is the natural beauty of Kamchatka that remains. The snow is still white, the rushing rivers still blue and clean, and dense forests of spruce, larch, aspen, and birch still teem with wildlife. There are the great volcanoes, including the giant, still-growing Klyuchevskaya (klyuh-CHEF-skah-yah), an infant less than 10,000 years old. The gigantic 1956 eruption at

While less than 10 percent of Russian industry is located in Siberia, there is a major mining and manufacturing region in western Siberia called the Kuznetsk (kooz-NYETSK) Basin (or Kuzbass) around Novosibirsk (noh-voh-seh-BEERSK), Siberia's largest city. Western Siberia also produces more than half of Russia's oil and gas. In fact, in the mid-1980s, the region produced 60 percent of all Soviet oil and 58 percent of its natural gas. Lumbering is another major industry in Siberia.

Not only is Novosibirsk Siberia's largest city, but, during the Soviet era, an enormous research and academic center called Akademgorodok was built there. It was unusually well supplied with housing, consumer goods, and cultural facilities to attract some of the former Soviet Union's most nearby Bezmyannaya was comparable to the 1980 eruption of Mount St. Helens in the United States. There is also the Valley of the Geysers in the center of Kamchatka's 500-mile-long volcano belt, where fumes and towering spouts of near-boiling water from underground thermal springs create a steaming, smoldering scene reminiscent of our planet's violent youth.

But even in Kamchatka, nature is under assault. The loggers who clear-cut the forests have been here since the Soviet era. Today, many of the logs that clog Kamchatka's ports are bound for Japan. The harm the logging has done is serious, as a local fishery inspector explains:

> Timber cutting has already severely damaged the watershed. Runoff is more rapid, causing floods and erosion. The water table drops. Lakes are becoming shallower, even drying up completely. Rivers are becoming silted. That has caused a decline in salmon spawning. This year we'll be allowed to catch only 3000 tons of salmon, compared to 10,000 tons ten years ago![6]

The oil rigs also have arrived along Kamchatka's west coast, and there are plans to mine for gold.

Preserving Kamchatka's unique and irreplacable natural beauty will not be easy. However, people like Sergei Alekseyev (ah-LEKS-eh-yef), director of a nature reserve in the center of Kamchatka, are doing their best. As Mr. Alekseyev puts it:

> We absolutely need to keep some places on the planet untouched, so they can serve as a benchmark for natural preservation. But the situation is such today that we have to find a compromise.[7]

talented scientists and researchers. For three decades, Novosibirsk thrived. However, after the collapse of the Soviet Union, hard times came to Novosibirsk, as they did to the rest of Russia, and many of its outstanding scientists and academics have moved elsewhere as a result.

Everything about Siberia seems to be big. During the czarist era—between 1891 and 1916—Russia built the Trans-Siberian Railroad across the region. The railroad is the longest railroad line in the world, stretching over 5,589 miles (9,000 km) from Moscow to the Siberian port city of Vladivostok (vlah-dee-vahs-TOCK). The construction of the Trans-Siberian Railroad, under the harsh conditions that exist in Siberia, was a brilliant engineering achievement. During the late Soviet era, a second

Vladivostok, which in Russian means "lord of the east," stands where the Trans-Siberian Railroad reaches the Pacific shore and is Russia's main Far Eastern port and a major naval base. Because of its coastal location, the climate of the city is comparatively mild.

line was added called the Baikal-Amur Mainline (BAM). Completed in 1989, the BAM is held together by four tunnels and over 3,000 bridges. The Bratsk Sea, the reservoir behind the huge Bratsk hydroelectric dam, is another manmade Siberian giant. It has an area of 1,930 square miles (5,000 sq km). Another giant that for many years cast a grim shadow over Siberia was the Soviet labor camp system of the Stalin era. Some of Stalin's largest and most brutal camps were located in eastern Siberia.

The southeastern corner of Siberia, along the Sea of Okhotsk and the Sea of Japan, is often referred to as the Far East Region. Because it is close to the sea, the climate of the region is humid and milder than elsewhere in Siberia. Farming is possible, especially in the Amur River Valley, and crops include wheat, rice, and soybeans. Other important industries are timber and fishing and fish processing. There are also several large shipbuilding yards and a large naval base in Vladivostok. Just off the coast is Sakhalin Island, whose still relatively untouched natural resources include oil, natural gas, and various metals. Across the Sea of Okhotsk, jutting out of easternmost Siberia, is the wild Kamchatka Peninsula. Kamchatka is a wildlife paradise. It also is studded by dozens of active volcanoes and therefore is often called Russia's "land of fire and ice."

NOTES

1. Quoted in Nicholas V. Riazanovsky, *A History of Russia,* 2nd ed. (New York: Oxford University Press, 1969), p. 3.
2. Quoted in ibid.
3. Wright Miller, *Russians as People* (New York: E. P. Dutton, 1961), p. 18.
4. The *New York Times,* January 21, 1994.
5. Quoted in Farly Mowat, *The Siberians* (Boston: Little, Brown, 1970), p. 123.
6. Brian Hodgson, "Kamchatka," in *National Geographic,* April 1994, p. 48.
7. The *New York Times,* October 28, 1992.

6

Politics and Government

*R*ussia has endured centuries of government that is bad or brutal, and often both. The country also periodically has swung back and forth between autocratic rule and anarchy. In the late 16th century, for example, after the cruel reign of Ivan the Terrible, Russia plunged into its "Time of Troubles," a period of internal turmoil and foreign invasion that lasted for 15 years. During the reigns of Peter the Great (1682–1725) and Catherine the Great (1762–1796), while ambitious rulers increased their personal power and waged wars to extend Russia's territory, great peasant rebellions burned their way across the broad steppe. When czarism finally collapsed during World War I under the hammer blows of military defeat and hardship at home, an attempt to establish parliamentary government produced chaos instead. That short-lived effort ended when the Bolshevik Party seized power. The Bolshevik attempt to establish a one-party dictatorship produced a devastating civil war that tore the country apart, while the Bolshevik victory resulted in a totalitarian regime in the decades that followed.

Even when Russia's government has been able to maintain order, its people have suffered from its policies. Since the time of Peter the Great, Russia's rulers have struggled to modernize their backward, sprawling realm and bring it into the ranks of the world's economically, socially, technologically, and militarily advanced countries. Change has come from the top, at the expense of those at the bottom. In the 18th century, Peter the Great's reforms pushed and pulled a reluctant Russia forward. But his wars and building programs were paid for by crushing taxes on the people, and many of his programs came to an end after his death. In the 19th century, although Alexander II freed the serfs, he left them tangled in a web of restrictions and mired in poverty. The policies of Sergei Witte, who served Czars Alexander III and Nicholas II, greatly expanded Russia's industrial base. But once again, the country's peasants and workers paid the bill through low wages and heavy taxes.

The Bolshevik Revolution and Stalin's industrialization drive of the 1930s shattered Russia's old order. The new Soviet regime intended to build the world's most advanced society. The Soviet Union did, in fact, become the world's second largest industrial power, and a military superpower. However, the human cost was catastrophic even by Russian standards; never had Russia's government waged such war against its people. Not even Ivan the Terrible or Peter the Great tortured Russia as Stalin did. And despite undeniable improvements in the three decades after Stalin's death, the Soviet government ultimately proved unable to keep the country from sliding into political, economic, and social decay. During the Gorbachev era, a serious attempt at reform misfired, leaving the economy in a shambles and the Russian people, along with the rest of the Soviet Union, once again with a falling standard of living.

Through all of this, Russia never had a chance to develop a democratic tradition. The czars ruled tyranically from above. During the last decade of the czarist era, Czar Nicholas II was forced to grant Russia a parliament, called the Duma, with limited powers. The Duma, which was elected by a system that greatly favored the nobility and wealthy, nonetheless was a modest beginning. However, the collapse of czarism brought about the Duma's demise as well. The Provisional Government's attempt to establish a genuine parliamentary government ended in November 1917 with the

Bolshevik coup. The Bolsheviks dared not prevent a democratic election for a Constituent Assembly planned by the Provisional Government before its collapse, but Lenin's government closed that assembly down by force after one day. Seven decades of Soviet totalitarianism followed.

Not until 1989, 71 years later during the Gorbachev era, would the Russian people get another chance to express themselves in an election. The election for the Congress of People's Deputies, while not entirely free, was an enormous step toward democratic government, but not enough to get the Soviet Union across the chasm between dictatorship and democracy. Reform had brought turmoil as well as democratic change. The Soviet Union collapsed, leaving Russia, shorn of most of the non-Russian population it had controlled since the days of the czars, to find a new and better way of governing itself.

Russian Politics in December 1991

When the Soviet Union collapsed, many people hoped that a new era of democratic politics finally could begin in Russia. They looked to Boris Yeltsin, president of Russia and the hero of the August coup, to move Russia toward democracy and a free-market economy. However, the hopes for a functioning democracy, capable of introducing necessary reforms in a systematic and effective manner, ran up against both the gravity of Russia's economic problems and the realities of its political situation. Post-Soviet Russia, the Russian Federation, was born with a government that was an unstable entity of ill-fitting parts. Its constitution dated from 1978, which made it a document suitable for masking the Communist Party dictatorship that existed at the time, but not very useful for governing an enormous new country with equally enormous problems. Since the late 1980s, numerous amendments to the constitution made it more cumbersome rather than capable of providing a framework for governing a country. One of the constitution's most glaring faults was that it offered little help in settling the dispute that broke out between President Yeltsin and the parliament over who had more power. One article of the constitution proclaimed that the Congress of People's Deputies was the "highest organ of state power," while another announced that the president was "the highest official in Russia."

Grafted onto the confusing constitution were several new institutions. The parliament—the 1,068-member Congress of People's Deputies—had been elected in 1990, when the Communist Party was still Russia's dominant political force. Boris Yeltsin, whom the Congress elected as its chairman and therefore as president of Russia, was still a party member at the time, as was Aleksandr Rutskoi (ruh-TSKOY), Yeltsin's running mate and Russia's vice-president. A smaller body—the Supreme Soviet—which was elected by the Congress to be Russia's day-to-day legislature, also was a stronghold of Soviet-era Communist officials. Not all of those elected in 1990 as party members were conservatives wedded to the old Soviet regime. Many, like Yeltsin himself, were reformers to some degree. However, overall more than half the members of the Russian parliament opposed Yeltsin's program of moving Russia to a free-market economy.

Boris Yeltsin, president of Russia and the first freely elected leader in his country's long history.

Boris Nikolayevich Yeltsin (1931–)

Boris Yeltsin was born in the village of Butko in the Ural Mountains, where Asia and Europe meet. He writes that his family on both sides "had plowed the land, sown wheat, and passed their lives like all other country people."[1] From almost the very beginning, Yeltsin faced a struggle to survive in a hard world. In fact, he barely survived his baptism when a priest, who was drunk, dropped him into the baptismal tub and forgot to take him out. When his mother noticed what had happened, she screamed and retrieved her infant child. Once the baby was revived, the priest calmly and, as it turned out, prophetically said, "Well, if he can survive such an ordeal, it means he's a good, tough lad—and I name him Boris."

Boris was indeed a tough lad. He was an independent child and a ringleader who was unafraid of getting into fights. Or, as he told a journalist, "I've always been a bit of a hooligan."[2] His broken "boxer's" nose is the result of a battle in which he was hit across the face with a cart axle. Young Boris, who even as a boy enjoyed taking things apart to see how they worked, also survived the explosion of a hand grenade he stole and then tried to disassemble with a hammer. That experiment cost him two fingers on his left hand.

Nor was young Yeltsin afraid to stand up for what he believed. At his graduation, he publicly criticized a teacher for humiliating and otherwise abusing her students. His outspokenness nearly cost him the chance to continue his education.

Yet Boris survived all his youthful escapades and became a civil engineer. He rose through the ranks of the Communist Party, eventually becoming the first secretary of the Communist Party organization in Sverdlovsk. In 1985, Mikhail Gorbachev brought Yeltsin to Moscow to head the party organization there, but, in 1987, Yelstin was fired for publicly criticizing Gorbachev for going too slowly in making reforms. Once again Yeltsin survived. In 1989, he was elected to the Congress of People's Deputies with an astounding 89 percent of the vote in his district. In 1991, when he was elected president of Russia, he became the first freely elected leader in his country's 1,100-year history. A few months later, he became the hero of the resistance to the August coup by hard-line Communists against Mikhail Gorbachev.

Opposing the parliament was the president of Russia, Boris Yeltsin. Yeltsin had broken with the party in a dramatic public resignation in July 1990. While the Congress of People's Deputies and the Supreme Soviet

In December 1991, Yeltsin took the lead in putting an end to the crumbling Soviet Union by forming the Commonwealth of Independent States with the leaders of Ukraine and Belarus. As of January 1, 1992 he was the president of an independent country, the Russian Federation.

Yeltsin's first term in office was stormy as he struggled to lead Russia from dictatorship and communism to democracy and free enterprise. Privatization and its problems, the violent showdown with the Duma, and the disastrous war with Chechnya [see pages 105–109] all increased the strains on Yeltsin and on Russia. At times Yeltsin seemed to be his own worst enemy, as he behaved in ways that reminded people of the Communist Party boss he once was. Still, most observers continued to regard him as essential to Russia making a successful transition to a democratic political system and free enterprise economy, especially when they compared him to Russia's other leading political figures.

The endless stress of dealing with Russia's many problems took its toll on Yeltsin. His health visibly declined. During 1995 he suffered two heart attacks, although this information was kept from the public. As his term as president drew to a close and rumors about his health circulated, many people questioned whether Yeltsin had the physical strength to undertake a second term. His falling popularity raised the issue of whether Yeltsin, healthy or not, could even win election to a second term. Somehow Yeltsin rallied his political supporters and marshaled his physical strength enough to win reelection to a second term in July 1996. His increasingly severe heart condition, which could no longer be kept secret, then forced him to disappear from public view. He was obviously a sick man at his inauguration in August.

In September 1996, Yeltsin announced that he would undergo heart surgery. The operation took place in Moscow in November. While a Russian doctor performed the operation, a leading American surgeon also was present. Yeltsin then attempted to return to work too quickly, which probably contributed to a dangerous bout with pneumonia. Yet he survived this ordeal also. And there was still enough spirit in Yeltsin to enable him to surprise both Russia and the world by making a strong physical recovery. Within several months he had returned to full-time duty. Russia's recovery from the turmoil of the preceding five years was the next matter on his agenda.

were creatures of the defunct Soviet system, the Russian presidency was a giant step away from that system. The credit belonged to Yeltsin. In June of 1991, he defied Mikhail Gorbachev and the Communist Party by organizing an election for the presidency of Russia. When he was elected with 57 percent of the vote, Boris Yeltsin became Russia's first popularly elected president in the country's 1,100-year history.

However, Yeltsin found that being elected by the people did not help him in his dealings with the parliament. It opposed many of his reforms, especially those designed to establish a free-market economy in Russia. Among Yeltsin's most formidable opponents was Ruslan Khasbulatov (has-buh-LAHT-of), the parliament's speaker. Another opponent who emerged during Yeltsin's struggle with the parliament was none other than Aleksandr Rutskoi, his vice-president. The tug of war between Yeltsin and the Congress of People's Deputies, in effect a struggle for power, began almost immediately. By April of 1992, Yeltzin's allies barely defeated an attempt to debate a motion of no confidence in the government. Both sides appealed to the Russian constitution to support their positions; the problem was that the constitution provided no definitive answer as to which side—Yeltsin or his opponents—was in the right.

Making life yet more complicated was a third branch of government created in July 1991: the constitutional court. Its job was to interpret and apply the Brezhnev-era constitution to post-Soviet Russia, an impossible task even if the parliament and president had not been at each other's throats. At first, Chief Justice Valery Zorkin appeared to act as a mediator between the two sides. However, gradually he began to side with Yeltsin's opponents, which intensified the political struggle and made it increasingly difficult to govern Russia.

Another fundamental problem the new Russia faced was the relationship between the central government in Moscow and the 21 regions set aside for ethnic minorities. By December 1991, these regions were called "republics." Along with 68 other territorial divisions of various kinds, the ethnic republics were leftovers from the Soviet era, during which they were considered autonomous republics. Altogether these republics made up 28.6 percent of Russia's territory and contained about 15 percent of its population. However, not all their population was non-Russian. In fact, over 45 percent were Russians, and they were the majority in nine of the republics. Nonetheless, Yeltsin and his government immediately faced pressure for greater autonomy from many of the republics, and two of them openly threatened secession. There was great concern in Moscow that Russia's unity was at stake. As Yeltsin himself put it in April 1993:

It is no secret that the country is gripped by a feeling of anxiety about the territorial integrity of the Russian state. Will it share the same fate as the USSR?[3]

As if these problems were not enough, Yeltsin faced challenges to his leadership from a wide variety of political parties and groups. At first, the most bitterly opposed to Yeltsin were hard-line communist groups loyal to the Soviet system of socialism and extreme Russian nationalist parties. However, they soon were joined by those who in August 1991 had been Yeltsin's allies. Two men stood above the others in terms of the role they played in the August coup and their influence in the months that followed: Khasbulatov and Rutskoi.

Ruslan Khasbulatov was a member of a minority ethnic group called the Chechens and became the speaker of the Russian parliament after Yeltsin was elected president of Russia. During the August coup, Khasbulatov was one of several political figures who came to Yeltsin's country home to compose an appeal to the Russian people to resist the coup. He also was the first to return to Moscow. However, during 1992, Khasbulatov turned against Yeltsin and allied himself with those opposed to the president's economic reforms. He demonstrated both cunning and skill in manipulating the parliament to frustrate Yeltsin's policies.

A similar pattern marked the relationship between Yeltsin and his vice-president, Aleksandr Rutskoi. Rutskoi was a tough ex-paratrooper and an Afghan war hero who stood side by side with Yeltsin during the August coup. His dramatic radio speech to the Soviet army was a crucial part of Yeltsin's campaign to keep the Soviet military from supporting the plotters. In August 1991, Rutskoi said:

> Comrades! I, an officer of the Soviet armed forces, a colonel, a Hero of the Soviet Union who has walked on the battle-torn roads of Afghanistan and knows the horrors of war, call on you, my brother officers, soldiers, and sailors, not to act against your own people, against your fathers, brothers, and sisters.[4]

But by 1992, Rutskoi was the leader of a political faction called Civic Union whose goal was to stop Yeltsin's economic reforms. As the months and disputes dragged on, the relationship between Russia's president and vice-president became increasingly antagonistic. In 1993, they reached the breaking point.

The President Versus Parliament: 1991–1993

The dispute between Yeltsin and the parliament after August 1991 was rooted in differing visions of what path of development post-Soviet Russia should take. Yeltsin wanted Russia to change to a free-market economy and copy the democratic systems of the West. The conservatives in parliament, most of whom were officials and bureaucrats during the Soviet regime, realized their jobs and positions would disappear under such reforms and therefore opposed them. Conservatives also mistrusted the West and rejected Western values. They wanted to preserve what Rutskoi called the "Russian idea," by which he meant Russian interests and values. The personal rivalry for power between Khasbulatov and Rutskoi on the one hand, and Yeltsin on the other, intensified these differences. The result was that Khasbulatov and Rutskoi broke with Russia's democratic forces and sided with the conservative camp.

The first crack began to appear in November 1991, when Yeltsin announced his policy of moving Russia to a free-market economic system as quickly as possible. At that time, he was able to get the parliament to grant him special powers for one year. In January 1992, Yeltsin took the necessary first step by lifting price controls on most goods. The rapid price rises that followed hurt many ordinary consumers, which in turn hurt Yeltsin's image and popularity.

The first serious break between Yeltsin and the Congress occurred in April 1992 when Khasbulatov opposed Yeltsin's economic program and led an unsuccessful attempt to limit Yeltsin's powers. By the summer, Rutskoi's newly formed Civic Union joined the fight against Yeltsin's economic reforms. The split grew wider in December 1992. Conservatives proposed a series of amendments to the Russian constitution to limit the president's powers. Yeltsin managed to head off that effort but, in return, had to agree to Yegor Gaidar's removal as prime minister. The new prime minister was Viktor Chernomyrdin (cher-nohm-IHR-din), a former Communist Party bureaucrat who once ran the Soviet gas monopoly. Chernomyrdin made it clear that he intended to put a brake on Gaidar's radical economic policies. The Congress also agreed to Yeltsin's demand that a referendum be held in April 1993 to allow the people to vote on the basic principles for a new constitution.

The Showdown and the Shootout

The struggle between the reformist president and the conservative parliament came to a head in 1993. Khasbulatov used the early months of the year to try to discredit Yeltsin and undermine his power. The big blow was struck at the March meeting of the Congress of People's Deputies. The Congress stripped Yeltsin of his emergency powers, attacked him for allegedly violating the constitution, and reneged on the agreement to hold a referendum on a new constitution. Yeltsin struck back on March 20. In a nationally televised speech, he announced what he called "special presidential rule," under which the Congress could not overrule his decrees. Six days later, Yeltsin's opponents narrowly failed in their attempt to impeach the president.

Both sides then drew back from the brink by holding a referendum, although not one dealing with constitutional principles. The results were a victory for Yeltsin. Over 64 percent of the voters turned out: 58 percent said they supported the president, and almost 53 percent—a surprisingly high number in light of the country's economic difficulties—supported his economic policies. However, the referendum did not end Russia's political deadlock. By September, the tension between President Yeltsin and his opponents in the Congress of People's Deputies was higher than ever. On September 21, declaring that the parliament and its large Communist bloc was making reforms impossible, Yeltsin dissolved it and called for new elections in December. The country, he said, had reached a "deadlock." The Supreme Soviet, the parliament's day-to-day legislature, immediately voted to remove Yeltsin from office and ordered security troops not to obey the president. To noisy applause, it swore in Aleksandr Rutskoi as Russia's acting president. Meanwhile, several hundred hard-line Communists gathered outside the parliament building, known as the White

House. They built bonfires and barricades and shouted their hatred for Yeltsin. This time, neither side drew back.

On October 2, stone-throwing demonstrators battled police in the center of Moscow. The well-organized crowd forced police to retreat. Meanwhile, Rutksoi, calling himself the "President of the Russian Federation," issued a statement that left no doubt an attempt to overthrow Yeltsin was under way:

> Everyone to the struggle against dictatorship. Let us not allow Yeltsin even the smallest chance of trampling Russia under him.[5]

The next day, an enormous crowd wielding clubs, metal pipes, and wooden planks smashed through police lines in a march to the White House, the parliament's headquarters. Armed parliament guards, firing in all directions, seized the office of the mayor of Moscow by driving trucks through plate-glass doors. The Russian flag at the office was ripped down and replaced by a red symbol of communism amid shouts of "It's our October revolution" (a reference to the Bolshevik Revolution) and "Hang that bastard Yeltsin." Two hours later, at Rutskoi's urging, a crowd tried to storm the building housing Moscow's main television complex. By the end of the day, at least 20 people were dead. It was the worst violence in Moscow since the Bolshevik Revolution of 1917. Russia stood on the edge of civil war.

At 6:30 P.M. on October 3, President Boris Yeltsin declared a state of emergency. He told the Russian people:

> Today the fate of Russia and the fate of our children is being decided. The forces of civil war will not succeed. We will triumph.[6]

Meanwhile, a crowd of 10,000 was gathering near the Kremlin to support Yeltsin. But his situation was precarious. In August 1991, the military had refused to back the coup against Gorbachev, rallying to Yeltsin and enabling him to emerge as a hero. Khasbulatov and Rutskoi, knowing that the military was demoralized and hurt by cutbacks in funding since 1991, expected that this time it would turn against Yeltsin. They were mistaken. Both the minister of defense and the troops he commanded remained loyal to Yeltsin. By the early morning of October 4, tanks and troops were in position in several key places in Moscow,

Russia's Parliament building, or White House, under siege during the October 1993 rebellion against Yeltsin.

including the White House. So were television crews from networks around the world, as millions of Russians and hundreds of millions of people worldwide watched in fascination and horror. Near the battle scene, Muscovites watched, some perched in trees, with a calmness that seemed out of place for a country on the brink of disaster.

Shortly after 9:00 A.M., pro-Yeltsin troops seized the first two floors of the building. As the battle raged, Yeltsin once again spoke to the Russian people, whom he addressed as "Dear Compatriots." The tone of the speech—in which the leader of Russia spoke frankly, asked for help and paid his respects to his fellow citizens—showed how far Russia had come since 1985:

> I am turning to you at this difficult moment.
>
> Shots are thundering in Russia's capital and blood has been spilled. . . .
>
> I know that it was a sleepless night for many of you. I know that you have understood everything. . . .
>
> Those waving red flags [the Communist flag] have once again covered Russia with blood. . . .
>
> I am asking you, dear Muscovites, to give your moral support to boost the spirits of the Russian soldiers and officers. . . . They have one task today: to defend our children, to defend our mothers and

fathers, to stop and neutralize the rioters and murderers. Moscow and Russia are awaiting your courage and decisive action. . . .

I am appealing to the citizens of Russia. . . .

I consider it my duty to turn to Muscovites. In the past day and night, our numbers have grown smaller. Let us bow to those who perished.

Many of you followed the call of your hearts and spent the last night in the center of Moscow, [guarding] the far and near approaches to the Kremlin. Tens of thousands of people risked their lives.

Your will, your civic courage, your moral strength have proved to be the most effective weapon.

I bow to you from my heart.[7]

At noon, clouds of black smoke rose from the White House as the most powerful tanks in the Russian army pounded the building with enormous shells. The people inside, at first so confident of victory, could not believe what was happening. "We were all stunned," one commented. "Nobody actually believed they [Yeltsin's forces] would actually fire shells at the Parliament."[8] Yet the firing continued until the top half of the White House was in flames. The firepower massed against the rebels was overwhelming and decisive. The surrender began at 5:00 P.M. and an hour later it was over. Khasbulatov, Rutskoi, and the other leaders emerged from their smoldering headquarters and were taken to prison. According to official reports at the time, about 150 people were killed and 600 wounded in the abortive revolt, but the toll soon rose above that figure.

Aftermath of the Revolt

In the week following his victory over the parliament, Yeltsin moved quickly to shore up his position. He banned 10 political parties and organizations and suspended 13 newspapers. Among the organizations banned were the National Salvation Front and Pamyat (PAH-myat), both extreme nationalist groups with openly Fascist leanings, as well as Aleksandr Rutskoi's People's Party of Free Russia and the Communist Party of Russia. Yeltsin also fired several high-ranking government officials, who had either supported the parliament or failed to support him, and suspended the Constitutional Court, which he accused of supporting the revolt. In addition, the Russian president suspended Russia's regional and town councils known as Soviets, many of which had sided with his opponents. He said they would be replaced by new, smaller elected assemblies to be known as dumas, a term which dated from pre-Soviet times.

In a gesture that was merely symbolic, yet of historic importance because of the symbol involved, Yeltsin canceled the changing of the military guard at the Lenin Mausoleum in Red Square. For 69 years—every hour of every day since January 26, 1924, except during World War II—the ceremonial change of the goose-stepping guards had taken place. Yeltsin offered no explanation for his decision, but for millions of Russians none was needed.

Most importantly, Yeltsin announced that there would be elections for a new parliament on December 12, 1993. The people would be voting for a two-house parliament known as the Federal Assembly. The lower house, called the State Duma, would have 450 seats. Half its members would be selected according to proportional representation: each party that received over 5 percent of the vote would get seats according to the percentage of votes it received. The other half of the State Duma's members would be elected by majority vote in 225 single-member districts, each containing about 500,000 voters. The upper house—the Federation Council—would be made up of two representatives elected from each of Russia's 89 territorial divisions, for a total of 178 members.

Several days later, Yeltsin added that when they elected a new parliament, the people would also vote on a new constitution. They would answer a simple question: "Do you Agree with the Constitution of the Russian Federation? Yes or No."[9] After all the wrangling prior to October 4, it took barely a month for Yeltsin's advisers to prepare a draft of the proposed new constitution that gave the president far stronger powers than before.

Political Parties and Groups

As the smoke slowly cleared after the October revolt, several major and over 1,000 minor political parties and groups crowded Russia's political stage. By early November, 21 parties claimed to have collected the required 100,000 signatures to compete in the upcoming parliamentary election. However, 8 were disqualified by Yeltsin's election commission on the grounds that they did not have the required signatures. The remaining 13 parties, ranged across the political spectrum and included the previously suspended Communist Party of Russia.

The party closest to Boris Yeltsin was Russia's Choice (after June 1994 known as Russia's Democratic Choice). It was led by Yegor Gaidar (guy-DAHR), an economist who served as Yeltsin's prime minister from June 1992 until being forced out by conservatives in parliament in December of that year. Thereafter, Gaidar served as first deputy prime minister and economics minister. Gaidar was a technocrat concerned with economic programs rather than a politician able to mobilize the public in support of new economic policies. Russia's Choice supported a rapid transition to a free-market economy and was a strong defender of human rights.

The second major party was Yabloko. The name was an acronym formed from the last names of its three main leaders, the best known of whom was the respected economist Gregory Yavlinsky. Since the word *yabloko* (YAH-bloh-kuh) means apple in Russian, the party had a unique and easily recognizable symbol. Yabloko also supported reform and the transition to a free-market economy, but at a slower pace than that advocated by Russia's Choice. Another major reformist group, the Russian Unity and Accord Party, also favored a slower pace of reform. One party that favored a faster pace of reform was the Democratic Reform Movement.

The Communist Party of the Russian Federation (CPRF) proved to be one of the remarkable success stories of Russian politics in the early 1990s. Immediately after the defeat of the August coup, Yeltsin had banned the old Soviet-era Communist Party from political activity in Russia and seized its property. However, its loyalists were permitted to organize new groups, and several new communist parties were back in business by 1993. The most effective of them was led by Gennady Zyuganov (zyoo-GAHN-of), a former high-ranking official in the defunct Soviet-era Communist Party. Not surprisingly, along with other communist groups, the CPRF opposed free-market reforms, saying the state should have a greater role in the economy. Zyuganov was a hard-line communist who blamed the West for the failings of the Soviet regime. His version of history included the assertion that after the Cuban missile crisis of 1962, when the West supposedly saw it could not defeat the Soviet Union militarily, it began a long-term campaign to destroy the Soviet Union by subversion. The CPRF had an interesting logo: the hammer and sickle of the old Soviet-era party with a new addition: the word "Russia." Several parties were closely allied with the CPRF. The most effective was the Agrarian Party, a group controlled by managers of Russia's collective farms.

The Democratic Party of Russia began its life as one of the more moderate parties opposing Yeltsin. Its most important leader was Nikolai Travkin, a construction engineer. Travkin's party opposed the dissolution of the Soviet Union in 1991. By 1993, it was one of the better organized of Russia's political parties. Travkin, known for his dynamic personality, had a reputation as a moderate with democratic leanings. However, one of the party's other leaders was Stanislav Govorukhin (guh-vah-RUH-kin), a filmmaker with extreme nationalist sympathies.

Standing out among the many extreme nationalist groups with Fascist tendencies was the Liberal Democratic Party (LBD). Its leader was a charismatic and volatile lawyer named Vladimir Zhirinovsky (zhee-reh-NOF-skee). The LBD, in its own way, fit the 18th century French thinker Voltaire's description of the Holy Roman Empire as "neither holy, Roman, nor an empire." Certainly the Liberal Democratic Party was neither liberal nor democratic, and, like many of Russia's other amorphously organized groupings in the early 1990s, it was barely a political party. Rather, it was the creature and vehicle of Zhirinovsky, a fanatical Russian nationalist, a vicious anti-Semite, and a unapologetic foe of democracy.

Although there were plenty of extreme nationalists in Russia, there was nobody in Russian politics quite like Zhirinovsky. More than any other public figure he seemed able to tap into the frustration and anger his countrymen felt over the collapse of their empire and the economic decline of their country. He used the language of hate and fear—denouncing the United States, Jews, and Russia's democratic politicians—to win the support of frightened and often desperate voters. Zhirinovsky was especially effective in attacking and mocking Yeltsin:

> One million wealthy and 150 million in chains. That's what Boris has brought you.
>
> They tried to apply Marx to us and that failed. Now they are applying Boris. How is that making you feel?
>
> O.K. We have tried it their way. Now try it mine. That is all I ask. Can I do it worse than they have? Can you honestly believe that I could do it worse?[10]

Vladimir Zhirinovsky, the ultranationalist opposition leader, whose bigoted and dictatorial views are considered a serious threat to the attempt to establish democratic rule in Russia.

An unusual political party that took shape during Russia's early post-Soviet years was the Russian Women's Party. It had its roots in the old Soviet-era Communist Party, but gradually developed its own identity during the 1980s. Its political outlook was a ragged patchwork of feminist and old-style Communist ideas, with a few twists such as a commitment to a "strong army" and state guarantees to soldiers and their families.

Election Results

The one-month election campaign was largely without spirit, except for Zhirinovsky's demagogic and flamboyant performance. The voters appeared uninterested, gloomy, and undecided about which party to support. Yeltsin refused officially to endorse any party, although it was clear that he supported Russia's Choice. Most of his energy was devoted to selling his constitution. Yegor Gaidar, the leader of Russia's Choice, proved to be a lackluster campaigner, while the reformers as a group were split into four political parties. Zhirinovsky, on the other hand, seemed to be in his element, especially on television. He pounded away with slogans about restoring Russia's empire and bringing order back to the troubled country. One of his most effective posters read, "I will bring Russia up off its knees." As election eve drew near, Gaidar issued a warning:

> You know, I do not have nightmares often. But sometimes I am afraid of coming to the parliament and seeing the same people there. The changes in representative power may not lead to a better result.[11]

Gaidar was right. The results shocked Yeltsin, Russia, and the world. In the party-preference vote, Zhirinovsky's party led the pack with about 23 percent of the vote. Russia's Choice came in a poor second with about 16 percent, while the revived Communist Party received 12 percent and their Agrarian allies about 8 percent. The other major parties, including the remaining reformist parties that generally supported Yeltsin, trailed with between 5 and 8 percent of the vote respectively. The Democratic Reform Movement, which had favored increasing the pace of economic reform, won only 4 percent of the votes. The votes from the 225 districts increased the strength of the reformist/Yeltsin block relative to both the extreme Nationalists and Communist forces, but nothing could change the fact that Yeltsin and the reformers had suffered a stunning defeat. While Yeltsin could point out that his constitution was approved by the voters, the victory was less than overwhelming: about 58 percent of those casting ballots on the issue voted for it.

Why had so many people turned against Yeltsin? Probably the single most important reason was the hardship they had endured because of economic reforms since 1991. By December 1993, most Russians were worse off economically than they had been under communism. They resented Russia's new rich—the small number of business people who had prospered in the fledgling environment. Rising crime, including organized crime, turned many people away from Yeltsin. So did the feeling of humiliation that came with Russia's loss of empire when the Soviet Union collapsed.

The impact of the election showed immediately in the shape of the new government. Missing from Yeltsin's new cabinet, announced in January, were Yegor Gaidar and other like-minded reformers. In their place were advocates of moving more slowly toward a free-market system. Prime Minister Victor Chernomyrdrin expressed a new caution toward economic reform when he commented that "the period of market romanticism is over."[12] At the same time, Russia's foreign minister, Andrei Kozyrev, began taking a harder line toward Russia's immediate neighbors and the West. This clearly was to satisfy voters who had voted for Zhirinovsky. In short, in making policy, the government had to consider what some people called the "Zhirinovsky factor."

The first meeting of the new parliament in January showed that Yeltsin's problems with Zhirinovsky were likely to be serious. In the Duma, Russia's Choice, bolstered by victories in the district elections, held 76 seats, the largest of any single party. Zhirinovsky's Liberal Democrats followed with 63 seats. Next came the Agrarian Party (55 seats), the Communist Party of the Russian Federation (45 seats), the Russian Unity and Accord Party (30 seats), the Yabloko group (25 seats), the Women of Russia Party (23 seats), and the Democratic Party (15 seats). What this meant was that together the reformers commanded less votes than a possible alliance between Zhirinovsky and the Communist/Agrarian forces. In fact, this "red-brown" alliance—red being the traditional Communist color and brown being a traditional Fascist color—materialized, at least on certain issues, when the Duma met. Zhirinovsky himself failed to get elected to the post of Speaker, despite noisy protests that included an order to the Duma members to "shut-up" and "get out of the hall." However, Yeltsin's forces did not get their way, either. The successful candidate was an antireform Communist from the Agrarian party, who was elected with Zhirinovsky's support. Meanwhile, the Federation Council elected a Yeltsin supporter as its chairman, but only after an intense overnight campaign to gather the necessary votes.

The New Constitution

When Russia began a new era in its history in 1992, it had no record of genuine constitutional government, that is, a regime where the government is genuinely limited by law. Neither the czars nor the Soviets operated under legal restrictions. The semiconstitutional experiment that began in 1906 collapsed in 1917, while the effort to build a constitutional state under the Provisional Government ended with the Bolshevik Revolution. The constitutions of the Soviet era were constitutions in name only; their main function was to mask dictatorial rule by the Communist Party.

In contrast, the 1993 constitution is the first attempt in Russia's history to define and limit state power. The document written by Yeltsin's staff, and approved by Russia's voters in December 1993, was a real constitution designed to create a government that operated according to law. It states the Russian Federation is a "democratic federative, law-governed state with a republican form of government."[13] It guarantees a wide range of human rights, including freedom of conscience, freedom of the press, freedom of movement, freedom from censorship, and the right to private property, including the right to own land. It also grants a range of social rights such as free education, free medical care, and protection against unemployment.

The constitution provides for a popularly elected president (but no vice-president), a government of ministers headed by a prime minister, a two-house legislature called the Federal Assembly and a Constitutional Court. The president has enormous power, far more then the presidents of the United States and other democratic countries. The constitution defines the president as the "head of state" and the country's "highest official." The president is also commander in chief of the armed forces. The president is elected for a four-year term (for a maximum of two terms) and has extensive powers. He nominates candidates for prime minister to the Federal Assembly, has wide latitude in appointing and dismissing ministers, and alone can call for referenda. The president, under certain conditions, can also issue decrees with the force of law (that is, they do not require parliament's approval), dissolve the State Duma (the lower house of parliament), declare a state of emergency, and temporarily curb civil rights. He also can veto legislation and can be overridden only by a two-thirds vote of both houses of parliament.

The government under the prime minister determines and carries out day-to-day policy. The prime minister is appointed by the president with the consent of the State Duma. The government drafts the budget for approval by the Duma.

The Federal Assembly is Russia's legislature. Its upper house, the Federation Council, is elected by the country's 89 regions and republics, with two representatives chosen from each. The lower house, the State Duma, is elected on a population basis. Half of its 450 deputies are elected from single-member districts; the other half is chosen according to the percentage of the vote competing parties receive in a national election. The parliament has the power to pass federal laws and amend the constitution. The State Duma can impeach the president, and the Federation Council can then remove him from office.

The Constitutional Court considers the constitutionality of laws and decrees. It is made up of 19 independent judges, appointed by the president and confirmed by the Federation Council, who cannot be dismissed from office. It reviews cases submitted by state bodies and must approve an impeachment proceeding against the president. Another important feature of Russia's new constitution is that it strengthens the federal government at the expense of the regions and republics. But perhaps no feature of the new constitution is more important than two that are *not* there. Unlike czarist-era statements, the 1993 constitution makes no reference to an official state religion. Unlike the Soviet-era constitutions, it makes no reference to an official state ideology.

The new constitution has its flaws, some of them serious. On some important points, it is vague or contradictory. One particular problem, according to many experts, is the placement of the parliament in the new overall consitutional order. At issue are the powers of parliament's lower house, the State Duma (or Duma, as it is generally called). When Yeltsin presented the constitution, some experts feared with considerable justification that the Duma lacked the powers to function as a genuine parliament, especially in light of the powers of the president. The Duma lacked the power to supervise adequately the activities of government ministers or to monitor the implementation and observance of the laws it passed. The war in Chechnya (che-CH'NYA) highlighted the limits of the Duma's powers and its internal divisions. At the same time, the Duma's hybrid electoral system, under which half its members are elected directly from districts and the other half are elected from party lists, had negative effects. The electoral system tended to undermine the cohesion of political parties, as members elected directly from districts often shifted from faction to faction. This in turn helped make the legislative process chaotic.

during its first years of existence the Duma often passed laws with contradictory provisions.

However, fears that the Duma would be largely ineffectual turned out to be exaggerated. Despite formal constitutional limits and its own internal squabbling the Duma managed to forge an important role for itself. While clearly a lesser power than the executive branch, the Duma, dominated after both the 1993 and 1995 elections by Yeltsin's opponents, proved to be anything but a rubber stamp. After 1993 the Duma avoided serious confrontations with the president. In Februrary 1994 it demonstrated it could stretch its consitutional powers when it pardoned the leaders of the 1991 coup against Mikhail Gorbachev and the October 1993 parliamentary revolt against Yeltsin. In 1995, for the first time since the Russian Federation came into existence, the Duma succeeded in adopting a budget before the deadline when it was to take effect. It established a track record with legislation in areas such as reorganization of the judicial system, the criminal code, and voting rights. Of the 462 laws the Duma passed between 1993 and 1995, Yeltsin signed 282 into law. The president in turn also tried to work within the new and developing system. As the Duma and the president groped for a workable way of governing their sprawling and troubled country, their competition and conflict at least were increasingly governed by mutually accepted political rules and limits.

Problems of Government under the New Constitution

While Russia's new constitution suggested the promise of better government, what was written on paper often was not translated into reality. In fact, even with its new constitution, Russia continued to be poorly governed. One problem was that many basic institutions that any government needs to govern did not exist; for example, in November 1994, the Duma passed a new civil code designed to regulate many types of legal relations between citizens. The code officially went into effect on January 1, 1995, but in a practical sense its impact was limited. This was because the country still did not have the judicial structures necessary for the code to work. It still needed a modern and efficient system of courts, a modern bar to define and regulate the activities of lawyers, and knowledgeable officials to staff the legal system. In addition, the new code did not cover most property in land. That huge gap would have to be covered by a new land code.

An even more serious problem was the central government's inability to collect taxes. During the Gorbachev era, Russia's tax collection system fell apart in what one observer had said "may be the biggest tax revolt in recent history."[14] Local and republic governments simply refused to turn tax money they had collected over to the government in the Kremlin. The impact of that tax revolt was crippling and certainly contributed to the eventual collapse of the Soviet regime in 1991. Yeltsin's attempts to remedy the situation after 1992 went poorly. The central government's tax service was badly over-matched given the huge job it faced. It did not have adequate information on taxpayers, either individual or corporate. It lacked a computer system capable of processing the information it did have.

As a result, by 1995 Moscow was able to collect only one-quarter of the taxes it imposed. Some of the country's largest companies, such as the giant natural gas company Gazprom, owed the equivalent of hundreds of millions, or even billions, of dollars. (By 1995, inflation had lowered the value of the ruble to almost 4,000 to the dollar, so these debts were measured in trillions, and hundreds of trillions, of rubles.) In 1997, Russia's tax service estimated that only 17 percent of corporate and other taxpayers provide payments fully and on time. About 49 percent occasionally complied, while 34 percent simply did not pay at all. The worst offenders were the country's biggest companies. Thus 72 companies, including Gazprom and the giant automobile company Avtovaz (which as of early 1997 owned $500 million), accounted for more than 40 percent of all tax arrears.

Meanwhile, local and regional governments raised funds to pay for their expenses but refused to turn over the required amounts to the central government. In 1994, only 7 percent of the taxes collected at the local level went to fund federal expenses. That figure was down from the 9 percent level of 1993, the year before the new constitution took effect.

Making matters worse, corruption ate at Russia's financial resources at both ends of the tax pipeline. Tax service employees were poorly paid. The salaries of those living in Moscow barely kept them above the poverty line. It was therefore no surprise that they readily took bribes for not checking a citizen's income declaration or ignoring that a business had hidden a major part of its income. On the other end of the pipeline, it was hard to blame local governors for refusing to send their required payments to Moscow. After all, it was very difficult, at least if one stayed within the law, for regional governments to get the money the central government by law was supposed to provide them. The "rules of the game" often required large bribes to Moscow officials in the finance ministry to free up the transfer of funds to the regions. The corruption was so bad that governors often hired private specialists in the business of bribery to do their work for them. Known as *zhuchki* (zhuch-KEE), "little beatles," these professional bribers and influence peddlers kept a percentage of the take, sometimes as high as 10 percent.

The Kremlin's efforts to get around its tax difficulties frequently made things worse. In the spring of 1994 the central government resorted to a measure used under both the czarist and Soviet regimes: it reestablished the old state alcohol monopoly. Because many Russians are heavy drinkers, that monopoly had once paid for a significant part of both czarist and Soviet budgets. Under the czars, people had referred to the national budgets as "drunken budgets." Now, almost eight decades after the fall of the czar, the government in Moscow once again was going to try to finance its operations by exploiting the country's destructive drinking problem. Another tactic was to place high and often unjustifiable taxes on foreign companies operating in Russia. Unlike Russian companies and taxpayers, foreign firms tended to pay their taxes; however, high or improper taxes discouraged foreign investment in Russia, which already was a risky business because of lawlessness, corruption, and general instability.

In addition to all these problems, Russia lacked the most basic prerequisite for effective tax collection: physical safety for its tax collectors. The dangers of the job led the government to create a special force in 1996 to collect taxes. Its motto was "We have weapons, and we know how to use them." Apparently, neither the weapons nor the motto were enough. During the first 8 months of 1997, 10 members of the tax collection service were killed on the job. Forty more were injured, while two were missing.

Another area where the new constitution did not make a sufficient practical difference involved Russia's security services. During both the czarist and Soviet eras, the Russian people suffered under the state's security services or secret police. The Soviet regime operated the world's largest secret police. Founded in December 1917, it was known by several names over the next seven decades; during the post-Stalin era that name, in translation, was the Committtee on State Security, or KGB. The KGB's many tasks included foreign espionage and spying on the Soviet people in order to ferret out and destroy any political opposition. With its hundreds of thousands of agents, troops, and bureaucrats, the KGB was the strong arm of the Communist Party that kept a tight grip on Soviet society until the Gorbachev era.

With the collapse of the Soviet Union, the KGB was broken up, but it was not reformed. Yeltsin divided it into five separate agencies, and he subsequently reshuffled or renamed several of them. The largest and most important of the successor agencies was the Federal Security Service (FSB)*, which was responsible for internal security. Symbolically, it continued to have its headquarters in Moscow in a foreboding building known as the Lubyanka, the dreaded old headquarters of the Soviet secret police. The second major successor to the KGB was the Foreign Intelligence Service (SVR)*. In 1993, in addition to the KGB's five successors, Yeltsin created yet another independent agency specifically designed to protect the president and his family called the Presidential Security Service (SBP)*. Its head was General Alexandr Korzhakov (kuhr-zhah-KOFF), at the time Yeltsin's closest friend and adviser. In effect, the SBP functioned as a mini–secret police for Yeltsin right in the Kremlin.

Nor was this all. Russia had a number of other security agencies inherited from the Soviet era, including the military's Main Intelligence Directorate (GRU)*, the ruthless and highly effective intelligence organization responsible for many Soviet espionage successes during the cold war. The problem as Russia began its post-Soviet era was that these agencies retained enormous powers and were not subject to parliamentary oversight. As Yeltsin increasingly became concerned with Russia's burgeoning crime problem, he gave its security services increased authority. That authority did little to reduce crime. Nor were the security agencies particularly successful in thwarting terrorist acts that grew out of the struggle against the secessionist region of Chechnya after 1994 (see pages 107–108). Furthermore, the security agencies themselves were tarred by corruption. More important, many observers considered them a threat to the newly won freedoms of the Russian people. A new law in 1995 gave the FSB increased investigative and arrest powers that, according to one

---

*Note: Abbreviations for government agencies correspond to their official Russian name, not the English translation.

expert, "even the old KGB would have envied."[15] The simultaneous firing of Korzhakov and the head of the FSB in mid-1996 changed some faces at the top, but it did nothing to change a situation that could easily undermine Russia's struggling democratic institutions.

The War over Chechnya

As the Soviet Union was falling apart in 1991, Russia faced its own problem with breakaway regions. The most serious secessionist movement developed in the repubic of Chechnya, which is located in the North Caucasus. The Chechens, a Muslim group, made up most of the republic's 1.3 million people. The warlike Chechens first clashed with the expanding Russian Empire in the late 18th century. Russia's conquest of the North Caucasus during the 19th century took five brutal decades. The Chechens, whom the Russians called the "Mountaineers," resisted fiercely and did not surrender until 1859. Among the Russian officers who fought them was the great writer Leo Tolstoy. He described their resistance and the heroism of their leader Shamil in his short story "Hajdi Murat."

Even after the Russian conquest, the Chechens did not give in. After decades of passive resistance, they tried unsuccessfully to claim their independence in the aftermath of the collapse of czarism in 1917. In 1944, Stalin deported the Chechens to Kazakhstan after falsely accusing them of mass collaboration with the Germans during World War II. In 1957 the Soviet government under Nikita Khrushchev finally allowed them to return to their homeland. Many Chechens then left Central Asia to return to the North Caucasus by foot.

The chaos that swept Chechnya during the last years of Soviet power provided an opportunity for an ambitious former Soviet military officer named Dzhokhar Dudayev (ja-HAR doo-DAH-jef). Born in Kazakhstan, he returned with his people to Chechnya in the 1950s, but he then spent most of his adult life far from the North Caucasus while serving in the Soviet air force. Dudayev finally returned to Chechnya to stay in 1991. In the fall of that year he seized power and gave that power a legal cloak by winning the presidency of Chechnya in a rigged election. On November 1, 1991 he declared Chechnya a sovereign and independent state.

This was a serious matter for the Yeltsin government; government officials worried that Chechnya's action could set off a chain reaction in the six other ethnic republics in the North Caucasus, five of which have large Muslim populations. They also worried about secessionist tendencies elsewhere in Russia. Nonetheless, for the next two-and-one-half years the Russian government, busy with other problems, did little to assert its authority in Chechnya. Dudayev meanwhile kicked sand in Moscow's face by allowing Chechen criminal gangs to base their operations in the republic. Among their illegal activities were arms smuggling and narcotics trafficking.

In June 1993 Dudayev dissolved the local Chechen parliament and began ruling openly as a dictator. Local opposition to him grew. By mid-1994 Moscow began putting strong pressure on Dudayev's breakaway regime, mainly by supporting groups rebelling against him. That tactic reached a dead end in November, when anti-Dudayev forces, despite assistance from Soviet security forces, failed to seize the Chechen captial of Grozny (GROHZ-nee). In December, Yeltsin sent thousands of Russian army troops into Chechnya to destroy Dudayev's regime and end the Chechen secession.

The question is why Yeltsin decided to strike in late 1994. It is true that the criminality originating in Chechnya was a serious problem. Russian officials sometimes bitterly referred to Chechnya as Dudayev's "free economic-criminal zone." Even more disturbing was the potential threat Chechnya's secesssion posed to Russia's unity. However, while these were serious matters, they were not so immediately menacing that they demanded quick military action. In fact, by 1994 there were distinct signs that Dudayev's grip on Chechnya was weakening. But Yeltsin had other concerns. He was deeply worried about his chances for reelection in 1996. A successful strike against Chechnya would enable him to steal some of the nationalist thunder that Zhirinovsky was using so effectively. Furthermore, some of his closest advisers promised him a quick victory. They included Korzhakov, the defense minister Pavel Grachev (grah-CHOFF), the head of the Federal Security Service, and the minister of the interior. Grachev even boasted that a regiment of paratroopers could take Grozny from Dudayev's forces in two hours. Yeltsin was convinced by this "party of war." In December 1994 he sent thousands of Russian troops into Chechnya.

The assault ran into trouble from the start. It was badly planned and the soldiers involved were poorly trained. When Russian tanks attacked the city of Grozny, Chechen guerrilla fighters cut them to pieces. Russian tanks became death traps when Chechen guerrilla fighters ambushed them and cut them off from help in Grozny's streets. The furious Russians responded by a massive air and artillery bombardment of Grozny that destroyed most of the city. At one point, more than 4,000 bombs and shells rained down on the city every hour. At least 25,000 civilians died during this assault, including many ethnic Russian inhabitants of Grozny who were unable to flee into the Chechen countryside. Russian army losses are still disputed; estimates range from 1,800 to 5,000 dead. The Chechens admitted to losing 3,500 men, although the actual figure probably is much higher. The main government center in the city fell on January 19, but the Russians did not establish complete control of Grozny until March 1995. By then the main battles of the war were being fought in Chechnya's towns and villages in the countryside. By the summer, the Russian army controlled most of the key points in Chechnya'a lowlands as well as several key mountain strongholds.

The Chechens countered by taking the war to Russian territory with spectacular and deadly acts of terrorism. In June, a Chechen force

A Russian soldier, a member of a tank crew, lies dead amid the rubble of Grozny on January 1, 1995 after a night of heavy fighting in the Chechen capital.

crossed the Russian border, traveled 200 miles undetected to the city of Budyonnovsk (buh-DION-nohfsk), and immdiately killed about 60 people. The Chechens then seized control of a hospital and took about 2,000 hostages, holding women hostages up to the windows and using them as shields. Yeltsin damaged his standing with the Russian people by leaving the country during the crisis to attend an international economic summit meeting with Western leaders. He left it to Prime Minister Chernomydrin to negotiate the release of the hostages, which Chernomyrdin did in front of the television cameras while millions of his countrypeople watched. By the time the raid was over and the Chechens retreated, 120 civilians were dead. A second raid into Russian territory in January 1996 finally led the Russian government to begin negotiations with the Chechens.

The two sides negotiated a cease-fire in July and then promptly broke it. In December, Russian forces took Chechnya's second largest city. They then held every major Chechen town. As the fighting spilled into 1996, Russian forces in April succeeded in killing Dudayev. Their triumph was short-lived, however. Fighting alternated with negotiations into the summer until August, when Chechen forces stormed back into Grozny. Once again, the demoralized Russian troops were unprepared, and the city fell to the rebels. It was a stunning defeat that showed Russia and the entire world how badly the Russian army had deteriorated since the collapse of the Soviet Union. Meanwhile, the death toll, Russian and Chechen, reached 100,000.

Once again the two sides returned to the negotiating table. This time the Russians could do little more than seek terms that would mask as much as possible their disastrous defeat. Yeltsin sent fomer general Aleksandr Lebed to deal with the Chechens. Lebed was a highly respected soldier and war hero who had recently retired from the military. He had been a presidential candidate in the 1996 elections (see pages 112–114) before switching his support to Yeltsin, who then appointed him to head Russia's National Security Council. The agreement Lebed negotiated called for a withdrawal of Russian troops from Chechnya. It left the issue of Chechnya's independence unresolved, specifying only for a five-year transition period. After that the people of the republic would decide its final status.

Russia began withdrawing its troops from Chechnya in December. In January 1997, Chechnya held a presidential election. The voters overwhelmingly chose Aslan Maskhadov (mahs-HAH-doff), a former Soviet army colonel and chief of staff of all Chechen forces during the war, as their republic's new leader.

Exactly what the August peace agreement meant depended on who was asked. Maskhadov had a reputation as a reasonable and moderate man, yet both he and more militant Chechen leaders left no doubt that after five years they expected full independence. Yeltsin and those around him were no less adamant that Chechnya, one way or another, would have to remain part of the Russian Federation. In late 1996 and early 1997, however, neither side was prepared to force the issue. The Russians were badly wounded and humiliated, and they had other serious problems to deal with. The Chechens, whose tiny republic was surrounded on three sides by the Russian Federation, lived in a land devastated by war that could never recover economically without Russian cooperation. What this meant was that the fighting was over, at least until the crucial unsettled issue of Chechnya's final status could no longer be avoided.

Political Conflicts and Contests: 1993–1996

Between 1993 and 1996, Russia took important steps in laying the foundations for a political system based on genuine elections. In December 1993, as mentioned earlier, Russian voters elected a State Duma. Two years later they once again elected a Duma. In June and July 1996 they chose a president in two rounds of voting. Rather than becoming apathetic, voters went to the polls in increasing numbers. While only about 50 percent of eligible voters cast ballots in 1993, about 65 percent went to the polls in 1995 and nearly 70 percent voted in the presidential elections of 1996. Fall 1996 also saw the election of 50 regional governors. All elections were held on schedule and according to law and, equally important, all sides accepted the results. Whatever the shortcomings of these elections, they represented a major achievement for a country with a history of centuries of czarist absolute power and seven decades of Soviet totalitarian rule.

Russia's second parliamentary elections took place after only two years because of rules Yeltsin proclaimed in late 1993 before the adoption of the new constitution. Thereafter, the Duma's term would be four years, unless, of course, the president dissolved the Duma and called for new elections. During that short first Duma term Russia's political turmoil continued. Although there was not much organized opposition to the war in Chechnya, the war still was extremely unpopular. The defeats and high casualties the Russian army suffered and the brutality of the tactics it used against the Chechens dismayed millions of Russians. A number of Russian mothers whose sons were fighting or missing in Chechnya bitterly denounced the war. The war undermined Yeltsin's popularity and the standing of the political groups that supported him. The strains of war also undermined Yeltsin's fragile health. The war's mounting cost as the fighting dragged on damaged the Russian economy and thereby increased the hardships of citizens of ordinary means who were struggling to make ends meet. The spread of organized crime, which produced several highly publicized murders of prominent people, also damaged Yeltsin and his supporters. A major shock ocurred in March 1995 when criminals murdered Vladimir Listev, a highly respected journalist who had recently been appointed as the head of Russian public television.

One of the most severe blows to Yeltsin's credibility with the Russian people occurred when the fighting in Chechnya reached into Russian-inhabited terrritory during the Budyonnovsk crisis of June 1995. Criticism of the Kremlin's "party of war" mounted. The Duma overwhelmingly passed a "no confidence" vote. To defuse the criticism and shield his government from the fallout from the Chechen war, Yeltsin in June dismissed three of his ministers associated with the "party of war." This changed enough minds in the Duma to prevent passage of a second no-confidence vote, which would have brought down the government and forced immediate new elections. Yeltsin's poor health forced him into the hospital in June, and again in October, which added to the general uncertainty.

Meanwhile, the country geared up for the scheduled parliamentary elections in December. The one clear thing at the moment was that the hopes of Russia moving toward a stable two-party system were not materializing. In 1993, 13 political parties had contested the election; in 1995, 43 parties fielded candidates. One factor promoting a bit of order was a new rule that to win a parliamentary seat in the proportional representation portion of the election a party had to win at least 5 percent of the vote. This rule was designed to eliminate small splinter parties, or at least to keep them out of the Duma.

The 1995 election brought some major changes to Russia's political landscape. Yegor Gaidar's party, Russia's Democratic Choice, the group most closely identified with the government's economic policies and the largest party in the old Duma, lost most of its support. It failed to get the 5 percent of the vote necessary to win seats in the proportional representation part of the vote. Russia's Democratic Choice ended up with only nine seats won in single-member districts. Zhirinovsky's LPD also lost strength. However, it still managed to finish second in the proportional representation race with over 11 percent of the vote. Just behind the LPD was a newly formed party called Russia Is Our Home led by Prime Minister Chernomyrdin. Russia Is Our Home was decidedly less impressive than it looked on paper; in reality it was more of a collection of people who clung together for political gain than a political party with a clear platform or direction. It had little grassroots support and was likely to disintegrate if Chernomyrdin lost his post as prime minister. The only other noncommunist party to top the 5 percent threshold was Yabloko, which now replaced Russia's Democratic Choice as the main supporter of reformist parties in the Duma.

The winner in the election was the Communist Party of the Russian Federation. Led once again by Gennady Zyuganov, the CPRF took more than 22 percent of the vote. As in 1993, it drew its main support from older people unable to adjust to Russia's post-Soviet economic realities. This gave it a larger base of support than any other party but also in an important way cast it as a party of the past. The CPRF's Duma seat total from the proportional representation race (99) and single-seat districts (58) was 157. This gave it just over a third of the Duma's 450 seats. Russia Is Our Home (45 and 10) was second in overall seats with 55, the LDPR (50, but only one single district seat) was third with 51, while Yabloko (31 and 14) was fourth with 45.

Among the parties with less then 5 percent of the vote, the Agrarian Party won 20 seats; Russia's Democratic choice won 9 seats; and a variety of other parties split the remaining seats. They included a new party called the Congress of Russian Communities, one of whose leaders was former general Aleksandr Lebed, which won 3.9 percent of the votes and five single district seats.

The CPRF's victory made itself felt in early 1996 when Russia's pro-Western foreign minister Andrei Kozyrev resigned. His replacement, Yevgeny Primakov (pree-mah-KOFF), previously head of the Foreign Intelligence Service, was considerably less friendly to the West than Kozyrev. He was a supporter of many policies followed during the Soviet era, including its support of Middle Eastern Arab dictatorships such as that of Iraq's Saddam Hussein. Anatoly Chubais, the first deputy prime minister who managed a key part of Yeltsin's economic reform program, also lost his job. His replacement was an unimaginative Soviet-era bureaucrat who previously headed a huge automobile factory. The shake-up also brought changes to several other ministries. The Duma then chose CPRF member Gennady Seleznev (seh-lehz-NYOFF) as its speaker, or chairman.

These developments were a prelude to the real contest: the 1996 presidential election. Both Yeltsin's popularity and his health were at a low ebb. His chances of winning reelection seemed poor. During the early months of the year Yeltsin and several of his political advisers, in particular Aleksandr Korzhakov, seriously thought of canceling the elections, provided they could find the right excuse. In the end, Yeltsin decided to run. So did nine other candidates, including Zyuganov, Zhirinovsky, Gregory Yavlinsky of Yabloko, and a new face in Russian politics, former general Aleksandr Lebed. There also was an old face, the former general secretary and Soviet president Mikhail Gorbachev, who decided to run although polls showed he would win less than 1 percent of the vote. With so many candidates in the field, it was virtually certain that none of them would win 50 percent of the vote. That meant there would be a first election round in June, after which the two leading candidates would face off in a second and final round in July.

The campaign began with Yeltsin trailing Zyuganov badly in the polls. The ailing president immediately took a daring step by puttting his former first deputy prime minister Anatoly Chubais (chuh-bah-EES) in charge of his campaign. Chubais did an excellent job of organizing the campaign and motivating the president, despite his poor health, to campaign hard. Another key player in the campaign was Tatiana Dyachenko, the president's younger daughter, who on many issues emerged as her father's closest adviser. Over the next 4 months, Yeltsin made an astounding 33 campaign trips. Equally important, he also made full use of his presidential powers to influence voters. The government spent billions of dollars to pay workers overdue wages or provide other services to voters that they

Gennadi Zyuganov, leader of the Communist Party of the Russian Federation, waves a red caranation as he marches with supporters toward Moscow's Red Square on May 1, 1997 in celebration of the traditional Marxist holiday May Day.

were unable to get before the campaign began. Russia's major private media networks, which were owned by his supporters, gave Yeltsin constant positive coverage. Other wealthy supporters who feared a Communist victory poured money into Yeltsin's campaign. Most journalists, who also dreaded a Communist regime, praised Yeltsin and attacked Zyuganov. Rock stars and other entertainers put on concerts throughout the country to win the youth vote for the president. At one of the concerts, in the provincial city of Rostov, Yeltsin joined a line of miniskirted young women and danced as the rock music blared. While Zyuganov took regular commercial airline flights, Yeltsin crisscrossed the country in his presidential jet.

Yeltsin's major campaign tactic was to switch the attention from Russia's economic problems and make communism the main issue. He warned that a Zyuganov victory would mean a return to dictatorship. Zyuganov helped his opponent by making increasingly hard-line statements as the campaign wore on. Helped by Zuyganov's failure to escape from the shadow of failed communism, Yeltsin's campaign steamroller and avalanche of spending produced results. Yeltsin won a plurality in the first round of the election, with 35.8 percent of the vote to Zyuganov's 32.5 percent. To guarantee victory in the runoff, the president turned to Lebed, who had finished a strong third with a surprising 14.7 percent of the vote. (Gorbachev finished seventh with .5 percent of the vote.) Yeltsin won Lebed's support by appointing him head of Russia's National Security Council, a step that suggested to many that Yeltsin favored Lebed as his eventual successor. The president also fired his unpopular defense minister, Pavel Grachev, and the equally unpopular Korzhakov, both of whom were closely identified with the disastrous war in Chechnya. In July, Yeltsin coasted to victory over Zyuganov in the runoff election, winning about 54 percent to Zyuganov's 40 percent. Among the other votes cast, about 5 percent voted against both candidates.

Yeltsin's Second Term

Yeltsin was inaugurated for his second term on August 9, 1996. During the ceremony he was pale and shaky and obviously very ill, but Yeltsin still had the strength to cut a potential rival down to size. At the end of August, Lebed negotiated the cease-fire in Chechnya that Yeltsin so desperately needed. The president and many of his advisers did not like the terms of the agreement, which they believed offered the Chechens too much; however, the demoralized condition of the Russian army left them unable to reject the agreement. Yeltsin waited until October and then fired Lebed from all his government posts. The next month, the president underwent heart surgery.

After his recovery, Yeltsin took another major step. In March 1997, he overhauled his government by firing several ministers and important new appointments. Two of the new additions indicated that Yeltsin once again planned to resume a vigorous reform program. The first was Anatoly

Prime Minister Viktor Chernomyrdin (center) is flanked by Yeltsin's two leading reformers, First Deputy Prime Minister Anatoly Chubais (left) and First Deputy Prime Minister Boris Nemtsov, during a session of the Russian Duma in October 1997.

Chubais, who once again became a first deputy prime minister. A week later Yeltsin appointed another first deputy prime minister. He was Boris Nemtsov (nehm-TSOFF), the young and vigorous governor of the Nizhnii Novgorod region east of Moscow. Just 37 years old, Nemtsov had won recognition for his market-oriented economic reforms that were widely considered the most successful in Russia. However, it remained an open question whether Nemtsov, even working together with Chubais, could duplicate his Nizhnii Novgorod successes on the much larger and more demanding stage the size of all of Russia.

Yeltsin's governmental overhaul did not solve any of the problems related to the governing of Russia. Nor did it end controversies surrounding Russia's top officials. In November the news broke that First Deputy Prime Ministry Chubais had signed a book contract worth $90,000 with a publisher connected with a major bank that had recently won a privatization auction for one of Russia's most valuable companies. Although the auction in question had been conducted fairly, the news of the book contract undermined Chubais's credibility. As a political storm swirled around Chubais in Moscow and damaged his ability to promote reforms, the government of Saratov (sa-ra-TOFF), a region along the Volga River, took a step of its own to push reform forward. It put into force a law, Russia's first, that permitted the sale of land, including agricultural land. Meanwhile, on January 1, 1998 the central government introduced a new ruble to replace Russia's old, inflation-cheapened currency. Each new ruble was worth 1,000 old ones, which meant that a dollar was worth about six rubles, instead of about 6,000. On March 5, there was another positive development when after months of bitter debate the Communist-controlled Duma finally passed the budget the Yeltsin government had submitted for 1998.

The budget agreement seemed to bring an element of stability to Russia's government, but not for long. On March 13, Yeltsin stunned his country and the world by firing his entire cabinet. The main targets of this shocking move appeared to be Prime Minister Chernomyrdin, First Deputy Prime Minister Chubais, and Interior Minister Anatoly Kulikov. Yeltsin probably decided to get rid of Kulikov, a staunch supporter of the disastrous war in Chechnya, and Chubais, who often was blamed for the hardship caused by economic reforms, because they had become political liabilities. His decision to dismiss Chernomyrdin was more difficult to understand. Chernomyrdin had been Russia's prime minister since December 1992. He had won repect for his job performance and had become a source of political stability. At the same time, he did not push economic change as far as most reformers insisted was necessary. Most observers guessed that Yeltsin acted to cut down a man who might challenge his authority and become a political rival. By 1998 Chernomyrdin was widely considered a potential candidate for president of Russia in the year 2000. This seemed to bother Yeltsin: even though he was constitutionally barred from running for a third term, Yeltsin was known to be considering ways to run again anyway.

To replace Chernomyrdin as prime minister Yeltsin chose an unknown reformist banker, 35-year-old Sergei Kiriyenko (kee-ree-YEN-kuh). Kiriyenko's appointment seemed to represent what Yeltsin wanted: a prime minister without a political base and therefore totally dependent on him. At the same time, the new cabinet, which included Boris Nemtsov as one of three deputy prime ministers and several other free-market advocates, appeared to signal that Yeltsin intended to push reform with renewed vigor. However, just five months later, on August 23, Yeltsin again suddenly turned Russia's political revolving door. Out were Kiriyenko and his entire cabinet. In, once more, or so it seemed, was the old reliable Chernomyrdin as acting prime minister. However, this time the revolving door spun out of Yeltsin's control. Russia's growing economic crisis (see chapter 7) and Yeltsin's own erratic behavior weakened him and emboldened his political opponents, including Gennady Zyuganov and the CPRF. The result was that the Duma refused to confirm Chernomyrdin. After a three-week standoff Yeltsin was forced to compromise and to accept Yevgeny Primakov, Russia's foreign minister since 1996, as the country's new prime minister.

Primakov's appointment was significant. He was a Soviet-era bureaucrat who was certain to modify the economic reform policies Russia had followed since 1992 and possibly reverse some of them. Primakov also was likely to toughen Russian foreign policy toward the United States and the NATO powers. Perhaps most significant, Primakov's appointment was Yeltsin's most important political defeat since he became president of Russia. In light of the president's uncertain health, it probably marked the beginning of the end of the Yeltsin era. That added a heavy dose of uncertainty to Russia's many troubles. Overall, in contemplating Russia's future as it approached the year 2000 there was far more reason for concern than optimism.

NOTES

1. Boris Yeltsin, *Against the Grain: An Autobiography,* trans. Michael Glenny (New York: Summit Books, 1990), p. 21.
2. David Remnick, *Lenin's Tomb: The Last Days of the Soviet Empire* (New York: Random House, 1993), p. 433.
3. Quoted in Ann Sheehy, "Russia's Republics: A Threat to Its Territorial Integrity?" in *RFE/RL Research Report,* vol. 2, no. 20 (May 14, 1993), p. 34.
4. Remnick, *Lenin's Tomb,* p. 467.
5. The *New York Times,* October 3, 1993.
6. The *New York Times,* October 4, 1994.
7. The *New York Times,* October 5, 1994.
8. The *New York Times,* October 6, 1993.
9. The *New York Times,* October 16, 1993.
10. The *New York Times Magazine,* June 19, 1994, p. 56.
11. The *New York Times,* December 11, 1993.
12. The *New York Times,* January 21, 1994.
13. The *New York Times,* November 9, 1993.
14. S. Frederick Starr, "The Paradox of Yeltsin's Russia," *The Wilson Quarterly,* Summer 1995, p. 69.
15. Amy Knight, "Internal Security and the Rule of Law," *Current History,* October 1996, p. 312.

7

Building a
New Economy

*T*he new Russia began its history carrying an immense economic burden. The old Soviet economy, upon which the life of the country had been based for 60 years, was in an advanced state of decay. Only bits and pieces of post-Communist free-market economy had managed to take hold. The country's standard of living was plunging. Making matters worse, although Russia could draw on the experiences of several Eastern European countries in moving from communism to capitalism, its size and historical experience made many of its problems unique. Russia had no model it could follow in making an extraordinarily complex and difficult transition from a planned to a market economy. Everyone from President Yeltsin on down was learning on the job.

In order to understand the economic problems Russia faced, it is first necessary to look at how the old Soviet economy worked, and did not work. It is also necessary to understand what happened to Russia's economy during the Gorbachev era, when the goal was to reform and restructure Soviet-style socialism.

The Soviet Economy

The Soviet economy was created by Stalin's industrialization drive that began in the late 1920s and peaked during the 1930s. The main features of that policy were: the abolition of private property and the free market, emphasis on developing heavy industry capable of building a modern military machine, the collectivization of agriculture, and a centralized planning system controlled by the government in Moscow.

The economy that resulted from these policies was riddled with problems. Prices, wages, what was grown or manufactured, and much more was controlled by the state, which rarely responded to consumer needs. There were no privately owned shops, independent professionals such as doctors or engineers, or service businesses to provide what the socialist economy failed to provide. The collective farm system was extraordinarily inefficient. It not only left Russia and the rest of the Soviet Union with six decades of food lines, but also without farmers willing or able to take any initiative to solve their problems. The planning system directed the country's most valuable natural resources and highly skilled people into industries that fed its military machine. Furthermore, the planning system was incapable of using the resources it had effectively, especially as the economy became more complicated after World War II.

There were, of course, some successes. By the end of the 1930s, the Soviet Union had a modern industrial infrastructure that produced many of the world's best tanks, artillery, and other weapons. Even during the Cold War era, planners could mobilize resources to build giant projects such as the Baikal-Amur Mainline, a new line on the Trans-Siberian Railroad. Some industries connected to the military or space exploration were among the best in the world. These, however, were the exceptions to the rule. Soviet leaders knew their country's socialist economy was overcentralized and inefficient compared to the economies of the capitalist countries.

Attempts at reform failed. Nikita Khrushchev's reforms of the 1950s and early 1960s ran aground on the rocks of his own poorly conceived programs and the opposition of Communist bureaucrats, who eventually overthrew him. Also, Khrushchev never questioned either central planning or the collective farm system. The Soviet central planning system continued to discourage innovation. Managers were rewarded for fulfilling production quotas, whether or not the products they made were of high quality or what the economy really needed. Under Brezhnev, after a short-lived attempt to increase efficiency, waste and corruption reached runaway proportions. About 20 percent of the grain and 40 percent of the potatoes rotted or spoiled before reaching the consumer, one-third of the natural gas leaked out of pipelines, and one-tenth of all oil produced was spilled. Workers, demoralized by low wages and poor consumer goods, had a saying: "They pretend to pay, we pretend to work."

As the Cold War dragged on, Soviet economic performance increasingly lagged behind that of the Western industrialized nations. Western producers had to introduce new technologies to stay in business; the Soviet planned economy had no corresponding incentive. By the 1980s, the technological backwardness of the Soviet economy, relative to the United States and its allies, threatened the Soviet Union's ability to keep up with Western military advances. It was clear that muddling through, as Brezhnev had done, had to give way to extensive reform. Economic reform, therefore, was the centerpiece of Mikhail Gorbachev's program after he came to power in 1985.

Gorbachev and Perestroika

Gorbachev's initial economic reforms caused more problems than they solved. They amounted to little more than using the same old methods to tighten up discipline, reduce corruption, and speed up production. Some of his programs, such as forming a mega-agricultural ministry out of several smaller ministries, actually increased the bureaucratic tangle that already hamstrung the economy. His antialcohol campaign, while intended to promote an admirable social goal, backfired when it decreased government revenues and angered many people. Meanwhile, the Soviet economy remained in the same Brezhnev-era rut.

More radical economic reforms beginning in 1987 had even worse results, as they often undermined the Soviet system rather than strengthened it. Factory managers received more authority to decide what to produce and what wages to pay. But there was no market to force them to produce efficiently or go out of business. Therefore, they often raised wages to keep their workers happy or stopped producing inexpensive goods, which often were the only products ordinary Soviet citizens could afford. These managers also found their supposed new freedom of action was limited because they still had to fulfill state orders that often equalled the entire production of their factories.

At the same time, Gorbachev did not move to dismantle the collective farm system. This made it impossible to increase food production and left in place one of the main dead weights holding back the economy. Nor did Gorbachev end price controls. He feared that if food prices were allowed to rise, he would face public discontent that might run out of control. He remembered 1962, when protests erupted after Nikita Khrushchev raised prices on meat and butter and that over twenty people were killed when troops fired on the demonstrators. Gorbachev also knew that price increases in Poland between 1970 and 1980 resulted in strikes and other protests that shook the Communist regime in that country to its roots.

Some sprouts of a new economy did manage to take root. In 1987, Gorbachev legalized what were called cooperatives: businesses run by groups of people. Cooperatives were permitted to run a variety of businesses such as restaurants, repair services, and taxis. Gorbachev also encouraged "joint ventures," in which Western companies invested in Soviet firms in return for part ownership. While these and other innovations helped create a nonstate economy that employed about 23 percent of Russia's workers by late 1991, the core of the Soviet economy continued to crumble.

In fact, by 1989, undermined by half measures that damaged the old central planning system but did not put enough new structures in its place, production was falling rather than rising in the Soviet Union. The standard of living of most ordinary citizens fell with it. Gorbachev, meanwhile, was unsure of what steps to take and faced opposition from a variety of political opponents no matter what he tried. He considered several reform plans, but never consistently followed any of them. One, proposed in 1990, called for drastic steps that would move the Soviet Union to a market economy in 500 days. However, in the end, Gorbachev bowed to pressure from Communist Party conservatives and refused to implement the "500 day plan."

By 1990, the Soviet economy was in critical condition. As one economist put it:

> It is not now a question of saving socialism, communism, or any other ism, it is a question of saving our people, our country.[1]

Yet nobody could stop the continuing economic disintegration. During 1991, production fell by 17 percent in the Soviet Union, a greater drop than during the worst year of the Great Depression in the United States. Because the government continued to print money to meet its expenses, the value of the ruble fell, a condition known as inflation. In the United States, it was considered a crisis when inflation reached 20 percent per year in the late 1970s. By the end of 1991, the inflation rate in the Soviet Union was 700 percent. The country's foreign debt, most of it borrowed from Western sources during the Gorbachev era, had climbed to over $80 billion. Spiraling inflation and growing foreign debt together were heavy shackles that dragged down an already weakened economy.

When the Soviet Union finally collapsed, that added yet another burden to Russia and the other newly independent states. Regions that had been tied together as part of one economy suddenly were separated by new international borders. Entirely new economic relationships would have to be worked out. Under these extremely difficult circumstances, Boris Yeltsin took charge of Russia and its collapsing economy.

Yeltsin, Shock Therapy, and Privatization: 1992–1993

The collapse of the Soviet Union meant the end of economic reform. Soviet socialism, the system Gorbachev had tried to reform, was dead. Yeltsin's policy was economic transformation to an entirely new system: a capitalist market economy. It was, and remains today, a herculean task, as large as Russia itself. It involved the creating or permitting of countless new institutions, patterns of behavior, and economic relationships, many of which remain in their infancy at the present time. However, several tasks had top priority. Prices had to be freed from state control. Laws had to be written to legalize economic activity that had been banned during the Soviet era. Russia's state-owned factories, farms, shops, and other businesses had to be privatized, that is, turned over from state to private ownership. In addition, many of Russia's military factories had to be converted to civilian use.

Yeltsin and his advisers believed that with the Russian economy already in such bad shape, they had to move ahead quickly. They also wanted to make enough basic reforms and create enough businesspeople with a

The new economics meets the new politics. This kiosk is one of thousands of similar tiny stores that have become a major part of Russia's new market economy. This particular kiosk sells a variety of liquor, cigarettes, and snack foods. Here both clerks and a customer pause in April 1993 to watch a television program on the summit meeting in Canada between Russian President Boris Yeltsin and U.S. President Bill Clinton.

vested interest in a market economy to make a return to communism impossible. They were well aware that many measures they were planning, such as allowing prices to rise, would cause hardships. At the same time, Yeltsin and his advisers were convinced that if they moved decisively, Russia could get its market economy working in the shortest possible time and keep hardships to a minimum. This program of drastic steps was called "shock therapy."

On January 2, 1992 Yeltsin plunged ahead. He lifted the Soviet-era price controls on most items. A number of necessities were excluded from the decree in order to protect lower-income people. They included bread, milk, medicines, public transportation, and vodka, the last item providing a telling commentary on the extent of alcohol abuse in Russia. At the end of January, another decree lifted restrictions on private trading. For the first time since the 1920s, all Russians could legally buy and sell.

The trading decree brought rapid and generally positive results. Russians responded quickly by setting up thousands of small stands, known as kiosks, along the streets of Russia's cities and towns. These kiosks sold a variety of consumer goods, mainly imported luxury products such as liquors, canned gourmet foods, and Marlboro cigarettes. Unfortunately, these items usually had prices many ordinary workers or people on fixed incomes could not afford.

Not everyone was pleased with the new situation. During the Soviet era, the differences in wealth had been hidden as much as possible. The well connected enjoyed their summer homes behind high fences and shopped in windowless stores to which ordinary people were not admitted. Now an array of tempting but unaffordable goods were tauntingly out in the open. This caused considerable resentment among people who had been raised with the idea that personal wealth violated the rights of the poor. As a clerk at one kiosk specializing in imported beer and vodka reported, "Little old ladies come and curse us all the time."[2]

However, the greatest impact of high prices on the people was in the shops where they bought their basic necessities. During January 1992, the first month without price controls, prices jumped by 250 percent. The pace slowed in the following months, but not enough to help most people. Yeltsin found this out firsthand in May, when he toured his native western Siberia. In Barnaul, a city on the Ob river, a crowd surrounded their president in a food store. One woman spoke for the others when she said:

These young Russian businessmen, ages ten and eleven, also are part of Russia's new market economy, as they sell Russian and American magazines from their makeshift stand.

> Oh, it's so hard to live. Our kids don't see anything good, nothing. It's very hard. Everything is so expensive.[3]

Although shock therapy was supposed to move quickly, its privatization component got off to a slow start. The problem was finding a method of transferring hundreds of thousands of businesses, including gigantic factories, from the state to individual ownership. The method that finally produced some progress was the voucher system, announced in August 1992 and enacted into law in September after a hard struggle in parliament. The program distributed what were called vouchers to each of Russia's approximately 148 million people. The people could then invest their vouchers in businesses that were being privatized. This system, Yeltsin optimistically promised the nation in a televised speech, would create "millions of owners, not a small group of millionaires."[4]

Despite ambitious goals, privatization continued to lag during the rest of the year, in large part because of the continued political struggle between Yeltsin and the parliament. However, in early 1993, Yeltsin managed to place strong advocates of privatization in important positions. The president also was boosted by the national referendum in April in which almost 53 percent of the voters approved of his economic policies, a degree of support that surprised many observers. These developments helped boost the pace of privatization, so that by the middle of the year, Russia had almost a million private or semiprivate businesses. They employed about a quarter of the labor force and produced a third of Russia's total output.

Agriculture remained one of the greatest barriers to economic progress. Yelstin wanted to promote private farming, but was unable to get the parliament to agree to a key step: allowing farmers to own and sell their land as they pleased. There also were opponents of privatization of the land outside of parliament. The most influential were managers of Russia's 26,000 collective farms who stood to lose their jobs if collective farming collapsed. They were joined by most collective farmers, who feared to go out on their own and also worried that they would lose what security and government help they had under the old system. One collective farm manager poignantly summed up the situation in the countryside and the problems Yeltsin faced in trying to put Russian agriculture on a new footing:

> But we simply are not ready. These people are just too afraid to leave the collective. We work badly, we live poorly, we lose money, but at least we still have the collective.[5]

Despite the web of restrictions that remained in force and hostility from their neighbors, during 1992, the first year of economic reform, about 180,000 farmers set up private farms. They had to work small plots of land that varied in size from region to region but averaged about 100 acres. Altogether, they farmed only 4 percent of Russia's farmland. Yelstin tried to give them and others who might be thinking of becoming private farmers some of the security they needed. That was why about three weeks after his October showdown with parliament, he issued a decree allowing farmers to own and dispose of land freely. The decree stated that all landowners would receive titles documenting their ownership. It also said that the state guaranteed the "protection of private property on land, as well as protection of property rights in all business transactions concerning land."[6] The constitution Russian voters ratified in December reinforced Yeltsin's decree by providing for private ownership in land. As a result, growth in private farming continued through 1993. By the end of the year Russia had about 280,000 private farms producing about 8 percent of the country's food. Another 30 percent of Russia's food came from the tiny private gardens tended by both collective farmers and city dwellers, a figure relatively unchanged from the Soviet era. However, neither Yeltsin's decree nor the new constitution, nor another decree he issued in 1995, settled the land issue. Serious obstacles to a free market in land remained. During the next few years, the Duma refused to pass the laws required by the constitution to put its provisions on land ownernship into effect. Overall, a small start had been made in the long and difficult task of re-creating a class of independent farmers to replace the one Stalin and the Soviet regime destroyed during the notorious collectivization drive of 1929–33. Given the time elapsed, the skills and traditions lost, and the difficulties of making a living on the land in 1990s Russia, there was no guarantee that he would succeed.

Economic Problems in the Mid-1990s

The program of voucher privatization officially ended on June 3, 1994. Even before that date there could be no disputing that privatization and shock therapy had changed Russia's economy. During 1993, the state's share of all economic activity passed a milestone when it dropped to 46 percent of the total, or less than half. Private businesses controlled about one-third of the total, while cooperatives accounted for most of the rest.

The privatization ministry, headed by the energetic Anatoly Chubais, had done an enormous job. More than 100,000 businesses were privatized in one form or another. They included everything from small shops to medium and large factories to enormous oil-producing companies. The 85,000 private shops were 70 percent of the country's total. Russia's 15,000 privatized factories employed more than 60 percent of its factory workers and produced more than two-thirds of its industrial production. Of Russia's 14,000 largest companies, 10,000 were privatized by the spring of 1994.

Furthermore, ordinary people had a share of the privatized companies. They had invested 138 million of their vouchers, helped by 600 registered voucher-investment funds run by experts. About 1 million people owned small businesses.

At the same time, privatization was less far-reaching than it looked on paper. As of June 30, 1994 about 21,000 large and medium-sized enterprises were joint-stock companies, that is, the company issued shares that people could buy, and ownership of the company was based on how many shares a person owned. Millions of ordinary Russians had traded their vouchers for shares in these businesses; however, they did not own *all* the shares. Although officially 70 percent of Russia's large and medium-sized industries were "privatized," the state kept a controlling interest in most of them by holding on to a certain percentage of the shares. It would take a second round of privatization to remove or reduce this important element of state control. Also, critical factories involved in military production were likely to remain under state control even after a new round of privatization.

In July 1994 President Yeltsin signed a decree authorizing a second round of privatization. In the new round, shares of enterprises would be sold to the highest bidder. The proceeds would be split between the government and the companies whose shares were being sold. The main advantage of this system was that it would provide the companies with funds they needed to modernize, while the government would get some desperately needed revenue. The main disadvantage, and it was a big one, was that the only people who would bid on these companies were the wealthy, particularly the new banking elite. Having accumulated great wealth in very questionable ways in only a few years, they now would be able to grab many of Russia's most valuable companies. The unequal benefits of economic reform, which until mid-1994 had created a few rich and many poor in Russia, would become even more extreme. Another important disadvantage emerged as shares of companies went on sale during 1995. The shares of some companies did not attract buyers, while company shares that were sold often brought a lower price than expected. This left both the companies and the government short of the revenues they had expected.

Still, there was some good news from the privatized sector. By mid-1994 some newly privatized firms were beginning to act like private companies. Under the Soviet regime, factories sold everything to the state at a fixed price and received additional cash when it was needed, regardless of whether they were making or losing money. By the spring of 1994, a study of 200 large, newly privatized enterprises showed that they were making it on their own. They had cut 20 percent of their employees to increase efficiency, although managers reported they would make further cuts if social services were available to care for the unemployed. The companies sold about 60 percent of their output to other private businesses. They also were changing their product line according to consumer demands, something that was unheard of during the Soviet era.

An example of successful privatization was the Koloros factory in Moscow, Russia's largest manufacturer of clothing dyes. Koloros set up a marketing department, something no Soviet-era factory ever needed, and convinced new customers to buy its dyes. It even opened a store that sells directly to consumers and established a financial division. Koloros invested some of its profits in new equipment to control pollution, although it still polluted the Moscow River flowing 400 yards from the factory. Its workforce was 15 percent smaller than before privatization, but, because of its success, its workers earned $200 per month, about twice the average in Moscow.

However, there was a lot more bad news than good news. Progress continued to be slow in agriculture. By 1994 the number of private farmers stagnated at about 280,000, and the percentage of the country's land they farmed did not rise above 6 percent. Private farmers were a part of Russian agriculture. They owned 25 percent of Russia's cattle, 28 percent of the pigs, and 38 percent of the sheep, all significant increases since 1991. However, 14,000 private farms—almost triple the number of 1992—closed down in 1993, often because they did not get paid for the grain they delivered. Private farmers also had to struggle against rising prices for machinery, livestock, and other materials. They had trouble getting the credit they needed to buy supplies. Meanwhile, the hard economic times that hurt so many Russians wore down many private farmers. During 1994 the number of failures increased. By the end of the year more private farms were being abandoned than created. Meanwhile, the collective-farm system remained in place and continued to operate inefficiently. While about one-third of the collectives officially reorganized as joint stock companies or cooperatives, they continued to operate as before. These problems hurt production. After grain harvests of 107 million tons in 1992 and 99 million tons in 1993, the grain harvest fell to 81 million tons in

Converting Military Factories to Civilian Use

In the 1940s, Obninsk, (OH-beensk) about 65 miles southwest of Moscow, was a tiny village. It then become the site of the project to develop a Soviet atomic bomb. Today, Obninsk is a well-kept city of 120,000, but also a city with an uncertain future. It contains 12 military research institutes and 1 factory, most of whose products go into nuclear reactors. The factory also produces a few circuit boards for the Polaroid Corporation of the United States. The jobs involved are among the very few in Obninsk that are not connected to the military, and in mid-1990s Russia, the military is being cut back. In 1992 alone, spending on weapons dropped 68 percent, while spending on research and development fell 50 percent.

The people of Obninsk are worried. As one highly skilled scientist put it:

> There's nothing else here. They told us we were on elite and set for life.[7]

The situation is little better in Novosibirsk, a city of 1.5 million people in Siberia, about 1,900 miles (3,059 km) from Moscow. Novosibirsk has been an academic, scientific, and military center since Soviet leader Nikita Khrushchev promoted its development in the 1950s. While there are more nonmilitary jobs than in Obninsk, about 80 percent of all industry in Novosibirsk works for the military. At the high-tech Oxide factory, the workforce has been halved due to cuts in military orders. Its director summed up the problems he faces in trying to save his factory and the jobs of workers:

> We've tried to minimize our losses, but we have no money for research or big investments into new [civilian] products. . . . But there's very little work. We do something. We're just polishing instruments right now. We need new inventions or modernization, and that takes capital.[8]

Some of Russia's military factories have managed to make a start in converting to civilian production. The huge Chkalov (chuh-KAH-loff) Aircraft Enterprise in Novovsibirsk, a manufacturer of advanced fighter aircraft, now also produces small civilian passenger aircraft. Even at Chkalov, however, it took a while to get started. At first, both managers and workers considered conversion "another crazy idea from Moscow." Then, an aircraft designer pointed out, "they stopped buying our airplanes, and it wasn't a joke."[9]

Another bright spot in the gloom that blankets military enterprises across Russia is the Luch Experimental Works in Podolsk, an industrial town about 15 miles (24 km) south of Moscow. Even before the Soviet Union collapsed, the Luch management formed a joint venture with a Swedish company. The factory began making machines to produce cardboard containers for milk and juice. By the time the Soviet Union collapsed, about two-thirds of the factory's production consisted of civilian goods. Other factories also have managed to convert their high-tech military skills to civilian use. In Izhevsk, an industrial city of 700,000 just west of the Ural Mountains, 70 percent of local production once went to the military. That has begun to change. Today, the 20,000 workers at the Motozavod military electronics plant turn out over 60 civilian product machines, including stereo tape players, disposable syringes, and cardiograms. The Radiozavod factory, which produced sophisticated military tracking systems, is making profits building high-quality bricks. Not everybody agrees with the idea of rushing ahead with converting military factories to civilian use. Critics argue that Russia's military factories and their skilled scientists and engineers are an invaluable technolgical resource that must be preserved to help Russia compete with foreign countries. They oppose, as one of President Yeltsin's advisers put it, "chasing away the experts and dismantling the equipment." Or, as one politician has noted:

> The point is not to lose the intellectual potential that we have. We can not simply take our expertise in electronics and turn it over to the production of pots and pans, although they are also useful.[10]

Russia, obviously, is not going to dismantle its entire military-industrial complex. However, drastic downsizing will continue. For most workers in military enterprises, the future will be difficult. A skilled middle-aged designer of optical instruments in Novosibirsk spoke for many when he sadly observed:

> I formed my world view long ago. What will I tell my kids? That's what bothers me. This new world seems to me selfish and grasping. Sure we were betrayed, and we feel it. But we were betrayed long ago.[11]

1994 and 63.5 million tons in 1995. This compared to a harvest of 86 million tons in *1913,* Russia's last full year of peace before World War I. The only exceptions to the gloomy agricultural news in 1995 were increases in potato and vegetable production. Only in 1996 did grain production inch up slightly, However, agricultural production as a whole fell that year by about 7 percent.

The problem of declining production was even worse for the economy as a whole. The wrenching changes from a planned to a free-market economy left thousands of factories without the state as their totally loyal customer and unwavering source of financial support. Without that support, these factories had to either cut back or stop production altogether. Companies producing oil and natural gas lacked the funds to make necessary repairs and modernize. The results between 1991 and 1994 were disheartening. By the spring of 1994, industrial production was only 49 percent of what it was in 1989. Oil production stood at about 61 percent of the 1988 figure and was falling at an increasing pace. Overall, Russia's gross domestic production declined every year from 1992 through 1996.

The problem with oil—and other industries as well—and what might be done to solve it, was illustrated by an oilfield in Muravlenko, in western Siberia. The local company lacked modern equipment and the cash to buy it, and production was down 20 percent. Forty percent of its wells were not operating at all. Fortunately, Texaco Oil, an American company, had its engineers on the scene and was investing $80 million in the region. But as one American engineer put it:

> This program is just a drop in the bucket. It'll take a lot of drops to make a significant difference.[12]

Some additional drops were on the way, such as a $350 million investment in another Siberian oil field by an American oil company, as part of a joint venture with a Russian company. As to what might restore Russia's ailing oil industry to health, the government's best guess was $8 billion, a figure many Western experts believed to be far too low.

One of the hardest hit sectors of the Russian economy was military production, once the pride of the former Soviet economy. As Russia cut back on military spending after 1991, its orders for weapons plunged. During 1992, military production fell by 42 percent; in 1993 the drop was

Siberia's oil reserves are among the largest in the world, but production has been falling because of outdated equipment and chaotic economic conditions. These oil workers are laying pipes on an oil platform in western Siberia.

29 percent. Such a decline in an industry that once employed 10 percent of Russia's workforce, including many of its most highly skilled scientists and engineers, was nothing short of a crisis.

By 1994, unemployment was one of the most urgent concerns of the Russian government. One of the first waves of unemployed people was made of employees of ministries of the former Soviet Union that were closed down. Factory cutbacks and closings soon added to the problem. As of early 1994, the official number of umemployed was about 1 million, or about 1.3 percent of the workforce. While that was a small figure compared to Western countries, it was high for Russia, which under the Soviet regime officially did not have unemployment. In fact, the real figure was certainly much higher. By the end of 1996, unemployment stood at over 9 percent. If the underemployed were included, the figure rose to

12 to 13 percent. The danger was that further industrial layoffs could drive the unemployment rate even higher.

Inflation was another problem that plagued the Russian economy in the early 1990s. During 1993, the rate of inflation was 200 percent per year. Yet that figure paled against the cumulative results of inflation that began under perestroika. During the Brezhnev era, the ruble officially was worth slightly more than a dollar, although on the flourishing black market, it was worth several times less than that. However, by 1994, it took 2,000 rubles to buy one dollar. By 1996, that figure was 5,000 rubles. By mid-1994, the Yeltsin government had brought inflation down to about 100 percent per year, and by 1996 inflation stood at 22 percent. While unacceptably high by Western standards, the 1996 inflation rate was a dramatic improvement over earlier years.

Economic reforms have brought hard times to those unable to adjust to a free-market economy. This elderly woman, who lives on a monthly pension of about $23, tries to make ends meet by selling her handmade, traditional peasant shoes called lapti. *Other elderly people who are unable to make things to sell must instead sell their personal possessions.*

In short, by the mid-1990s, Russia had left its old Soviet economy and some of the problems associated with it behind. But the transition to free-market capitalism was proving painful, and there was no guarantee that it would be successful. Shock therapy and privatization in Russia had created a small group of the newly rich. They were entrepreneurs or wheeler-dealers able to operate in a system still in the process of writing its rules. They could be seen in fancy stores buying expensive clothing or in automobile showrooms spending $50,000 or $100,000 for imported luxury cars. At the same time, economic change had created many new poor, people who lined the streets of Moscow or St. Petersburg selling their possessions in order to have some money to buy food. As of 1994, the real income of the Russian people as a whole was barely half (53 percent) that of 1991. Forty million of those people, one-fourth of the population—lived below the subsistence level. As one 81-year-old war veteran complained:

> Before, our pensions were small, but it was enough for food, and something extra, like clothes. Now it is just enough for a diet of half-starvation.[13]

Of course, there still were many Russians, especially the younger people, who saw what was happening as necessary to achieving a better life. A 25-year-old mother of two observed:

> For 70 years, people got paid the same no matter how well they worked. Now we live day by day, with everything changing, so you never know what anything will cost. Some want to go back because it was easier. But we also see a little into the future where people with good qualifications and hard work can find their place.[14]

To which her husband added:

> I think it's much better to live through this change and suffer now. To go backward again would be horrible, absolutely horrible.[15]

Russia's new market economy means that foreign goods are increasingly available to consumers who can afford them. In February 1993 Levi Strauss and Co., the famous American maker of jeans, opened its first store in Moscow. Hundreds of people waited to get in to pay $50, several months salary for an average worker, for a pair of Levi jeans.

The Russian Economy in the Late 1990s

Six full years after the start of Yeltsin's free-market reforms the Russian economy was anything but a model for capitalist development. There were a few good signs on the country's economic landscape: thriving small businesses, some successful privatized factories, private farmers who were bucking the odds and making money. However, these healthy shoots on Russia's economic landscape were scattered among decaying old growths such as failing factories, inefficient farms, extreme inequalities between rich and poor, widespread corruption, and other serious problems. Russia's new wealthy continued to send their capital abroad, rather than investing it in Russia. Thus, during 1996 over $22 billion that the Russian economy desperately needed left the country. This was 10 times the amount foreigners invested in Russia that year. The best that could be said was that after six years of shrinking, it appeared that the economy had hit bottom.

Perhaps no single development caused more anger among ordinary Russians than the shocking concentration of wealth that developed during privatization. Yeltsin admitted as much in a speech in September 1997, when he acknowledged that a small group of bankers and businesspeople had taken control over much of the economy, creating a huge gap "between rich and poor and spawning a corrosive popular cynicism."[16] A Moscow newspaper put it more bluntly when it stated that the "main struggle [in Russia] is over the question of who are the masters in the country—the money tycoons or the Government."[17]

During 1997 Yeltsin's new team of economic reformers, led by first deputy prime ministers Anatoly Chubais and Boris Nemtsov, made a serious attempt to correct past abuses. One of Nemtsov's first targets after taking office in March was to force the giant Gazprom natural gas company to pay its overdue taxes of $2.6 billion. In August, as part of the new round of privatization, the government held an auction for 25 percent of the shares of Svyazinvest (SVYAZ-in-vest), the country's telecommunications monopoly. Unlike in the past, there were no insider deals, and the shares went to the highest bidder. The problem was that the highest bidder was one of Russia's largest banks and that it outbid another huge bank for the prize. In other words, even at fair auctions, the shares of Russia's largest and most valuable companies would be bought by the same people who already held much of Russia's wealth. The concentration of wealth in a few hands would therefore continue and even intensify.

Meanwhile, 1998 brought yet another wave of economic trouble. Between January and June Russia's overall economic output remained stagnant, and that turned out to be the *good* news for the year. In early May, just as the Kiriyenko government was getting its feet wet, the Russian stock market plunged, triggering an economic crisis. Neither the government's emergency package of tax increases combined with spending cuts nor a commitment by international lenders to loan Russia $22.6 billion could save a sinking ship. In mid-August, the government announced it would let the value of the ruble fall from its current level of 6.3 to the dollar to as low as 9.5 to the dollar. It also defaulted on—that is, said it could not repay—a large part of its foreign debt. By the fall Russia's economy, and its long-suffering people, were being battered by huge debt, soaring prices, shrinking food supplies, and the menacing prospect that matters might easily get even worse.

In September the job of rescuing the country from its worst economic crisis of the post-Soviet era fell to the newly appointed prime minister, Yevgeny Primakov. Primakov had little experience in economic affairs, and on taking office he said little about specific measures he might introduce, but his background as a Soviet-era bureaucrat made it clear that Russia's era of undiluted free-market reforms was over. While a return to a Communist-style planned economy was impossible, the government could be expected to regulate economic life far more actively than at any time since 1991.

NOTES

1. Quoted in Richard Sakwa, *Russian Politics and Society* (London and New York: Routledge, Chapman, and Hall, 1993), p. 205.
2. The *New York Times*, October 19, 1993.
3. The *New York Times*, May 28, 1992.
4. Quoted in Sakwa, p. 231.
5. The *New York Times*, November 17, 1991.
6. Quoted in *The Boston Globe*, October 28, 1993.
7. The *New York Times*, December 13, 1993.
8. Ibid.
9. Ibid.
10. The *New York Times*, February 24, 1992.
11. Ibid.
12. The *New York Times*, November 26, 1993.
13. The *New York Times*, November 13, 1993.
14. The *New York Times*, July 20, 1992.
15. Ibid.
16. The *New York Times*, September 25, 1997.
17. Ibid.

8

Daily Life

*R*ussian daily life has been changing in many ways since perestroika began in 1985, and the process has accelerated since December 1991. These developments are the result of the collapse of Soviet totalitarianism and Russia's attempt to establish a free and open society. For the first time in decades, Russians are free to think, speak, and write as they please. They can practice religion without fear of the authorities and decide how to educate their children. If they have the money, they are free to travel abroad. If they have the skills and initiative, they have the opportunity to prosper economically.

However, freedom in Russia, where old institutions collapsed before new ones could be built to take their place, also means that the state no longer provides the economic and social safety net of the Soviet era. Russians, therefore, must look out for themselves as never before in their lives. For those who can not adjust to the new conditions and freedoms, daily life, which once seemed dreary and boring, but also was manageable, has become harsher and often a struggle to survive.

At the same time, Russians still do many of the things they enjoyed not only under the Soviets, but under the czars as well. Traditional Russian sports, entertainment, forms of worship, and customs remain alive in the daily lives of millions of people. In some cases, such as religious worship, the Russian people have leapfrogged backward across 70 years of Soviet rule and returned to traditions suppressed but not forgotten. In their daily lives, the Russian people have been seeking to forge a combination of old and new that will enable them to cope with troubled, difficult, but also hopeful times.

Surviving on the Capitalist Frontier

Prior to perestroika, living standards in Russia generally were far lower than in the West. A significant percentage of the population—between a quarter and a third according to Soviet statistics—lived in poverty. At the same time, people could be confident they would not lose what little they had. There was no serious fear of losing one's home or job and, therefore, little incentive to save for a rainy day. In their daily lives, Russians had to search, scrounge, and stand endlessly on line to get their daily food and necessities. But during the post-Stalin era, their lives at least were reasonably secure.

Since the transition to a free market began, Russians have had to learn to fend for themselves much more. For those unable to adjust to the new economic conditions, including many elderly people on fixed incomes, that has meant selling their valuables and heirlooms on the sidewalks of Russia's cities. For others, it has meant being on the move. One technique is to travel to provincial cities where certain consumer goods are manu-factured and return with them to metropolitan areas, where they can be sold at a profit. Sometimes, all that is required is moving consumer goods from one part of town to another. At other times, it is necessary to go abroad. Marina, a 21-year-old fashion designer, makes regular trips to Turkey. Her investment is about $225 for travel and $2,000 to buy Turkish-made clothing. After selling her stock in the street markets of her hometown of Ivanovo, about 350 miles (564 km) from Moscow, she pockets a profit of $1,500.

Most Russians who do business by traveling operate on a much smaller scale. Thousands go to Poland, where during a week's stay they sleep outdoors or in seedy hotels, eight to a room. They sell the goods they have brought in flea markets, and, with their earnings, they often buy other products to sell back in Russia. Valentina, 45 years old, explained why she endured the 17-hour train ride from Moscow to Warsaw:

> I pick up a little money. I can get enough to buy some things for the children. And I bring home some cosmetics, some jewelry, Japanese tape players. They sell big in Moscow.[1]

A good guess is that in 1997 there were as many as 10 million "shuttlers," as they are called. Most of them traveled back and forth between Russia and either Turkey, Poland, or China. The goods they imported competed directly with Russian-made products and were one reason that imports held about 60 percent of the local market for consumer goods.

While some Russians still are critical of those who buy and sell for a profit, another youthful entrepreneur explained the situation Russians faced this way:

> Too many people are still sitting and waiting—for the government to change, for subsidies, for bread. But if you just move a little bit faster here and use your brains, you can get what you want: a car, a flat, whatever.[2]

Some Russians manage to add to their incomes without leaving home. During the first year of free-market prices, Natasha, a young mother of two, began adding to the income of her husband, Mikhail, by making dresses on the German sewing machine her father-in-law gave her as wedding present. She began by sewing a leather jacket for a friend:

> It came out all right and then it was one thing after another: some dresses, and a man's coat. Then I wanted a coat, so I bought material enough for two . . . and sold one . . . and then bought more material.[3]

Another method of adjusting is to change professions, often to an occupation undreamed of only a few years ago. Typical of those who managed that transition is Boris, a 50-year-old former scientific researcher from Moscow. Today he owns a small shop where, among other things, he sells porcelain, furniture, and French brandy. Younger people, particularly those with a higher education, make the change-over in another way: they never enter the profession for which they have prepared. Thus, at the age of 27, Maxim, a graduate chemistry student, abandoned his studies to go into the business of desktop publishing. His father, Pyotr, himself a director of an important chemistry institute, was "disappointed" because his talented son was close to getting his doctorate. However, the son's business has been successful, while the father, who also must adjust to changing times, searches for private contracts to keep his institute alive.

Russia's writers and artists have been forced to make drastic changes in their lives to adjust to new conditions they face. Under the Soviet regime, authors could not write as they pleased if they wanted state support. However, those prepared to make a compromise with artistic freedom enjoyed state funding. Today, the state no longer provides cooperative artists free use of summer homes or access to quality health care for their families and schools for their children. They must find customers for their novels, stories, and plays, and that is increasingly difficult as publishing houses struggle, often unsuccessfully, to find a niche in the new marketplace.

The story is no different for artistic institutions. The Moscow Choreographic School, a renowned ballet school whose graduates dance for Russia's best troupes, typifies the problem. While the Russian Ministry of Culture still provides a majority of its budget, the school must find outside support to pay its bills. The search for funds takes the school's 78-year-old director Sofiya far afield. She not only gets support from Russian businesses, but receives contributions from foreign firms like the Russian office of the Chiquita Banana Company. It provides fruit to balance the diets of the school's 600 students. At the same time, Sofiya stresses that while change is unavoidable, Russia must hold on to the best of its past:

> Naturally, our whole life is changing where the economy is concerned. But where creativity is concerned, where Russian ballet is at stake, this will not change.[4]

Youth

Russia's youth began to change its behavior and interests dramatically during the 1970s and 1980s, as modern communications increasingly exposed them to Western cultural influences. During those decades, millions of young people in the Soviet Union began to reject what they considered the spiritual emptiness and hypocrisy of Soviet life. An underground youth culture developed, based in part on rock music and drugs, but also on other practices and ideas filtering in from the West, such as mysticism and yoga.

The boredom and neglect that marked the lives of millions of Russian adolescents during the late Soviet era led to many problems. Some young people organized themselves into vigilante gangs that looked for excuses to fight and beat up innocent people. There also were groups called *fanaty* (fah-NAH-tee) ("fanatics") who supposedly were avid supporters of popular soccer teams. In reality, the *fanaty* were unruly troublemakers, less interested in sports than, as one 18-year-old put it, in the desire for "self affirmation and to set oneself apart":

> One night I had no idea how to occupy myself. I went to the movies.
> Some film! Am I crazy to go to a movie like that? Then I ran into some
> kids. They offered me tickets to a disco in a club. . . . I met some
> companions. These kids invited me to a cafe and they said they were
> "fanatics." I liked it. And I became one of them.[5]

Aside from senseless violence, alcohol and drug use increased among young people during the late Soviet era. Drug use spread as young Russian soldiers returned home from fighting in Afghanistan in the 1980s. As in the West, the young drug users developed their own subculture and vocabulary. In fact, young Russians and Americans both used the word "grass" (in Russian, *trava* [tra-VA]) for marijuana.

All of these problems spilled over into the post-Soviet era, where they were made worse by turmoil and hard times. Russia's falling standard of living hurt Russia's children more than any other group. Their health worsened because their parents could not provide them with decent diets or pay for necessary medicines. Thousands of children have ended up homeless because they were abandoned by their families or ran away

Among the most tragic of post-Soviet Russia's social problems is the explosion in the number of homeless children. These children are in a dilapidated orphanage in Moscow that gives them two weeks of counseling and then atttempts to reunite them with their families.

from home. To survive, they have joined gangs and drifted into crime in order to survive. A Russian social scientist sadly pointed out that children

will do anything to escape from poverty. At best they sell newspapers; at worst they steal. Property crimes predominate among teenagers, and they are rising catastrophically. We now have ten- and eleven-year-old thieves and fourteen-year-old prostitutes.[6]

Along with terrible problems, the collapse of communism brought new opportunities to some of Russia's youth. The August 1991 coup against Gorbachev provided the chance and challenge to stand up for freedom, and thousands of young people did just that when they rallied to Yeltsin's defense. The transition to a market economy was an opportunity for those

There are thousands of homeless children living on Russia's streets, where many steal or commit other crimes to get money to stay alive. This boy, named Roman, said he stole something to drink from a woman because, "It was hot and I was thirsty."

not tied into the old system to make a fresh start. Many young people, with no careers to give up and little to lose, seized that opportunity. Speaking in the summer of 1992, a journalism student summarized the ambivalent state of mind of Russia's young people as they struggle to make it in a new and harsh world:

> There are so many people here who have become so pessimistic; they're in a state of depression. They're leaving their jobs, they're dissatisfied, they're unhappy with the prices, with the lines. And yet I also see a big wave of enthusiasm, a desire to change things, and things have turned around really quickly.[7]

Health

The Soviet health care system that took care of the Russian people for decades was trumpeted as one of socialism's great achievements. The system was free and covered all Soviet citizens. It extended from Moscow and other major cities to the mountains of the Caucasus and the remotest reaches of Siberia. In theory, the Soviet socialized medicine provided equally for all its citizens. The Soviet Union had more doctors and hospital beds per capita than almost any country in the world, including the United States. It is also fair to say that during the 1930s and 1940s, the newly installed Soviet health system was a significant improvement over what had been available in Russia before 1917.

However, by the 1980s, Soviet health care, like the rest of the Soviet system, was rife with corruption and problems. Many doctors were poorly trained or completely incompetent. While the hospitals that served Communist Party officials and other well-connected people were well equipped and provided quality care, hospitals that served ordinary people often were scandalously underfunded and poorly equipped. Some even lacked running water and proper sewage systems. By the 1980s, most people had to bribe their way into a good hospital and then pay for everything from a doctor's care to basic drugs. In other words, there was no such thing as "free" medical care, at least quality care, in the Soviet health care system. One reason that doctors took bribes is that their salaries were pitifully low. The most rudimentary medical supplies, such as syringes, were in short supply or unavailable. As with almost everything else in the Soviet Union by the 1980s, a second "black market" medical system, for which citizens had to pay, existed alongside the official, and totally inadequate, socialist system. Poor health care was one reason that the life expectancy dropped in the Soviet Union during the 1970s, while the infant mortality rate rose.

The end of the Soviet Union brought Russia's health care system to the brink of collapse. As one nurse in Moscow complained:

> There's a lack of medicines, disposable syringes, cotton, bandages. We don't have anything to treat the children with.[8]

One reason for the shortages was that the struggling Russian government was not spending what was necessary on health care. In mid-1992, the minister of health admitted that the country was spending less than half of what was required. Meanwhile, as inflation mounted, the price of medicines and medical equipment rose with it, making the budget crunch even worse. The situation became so serious that in mid-1992 thousands of health care providers took what for them was an unprecedented step: they went on strike to get more government support for health care.

The crisis in Russian medical care led to an epidemic of the deadly disease diphtheria in 1992 and 1993. The outbreak began in Moscow and St. Petersburg and then spread to the outlying parts of Russia and other countries of the former Soviet Union. One cause of the epidemic was that growing numbers of poverty-stricken people, wandering from place to place, were spreading the disease. However, a partial breakdown of Russia's inoculation program also was at fault. Many children were not receiving their initial inoculation on schedule, nor were adults between 20 and 50 receiving necessary booster inoculations.

As for the doctors and other medical practitioners, they began supplementing their regular incomes by taking on private patients. In December 1993, a 31-year-old pediatrician explained he had the money to shop for toys with his young son because he "earned about 10 times as much on the side." However, when asked if the worst was over for Russia he quickly said, "No, not at all, not yet."[9]

The pediatrician's grim prediction was born out over the next several years. Between 1992 and 1997, about 3.5 millon Russians under the age of 60 died. That kind of loss normally is associated with terrible famines

Summer at the *Dacha*

A *dacha* (DA-chuh) can be almost anything from a shack to a multisto-ried mansion. It can lack electricity and running water or boast ameni-ties such as an indoor swimming pool and an escalator leading down to a private beach. It can sit on several acres of land and be hidden from view by a high fence or by on a tiny plot squeezed next to other small ramshackle structures. Whether humble or luxurious, a dacha—the word means sum-mer home in Russian—is something many Russians have and most Russians want. It is a vital getaway from the crowded, tense, and hectic life of the cities. It is a place to grow fruits and vegetables in a garden, enjoy the company of family and friends, and relax amid the beauty of nature. Spending the summer, or at least weekends during the summer, at one's dacha is a crucial part of life for millions of Russians.

During the Soviet era, party leaders enjoyed vacations in luxurious dachas from the woods around Moscow to the shores of the Black Sea. Nikita Khrushchev was at the dacha on the Black Sea when the plot that overthrew him was put into action, as was Mikhail Gorbachev during the unsuccessful coup of August 1991. Not far from Moscow, a collection of luxurious dachas at a place called Zhukovka was a summer escape for the Communist Party elite, while many leading Soviet artists relaxed at a dacha colony called Peredelkino.

Far more modest is a dacha community along the Volga River about 430 miles (692 km) east of Moscow, just west of the city of Kazan. It is where

or long wars. It meant that the death rate among working-age people in 1990s Russia was higher than in the *1890s*. The death toll was especially devastating among men. Between 1990 and 1994, the life expectancy of the average Russian male fell from 63.8 to 57.3 years, a disastrous decline by any standard. The life expectancy for females also fell, although at a slower rate. According to the World Health Organiztion, by 1997 Russia had the greatest gap in male/female life expectancy—14 years—of any country in the world. President Yeltsin himself warned that if something were not done to reverse the situation, Russia's population would drop by 30 million in the next 50 years. As one demographer put it, "No country can survive such patterns for very long. . . . it has to stop or the consequences will be too awful to predict."[10]

Mikhail, a manager of a helicopter factory, and his wife Lyudmilla vacation, often with their grandchildren. The dachas here generally have electricity and running water. All, of course, have the obligatory garden. As Mikhail observed:

> I knew I would never garden; the whole idea paralyzes me with boredom. So, of course, now I garden.[11]

Mikhail and Lyudmilla often go mushroom hunting, a favorite activity that generally begins before dawn. They also enjoy relaxing in a *banya*, a wooden bathhouse in which a wood-burning stove heats stones used to create steam, that is found next to many dachas, even modest ones.

Unlike life in the city amid dreary blocks of apartment buildings, dachas in the woods have long been places where Russians could assert their individuality. Feliks, a retired army colonel, has a rather unique dacha he built himself out of brick. His banya is unusually large and well made. Feliks has turned his plot of land into a small farm, complete with a well, an irrigation system, greenhouses, and a chicken coop. He grows a surprising variety of crops in his garden from tomatoes, cucumbers, and parsley to raspberries, blueberries, and melons.

During the Soviet era, dachas were refuges from the conformity and sterility of life under communism. Today, they are islands of peace in a turbulent Russian world turned upside down. Regardless of the political and economic systems they live under, Russians are unlikely to give up their dachas.

Housing

Valentina is a frail 73-year-old invalid, unable to rise from her bed without help. Like about 20 percent of the Russian population, she does not have her own apartment, but shares what is called a communal apartment with several other single people or families. The 22-room apartment is in a 19th century Moscow building and has five kitchens and four toilets. At peak occupancy, it held no less than 72 people. In the late 1980s, the hot water disappeared; a bit later, so did the cold water. By late 1993, tenants were using buckets of water to flush their toilets. For over a year and a half, no maintenance workers came to the city-owned apartment to fix its broken windows or missing light fixtures.

Russia began the post-Soviet era with a severe housing shortage. The crisis began in the 1930s, when the Stalin regime built virtually no housing for millions of workers pouring into urban areas. A crash building program under Khrushchev alleviated some of the problem, but did not solve it. Furthermore, the attempt to build housing as cheaply and quickly as possible produced shoddy buildings that started falling apart almost as soon as they were built. While housing construction continued under Brezhnev, the pace did not match the effort of the Khrushchev years or the needs of the people.

Most Soviet housing that Russia inherited in 1991 was government owned, especially in urban areas. There were some cooperative units; private housing was mainly in rural areas. The one advantage of the Soviet system was that state housing was heavily subsidized. Rent cost the average family as little as 4 or 5 percent of its budget.

Beginning in 1992 the government's goal became to privatize housing. By the end of 1993, about 35 percent of stated-owned apartments were the property of their occupants. Meanwhile, in the private sector, businesspeople set themselves up as brokers to bring buyers and sellers together. That was fairly simple when one family or person occupied an apartment, but communal apartments presented a special challenge. One technique brokers used for communal apartments was to find their residents small, individual apartments and then buy the larger apartment as it was vacated. It was then renovated and sold at a profit to wealthy Russians or foreigners.

Some individuals avoided brokers and entered the marketplace on their own to improve their living situations. One method was trading apartments. A typical would-be trader ran the following advertisement: "3 = 1 + 2." It meant that someone, possibly a divorcing couple, had a three-room apartment it wanted to trade for two apartments, one with one room and one with two. Some trades, organized by enterprising individuals, involved as many as six or more families.

At the same time, a private construction industry began to fill the gap in available housing. Developers started building large projects, often on the outskirts of cities. In addition, foreign firms seeking business became involved. For example, late in 1992, an American firm began building a $88 million, 478-unit townhouse development called Rosinka about 15 miles (24 km) from Moscow. However, as with many products in Russia's new market economy, the new housing development was strictly upscale. Its homes were far beyond the means of the great majority of Russians who need them most. Overall, private housing more than doubled between 1992 and 1995.

Publicly funded housing also was being built. However, because of corruption, much of that housing has been sold to private buyers. To help those who remain tenants in an era of rising rents and maintenance costs, the Moscow city government began a housing allowance plan. As with many plans to ease the transition to a market economy, Moscow's program can reach only a small percentage of those in need.

By the second half of the 1990s, a housing market Americans would recognize existed in Russia. In Moscow and Leningrad, housing prices vary according to when they were built and where they are located. Apartments in buildings built during the Stalin era are more expensive than those in the shoddy buildings built under Khrushchev and Brezhnev. In Moscow, the most expensive apartments are in the center of the city. In St. Petersburg, the most desirable neighborhoods are in the city's historic center. Meanwhile, prices rose rapidly; during 1993 alone their cost in dollars (not rubles) quadrupled.

Russian housing as a whole in the second half of the 1990s amounted to a mixed system. About 40 percent of all apartments were part of the old Soviet-era system. They were still owned and managed by cities and town government or by former Soviet enterprises, such as large factories. These governments and enterprises continued to provide their tenants with Soviet-era subsidies. This meant that rents were only a small fraction of what they would be if the apartments were rented on the open markets. Tenants therefore held on to their apartments as long as they could. If they moved elsewhere, they tried to pass them on to their children. The rest of Russia's housing stock was part of the free-market system. About 25 percent of all housing consisted of apartments that had been privatized, while another 25 percent was private construction. The remaining 10 percent of Russia's homes were cooperatives in which the residents of a building shared a common space but were responsible for this individual units.

The main issue facing the government by 1997 was how fast to cut subsidies and move to a complete free-market system. The Yeltsin government, with Boris Nemtsov leading the charge, was pushing to end subsidies by 2003. Many politicians, including non-Communists, opposed this on the grounds that ending subsidies would hurt poor and working people who had been hurt too much already by free-market reforms. Yuri Luzhkov (loosh-KOFF), Moscow's powerful mayor and potential presidential candidate in 2000, was the most prominent non-Communist advocating a more gradual approach. But even Luzhkov recognized that he at best could fight a holding action. His plan called for ending subsidies in Moscow in 2006, three years later than Nemtsov proposed.

Sex and Sexuality

For six decades beginning in the 1930s, the Soviet regime permitted virtually no discussion about sex and sexuality. Films and books were heavily censored. Children received almost no sex education in the schools. In 1991, 87 percent of Russian children reported their parents had never spoken to them about sex. No books or manuals about sexuality were available to adults until the 1970s. Contraceptives were very difficult to obtain. The lack of contraceptives was the main reason that after 1955, when abortion was legalized in the Soviet Union after a ban of 21 years, it became the main form of birth control among Russian women. It was not unusual for Russian women to have six or more abortions.

During the Gorbachev era, the policy of glasnost led to considerable change. Classic Western books with sexual themes, such as Vladimir Nabokov's *Lolita* (Nabokov was a Russian émigré whose family left Russia after the Bolshevik Revolution) and D.H. Lawrence's *Lady Chatterley's Lover*, finally were published in the Soviet Union. An important sign of the changing times was the publication of a book on sexuality for married couples. It became an immediate best seller. Films also reflected the new openness regarding sex. In 1989, *Little Vera*, a film about the hardships of Soviet working-class life, shattered existing Soviet cinemagraphic taboos by dealing frankly with the issue of youthful sexuality.

Despite years of censorship and the refusal to discuss the topic openly, post-Soviet Russia faces many of the same trends in terms of sexuality that are present in the West. However, it has less resources to deal with the problems they cause. The earlier sexual maturation of teenagers and their earlier interest in sex has contributed to rising rates of out-of-wedlock births and the spread of sexually transmitted diseases. Although the Soviet Union's isolation delayed the arrival of the international AIDS epidemic, the dreaded disease is spreading in post-Soviet Russia.

Today in Russia, premarital sexual relations and unmarried people living together are more common and increasingly accepted by society. There is greater discussion about and increasing recognition of the importance of sexual gratification to a stable marriage. Russians are showing a growing interest in erotic material of all sorts, from serious art to crude pornography. Homosexuality is openly discussed, and homosexuals are beginning to protest against discriminatory treatment. While many Russians approve of some or most of these trends, others vigorously oppose them as yet another negative influence of the West. Whatever Russians think, their country is likely to be much more open about sex and sexuality than ever before in its history.

Sports and Recreation

Russians are enthusiatic participants in sports. They enjoy soccer, hockey, gymnastics, basketball, track and field, and many other physical activities. During the Soviet era, the state supported a massive and highly successful program designed to create world and Olympic champions. The program produced some of the world's greatest gymnasts, hockey players, weight lifters, and track athletes.

Reading is another favorite Russian pastime. Russians in general spend far more time reading books and newspapers than Americans do. Millions of Russians also are devoted chess players, and their country has produced a large percentage of the world's greatest players.

Eating and drinking with friends is another favorite Russian form of relaxation. Russians use any holiday as an excuse to enjoy a feast. Traditionally, Russians have not shared the concern Americans and western Europeans have with being thin. Their diet—over two-thirds of which consists of grain, potatoes, fats, oils, and sugar—is much higher in calories than the American diet. As a result, once they pass their teenage years, Russians tend to put on weight.

A major change in the way Russians enjoy food has occurred in recent years. During the Soviet era, all restaurants were state-owned and known for their terrible food and even worse service. There also were very few of them: only 25 restaurants for the 5 million residents of St. Petersburg, for example. With the end of communism, restaurants have sprung up all over Russia providing good food and service, although often at prices few Russians can afford.

The downside of Russia's love of eating and drinking is the country's alcohol problem. Travelers from Europe, as early as the 16th century, commented on Russian drunkenness. Russians have long been the world's largest consumers of vodka, a powerful alcoholic drink. Vodka, in practice, is the Russian national drink. It is common for Russians, especially men, to show their friendship for each other by drinking together until they are completely drunk. Per person, Russian consumption of alcoholic beverages doubled between the 1960s and the 1980s. By the 1980s, alcoholism was directly responsible for tens of thousands of deaths. Gorbachev's attempt to stem the tide of alcoholism failed. It remains one of the most serious day-to-day social and health problems in contemporary Russia.

Religion

Before 1917, the great majority of ethnic Russians belonged to the Russian Orthodox Church. During the Soviet era, one of the major goals of the regime was to put an end to religious faith of all kinds, including Russian Orthodoxy. The Soviet leadership, like all Marxists, considered religion to be a primitive superstition, the "opiate of the people," as Marx had put it. In addition, the Communist Party considered itself the source of all truth and did not want any challenges to its authority, including challenges that easily could grow out of religious faith. The Soviet regime, which officially was atheist, therefore attacked all religious organizations, including the Russian Orthodox Church. It seized church property; destroyed or closed churches, synagogues, and mosques; and, with limited exceptions, forbade religious instruction. Communist-run organizations like the "Living Church" and the "League of the Militant Atheists" were used to lure people away from their religious faiths.

Among the houses of worship destroyed under Stalin was the famous Cathedral of Christ Our Savior in Moscow. It was dynamited to rubble to make way for what was supposed to be the world's tallest building, which was never built. Eventually, a huge outdoor swimming pool was built on the site. Russia's best known church, Moscow's St. Basil's Cathedral, barely escaped Stalin's wrecking ball.

By the late 1920s, the leadership of the Russian Orthodox Church (ROC) reached an accomodation with the Soviet regime. The ROC thereby secured a privileged position among Russia's religions and did not suffer as much as smaller religious groups, especially the Jews. Jews had been subject to severe discrimination and violent persecution under the czars. Under the Soviets, Jews and Judaism endured several waves of particularly brutal treatment, including during the late 1940s—when Stalin had many Jewish cultural figures murdered—and from the mid-1950s through the early 1960s, when three-quarters of the remaining synagogues in the Soviet Union were closed.

Despite all the persecution and destruction, the Soviet regime could not entirely uproot religion. The Russian Orthodox Church and other religious groups were allowed to operate on a limited basis under careful state control. They continued to attract believers. During the late Soviet era, as many as 30 million people were reported to be attending church. Although many of them were elderly, young people also showed interest in their religious roots. One sign of the religious revival was the noticeable increase in church weddings; another was the increasing number of children being baptized.

During the Soviet era, the regime eased the pressure on religion several times, most notably during World War II, in order to win support for the struggle against Nazi Germany. However, not until Gorbachev and glasnost did the Soviet regime take serious measures toward restoring genuine religious freedom. A landmark step in that direction occured in 1988, when the regime permitted celebrations marking the 1,000 anniversary of Russia's conversion to Christianity.

Great changes took place after the collapse of the Soviet Union and Russia's emergence as an independent state. For the first time in Russia's 1,100-year history, the country officially was a secular state. It adopted the principles of separation of church and state and religious freedom for all groups. Not only the Russian Orthodox Church, but other Christian churches, Jews, Muslims, and other religious groups officially received the right to practice their religions.

Religious revival: After decades of official atheism, millions of Russians are openly returning to their religious beliefs. Here, women carry an icon during a celebration two weeks after Russian Orthodox Easter in Moscow.

Freedom of religion led to a religious revival. Thousands of churches and other places of worship were returned to the control of religious authorities and permitted to reopen. Monasteries that the Soviets had seized and used as factories or museums once again were filled with monks and echoed with melodies of medieval religious chants. Among the religious landmarks returned to church authorities were the cathedrals in the Kremlin and St. Basil's Cathedral in Red Square. Russian Orthodoxy remained the leading religion in Russia. It had over 60 million believers and over 6,000 newly reopened churches and monasteries. However, the Russian Orthodox Church was not without its problems. Its reputation was tainted by its cooperation with the Soviet regime; many of its clergy were accused of having worked for the KGB. Its long history of tension with the Roman Catholic Church continued, although much of that struggle was focused in Ukraine, rather than in Russia. Some of its clergy became associated with extreme Russian nationalist groups that were both antidemocratic and oppose freedom of religion.

In fact, some aspects of Russia's religious revival disturbed the Russian Orthodox Church. It faced competition from other religious faiths. Some, like the Baptists, Seventh-Day Adventists, and Pentecostalists, have a presence in Russia that dates back long before the Bolshevik Revolution. Other groups were new. By the middle of 1993, at least fifty foreign organizations and 1,000 foreign missionaries were active in Russia. They ranged from the American evangelist Billy Graham, who filled a huge stadium in Moscow when he preached there, to Catholics, the Jehovah's Witnesses, and the Reverend Sun Myung Moon's Unification Church. The Russian Orthodox Church considered these missionaries a threat. In 1993, it pressured the Russian parliament to pass a law requiring foreign religious organizations to register with a government board. Patriarch Alexei II, the spiritual head of the Russian Orthodox Church, supported the law on the grounds that there must be controls on who is allowed to preach to the Russian people. Both human rights activists and non-Orthodox religious groups criticized this retreat from the Russian government's original policy of religious freedom.

A much more controversial measure strongly supported by the Russian Orthodox Church became law in fall 1997. It gave a special status to "traditional" religions, which were defined as religions recognized 15 years earlier when Russia was part of the Soviet Union. Aside from the Russian Orthodox Church, the religions that recieved such status were Judaism, Islam, and Buddhism. It allowed them to own property, control radio and television stations, run schools, receive tax exemptions, and enjoy other privileges. Other religions would have their activities limited by a series of regulations. Among the religious groups that did not qualify under the 15-year rule were Catholics, evangelical Protestants, and independent Orthodox sects. Yeltsin at first vetoed the bill on religions but then signed it into law after the Duma, having modified it slightly, passed it overwhelmingly. The law's main redeeming factor, according to many critics in both Russia and the West, was that it was vague on key points. Authorities therefore might decide to apply it loosely and minimize its effects on freedom of religion.

Russia's religious revival extended beyond Christianity. Although Russia's Jewish community shrank as hundreds of thousands of Jews immigrated, mainly to Israel, Jews who remained in Russia began restoring their religious life. Many Jews, long denied the right to learn anything about their religion and history, started attending schools and summer camps. They worshiped in reopened synagogues. However, anti-Semitism remained a powerful force in Russia, despite the efforts of President Yeltsin to oppose it. Several fires at Jewish institutions, including one that destroyed a Moscow synagogue, stood as grim evidence that religious bigotry remained a powerful force in Russia.

Russia's Muslims also participated in the country's religious revival. Hundreds of mosques were opened in Muslim regions, teachers arrived from abroad to provide religious instruction, and young poeple went to foreign Muslim countries to study. The Muslim revival caused tensions that are political rather than strictly religious in nature. There was concern that minority Muslim ethnic groups in Russia would establish ties with the newly independent Muslim republics of Central Asia or other foreign Muslim groups and eventually threaten the unity of the country. A conference in April 1992, organized by the Islamic Renaissance Party, which stressed such ties, intensified these concerns. Yeltsin responded in June 1992 by calling on his country's Muslims to help build "a single Russian community, strengthening civil peace and national accord."[12] Russian leaders at the time were worried about secessionist movement in three of Russia's autonomous republics with large Muslim populations: Tatarstan in the Volga region and Chechnya and Bashkortostan in the North Causasus region. Their worst fears eventually were realized in Chechnya, where Chechen separatists appealed to the idea of Islamic solidarity to solidfy their movement. One result of the war in Chechnya was the growth in the role of Islam as a political factor in other predominantly Muslim parts of the North Caucasus.

Overall, religious life has flourished in post-Soviet Russia. Patriarch Alexei II has often said that "the greatest wound inflicted by the Communist dictatorship was the lack of spirituality."[13] While not everyone agrees with the Patriarch about which of Russia's Communist-inflicted wounds are the greatest, it seems clear that Russia's wounded spirituality has begun to heal.

Education

"How are educators who themselves do not know what freedom is going to educate free people?" a Russian mother asked.[14] Other unanswered questions that plague Russian education include, How will children be trained for jobs in a free-market society rather than one dominated by the state? How will an economically strapped Russia be able to pay for quality education for all its children? How will Russia hold on to what it did best during the Soviet era—such as teaching science, math, and foreign languages—while introducing new ways of instruction that encourge democracy and independent thinking?

Soviet education had its successes. It turned a largely illiterate country into a highly literate one; illiteracy in Russia dropped from 72 percent in 1913 to between 1 and 3 percent in the 1980s. It trained many highly skilled technicians and scientists. The educational system was free, including its highest levels. By the end of the Soviet era, all children received at least eight years of free public schooling; in the large cities they received 10 or 11 years. The Soviet regime increased the number of universities in Russia from 12 to 52 and the number of higher educational institutions from 105 to over 840.

At the same time, Soviet education was taught through the prism of Marxism/Leninism. History, geography, literature, and other subjects were saturated with the Marxist view of the world and the Soviet dictatorship's version of the truth. As a result, Soviet education was filled with distortions and outright lies about Russia's history and culture, as well as about the rest of the world's. The central goal of Soviet education was to create the "New Soviet Man" and the new "Builders of Communism," people totally committed to the Soviet dictatorship and its collective way of life. In that key endeavor, as the events of the late Soviet era were to show, it failed completely.

Soviet education was highly centralized. The state controlled all the schools. It determined the curriculum, teaching methods, textbooks, and even the uniforms most Soviet children wore. Discipline and control were reinforced by party-run youth groups to which most children belonged: the Octobrists for ages five to nine and the Pioneers from ages 10 to 15. These groups received their guidance from the Komsomol (kum-suh-MOLL)—the Communist Youth League—which enrolled upward bound and politically correct youths between ages 14 and 28.

Today, as with virtually every other aspect of life, Russia is in the throes of a difficult transition in education. Private schools, including religious schools, once again are permitted and they have sprung up in every major city. Their teaching methods usually are less regimented than they were in the old Soviet schools. Teachers are among the best available, as their pay generally is much higher than public school teacher salaries. However, many of the best schools in cities like Moscow and St. Petersburg are expensive and beyond the reach of all but the most wealthy Russians.

There still are some excellent public schools, the descendants of elite schools set up during the Soviet era. These schools also have adjusted their teaching methods. One mother whose child attends elite School No. 11 near Moscow, contrasted her own education to what her child receives:

> We were beaten down. We avoided teachers. We never asked them questions. . . . These kids are completely unfettered.[15]

However, the situation at School No. 11 is the exception. Because education's share of the state budget fell after 1970, many of Russia's schools are in terrible shape. By the late 1980s, a fifth of the students attended schools without central heating, 30 percent of the schools lacked running water, and 40 percent did not have an indoor toilet or indoor gymnasium. Many schools lacked necessary textbooks. Russia's higher education institutions were short of money to pay basic costs.

During the 1993–94 academic year, the Russian government began introducing a new post-Communist curriculum in its public schools that it hopes will prepare its children for life in the new Russia. As of mid-1994, less than one-third of the country's 67,000 schools had adopted it. The immediate future will be difficult, especially for a country that prided itself on its outstanding educational system. Russia's minister of education summed up the situation when he said:

> You can hear that our schools are fantastic now or that they are the worst, and both will be true. We are in a transitional phase.[16]

The Fast Life in Moscow

The reforms and rapid change that swept Russia after 1992 changed the lives of millions of people in virtually every part of the country. But nowhere was the change more dramatic or evident than in Moscow. For centuries, Russians saw Moscow as a symbol of their country's traditional values and considered the city Russia's "soul." However, after 1992 the

Part of the new capitalist Moscow scene, workers at McDonald's applaud the second anniversary of the opening of the American fast-food restaurant in January 1992.

pace and extent of change created what amounted to a new lifestyle in Moscow, one that had nothing to do with Russian traditions or spirituality and everything to do with materialism and foreign influences.

Moscow's fast life was fueled by money. It was the headquarters of the huge banks and small group of business leaders who used privatization to grab control of an enormous share of Russia's wealth. In 1997 about 5 percent of Russia's population, about 10 million people, lived within Moscow's 400 square miles. Yet Moscow controlled more than 70 percent of Russia's capital and produced over a third of its gross domestic product. While Russia's overall economy was declining, and continued to decline sharply in some regions, Moscow's economy was growing at the impressive rate of 6 percent per year. The city had far more cars and small businesses per person than the rest of Russia. Among Russia's cities, only Tiumen (TYOO-mehn), in the center of Siberia's oil region, had an income per person that was close to Moscow's. St. Petersburg's per capita income, in comparison, was less than one-third that of Moscow. All of this was evidence that Moscow, rather than stimulating economic development in the rest of the country, actually was draining wealth from its outlying cities and regions. Moscow also receives the lion's share of foreign investment, well over 50 percent. In mid-1997, for example, McDonald's, the giant American fast-food chain, opened its 13th outlet in the city.

By the second half of the 1990s, Moscow's new young rich, its "New Russians"—such as bankers, real estate developers, executives of giant Moscow-based businesses, and mobsters of all sorts—lived on luxurious apartments that easily could cost $10,000 per month. They rented mansions in the countryside that cost tens of thousands more. They ate in expensive restaurants and frequented exclusive nightclubs where virtually anything was available for a price, always protected, of course, by squads of bodyguards. The New Russians drove expensive foreign cars, ate and drank gourmet foods and liquors, and vacationed at the world's fanciest resorts. Moscow, as an American journalist reported, was a city of "cash, crime, and corruption. Suddenly, Moscow has become brasher than New York [and] faster than Tokyo."[17] A joke summed up how many Russians view the life of the "New Russians":

> One New Russian says to another, "I just bought the most fantastic tie in Paris. It cost three hundred dollars!"
> "Oh really?" says the other proudly. "I just bought the same tie for *four* hundred dollars!"[18]

What Moscow has in common with the rest of Russia is that it also has grinding poverty. It is a city where elderly pensioners struggle to survive by earning $15 per month gathering bottles on the streets. The poor crowd into rooms in apartments they share with other families, dreading the prospect that the apartment will be privatized and they will become homeless. And between the rich and poor, Moscow's growing middle class is starting and developing small businesses, working in offices and shops, and somehow managing to get by. Never, it is fair to say, has Russia seen anything like the fast life of 1990s Moscow.

NOTES

1. The *New York Times,* March 30, 1993.
2. The *New York Times,* March 9, 1994.
3. The *New York Times,* July 20, 1992.
4. The *New York Times,* January 13, 1994.
5. Quoted in Michael Rywkin, *Soviet Society Today* (Armonk, N.Y.: M. E. Sharpe, 1989), p. 155.

6. Quoted in Anthony Jones, "The Educational Legacy of the Soviet Period," in *Education and Society in the New Russia,* ed. Anthony Jones (Armonk, N.Y.: M. E. Sharpe, 1994), p. 10.

7. Deborah Adelman, *The "Children of Perestroika" Come of Age* (Armonk, N.Y.: M. E. Sharpe, 1994), p. 66.

8. The *New York Times,* May 9, 1992.

9. The *New York Times,* December 4, 1993.

10. The *New York Times,* June 8, 1997.

11. The *New York Times,* August 20, 1993.

12. Quoted in Karen Dawisha and Bruce Parrot, *Russia and the New States of Eurasia* (Cambridge, England and New York: Cambridge University Press, 1994), p. 99.

13. The *New York Times,* April 26, 1992.

14. Quoted in Anthony Jones, ibid., p. 14.

15. The *New York Times,* May 29, 1993.

16. The *New York Times,* May 22, 1994.

17. Michael Spector, "Moscow on the Make,: *New York Times Magazine,* June 1, 1997, p. 50.

18. Quoted in David Remnick, *Resurrection: The Stuggle for a New Russia* (New York: Random House, 1997), p. 181.

9

Problems and Prospects

As post-Soviet Russia struggles to establish democracy and a free-market economic system, it simultaneously must contend with other serious and dangerous problems. Some problems, such as the rising wave of crime or environmental destruction, are constantly discussed because they touch almost everybody's daily life. Others, such as the difficulties faced by the scientific community or Russia's relationship with the newly independent states that made up the former Soviet Union, are less visible, but their resolution is still critical to Russia's future. Together they constitute a tremendous burden on the new Russia and its people.

Crime

At 2:00 P.M. on July 19, 1993, seven men burst into an automobile showroom in the center of Moscow, machine guns blazing. In the shoot-out with security guards that followed, four people died. Two weeks later, gunmen killed four people when they fired into a downtown office building. A week after that, machine-gun fire claimed three more victims in a Moscow office. In May 1994, a member of parliament was gunned down outside his Moscow apartment. Four days later, another member of parliament shot and killed a would-be assassin in a battle of assault rifles.

By mid-1994, Russia was reeling from daylight robberies, gangland shoot-outs and murders, an epidemic of muggings, and even bombings in crowded pedestrian areas. Moscow residents were being kidnapped and terrorized so they would give up their apartments, or murdered if they refused. In June, the deadly violence ratcheted upward yet again when a huge car bomb shattered a sunny Moscow afternoon. The explosion decapitated the driver of a nearby limousine (the bomb was aimed at the limousine's owner), destroyed a fruit stand, and blew out all the windows of an eight-story building across the street. One witness, a man working across from where the explosion took place, spoke for a frightened and angry citizenry:

> I didn't mind when they [the gangsters] waited for each other and shot it out. Now the mafia has started killing each other with bombs that can also kill everyone else. It's disgusting.[1]

Crime, in particular organized crime, may be the most powerful and dangerous force to emerge in Russia from the wreckage of Soviet communism. Boris Yeltsin has called it a "superpower," and added that "Crime has become problem number one for us."[2] Millions of Russians agreed with Yeltsin. One opinion poll in 1993 found that almost half of them feared crime more than unemployment. A 1994 poll revealed that 91 percent of all Muscovites feared for their daily lives and that one in three had been in a life-threatening situation during the past year. Like the witness to the car bombing, they worried their country was falling prey to organized criminals they called the "Mafia."

As with so many difficulties Russia faces today, its problem with organized crime grows out of its Soviet past. Beginning in the 1960s, an enormous black market developed in the Soviet Union that supplied the population with many goods the Communist economy did not provide. Hundreds of large criminal gangs controlled sectors of that trade, and they often operated with the cooperation of corrupt government officials. It was during that period that Russians began to talk about what they called their "Mafia."

The criminal gangs grew stronger during the Gorbachev era. They were able to threaten and often control small businesses that began to operate during the late 1980s. After 1991, as the ability of the government in Moscow to control Russia weakened, criminal gangs flourished. By 1994, there were over 5,000 gangs in Russia, 10 times as many as in 1990. The Russian ministry of the interior estimated that these gangs controlled one-third of the sale of all goods and services in the country. The United States CIA reported that criminal organizations controlled 40,000 state and private enterprises in Russia. Criminals controlled as much as 50 percent of all private businesses. They used bribery, kidnapping, and murder to assert and expand their influence. Not only were the criminal gangs interconnected with Russia's emerging free-market economy, they cooperated with and had ties with government officials at every level. As one businessman and politician, himself the object of two failed assassination attempts in one year, put it:

> It is not just the ties between business and organized crime that worry me. I am far more worried about the links between the Government and organized crime.[3]

Russian organized crime presented many dangers, including the growing network of contacts they were establishing with similar organizations in other countries in Europe and the United States. Russian gangs used these contacts to move into the international drug trade. They also dealt in a staggering variety of goods, from drugs to raw materials to weapons stolen from the Soviet armed forces. However, two aspects of Russian organized crime stood out as dangers far worse than ordinary criminality.

One terrifying nightmare was that gangs, with the help of corrupt officials, would steal nuclear material in Russia that could be used to make an atomic bomb. Such material would find many buyers, especially aggressive Islamic countries such as Iraq and Iran or Middle Eastern terrorist organizations linked to them. Then in the spring and summer of 1994, the nightmare became a real threat. Four times in four months, police in Germany seized samples of highly enriched nuclear material—uranium 235 and plutonium 239—that could be used to make a nuclear bomb. Among the people arrested was an agent of Iraq, a country known to be interested in building an atomic bomb. The Germans concluded that the samples were smuggled out of Russia and warned that "international organized crime—a real atomic mafia—is at work here."[4] The director of the United States Federal Bureau of Investigation (FBI) called the spread of

Fighting crime: These anti–organized crime policemen are taking no chances. They are protected by bulletproof jackets as they guard an alleged drug dealer, who was arrested with more than 30 other dealers in a town about 25 miles (40 km) from Moscow.

nuclear weapons through thefts by organized crime "the greatest long-term threat to the security of the United States."[5] A German expert warned:

> It will take intense international cooperation among all of us—at the highest levels of the United States Government, the Russian Government, and here in Europe—to get control of this.[6]

That clearly was not going to be easy. Russia's supply of nuclear bomb material was not only in military installations, but was also scattered over dozens of research institutes, weapons labs, power plants, and other facilities. Many of these facilities were and remain vulnerable to theft. The country possessed about 170 tons of plutonium and over 1,000 tons of highly enriched uranium, and some of it was lost or otherwise unaccounted for. One expert estimated that it would take $1 billion and at least five years to bring the system under control. Meanwhile, a leading Russian physicist noted that, "It is possible to buy anything in our country, including weapons and samples."[7]

The second great danger posed by runaway criminality in Russia is that it would undermine democracy. The Russian people were dealing not only with organized crime, but with muggings and other violence that made Russian cities unsafe, even in broad daylight. To millions of Russians, democracy was associated with violence and gangsterism. Criminality was making their lives, already so difficult because of economic hardship, almost unbearable. As they struggled to make ends meet, ordinary Russians were taunted by wealthy criminals cruising around town in expensive imported cars and enjoying expensive clubs and restaurants. In the election of December 1993, many frustrated and angry voters turned to Vladimir Zhirinovsky and other antidemocratic politicians who promised to use force to restore order. The criminality that pervaded the new "democratic" Russia was turning ordinary Russians against democracy. One journalist spoke for many when he told an American visitor:

> To tell you the truth, if someone were to stage a coup tomorrow, I would not know what or whom to defend.[8]

It was in response to the increasingly threatening situation that Boris Yeltsin issued an anticrime decree in June 1994. It came after a weekend in which Moscow was ravaged by a dozen bombings and eight contract killings. The president told the Russian people the time had come to strike back at what he called "criminal filth." His decree suspended some of Russia's basic new civil rights. It allowed the police to arrest and hold people in prison for almost any reason and search homes without evidence of a crime being committed. Police also could go through the bank accounts of anyone suspected of ties with organized crime without a court order and use their findings in trials. It also called for using the army in cities like Moscow and St. Petersburg to combat crime.

Yeltsin's crime decree immediately was criticized for going too far and threatening the civil rights of all citizens while attempting to combat criminals. Many people doubted the law could be effectively put into practice. Yet one official summed up the gravity of the situation when he told reporters that "I am convinced that society will accept the most brutal measures against crime."[9]

In fact, Yeltsin's decree had little immediate impact. In 1997 an international study cited Russia as the fourth most corrupt country in the world. Criminality even was corrupting Russian popular culture. Gangsters increasingly were the heros of popular books and films. Well-known entertainers performed at the parties of prominent gangsters. Expressions that once referred to life in prison were used by the media to describe the normal condition of Russian society. Russia in the late 1990s seemed as far as ever from establishing the orderly rule of law, which everyone agreed was a necessary prerequisite for a stable free-market economy and a workable democracy.

Environment

For seven decades, the Soviet government stressed economic development at any price. Because they lived under a totalitarian dictatorship, people in the Soviet Union could not stop the construction of factories, dams, irrigation canals, or other projects that often damaged the environment. The result of Soviet policies has been nothing less than environmental devastation in every former Soviet republic, including Russia. The air, water, and land have been poisoned. As President Boris Yeltsin told his people, "We have inherited an ecological disaster."[10]

One of Russia's greatest natural gifts is her rivers, yet after 70 years of communism, every major river in the country is polluted. The prime example is the once mighty Volga, the river the Russians call their "Dear Little Mother." The Volga, which once flowed freely from north of Moscow to the Caspian Sea, has been bottled up behind massive dams and turned into a string of hundreds of lakes and reservoirs. Water that once took five days to flow from Rybinsk, north of Moscow, to Volgograd, in the south near the Caspian Sea, now takes 500 days, almost two years. Along the way, it is polluted by millions of tons of wastes from 200 major industrial complexes. Millions of the Volga's fish have died, and many of those that live to be caught have been teeming with worms. As the river approaches the city of Kazan, east of Moscow, its shores are lined with dam-flooded forests. Farther south, near Saratov, Russia's "Dear Little Mother" is clogged with green algae, which feeds on agricultural runoff.

All of this filth pours into the landlocked Caspian Sea, the world's largest inland body of water. The Caspian is also the most important source of Russia's famous caviar, or sturgeons' eggs. The sturgeon are further threatened by pollution from oil wells in the Caspian, as well as other industrial plants along its shores. The ecological degradation is equally serious in the nearby Black Sea, whose 2,500-mile (4,025-km) coastline Russia shares with five neighbors, including Ukraine and Georgia, both formerly part of the Soviet Union. Polluted by Russia's Don River and 60 other rivers and streams, the Black Sea's waters are losing their oxygen and its fish are disappearing.

Far to the north, the Kola Peninsula by the White Sea has been turned into one of the most poisoned places on earth. Once a land of pine forests filled with wildlife and pristine rivers rich with fish, the Kola is the victim of two of the world's largest and filthiest nickel smelters. Its pine and birch forests are wastelands of tree stumps, and its rivers now flow with poisonous metals. The workers in the Kola's factories and mines suffer from heart disease, lung cancer, lead poisoning, and emphysema. Local women have one of the highest rates of miscarriages in the world, and a quarter of the region's babies are born with serious birth defects. A local ecological expert summed up what has happened to the region he loves:

> In Russia today, it is difficult to say which is the worst place, the dirtiest, and the most dangerous place. But what has happened to the Kola peninsula is a disaster on any scale.[11]

Siberia, Russia's great frontier with an area larger than America's lower 48 states, is an ecological disaster on an even larger scale. The snow in the Kuzbass industrial region lies blackened on the ground from the emissions of factories and mines. Large stretches of Siberia's great rivers—including the Ob, Yenisey, and the Lena—are polluted. Even the seemingly endless taiga is threatened. Several areas already suffer from deforestation. Meanwhile, a South Korean logging company has begun cutting vast tracts, and other foreign loggers wait in the wings, ready to take advantage of Russia's desperate financial needs.

In almost every part of Russia, the situation is equally disturbing. In the city of Magnitogorsk in the Urals, where Stalin ordered the world's largest steel mill to be built, gas and dust that spew from smokestacks have left a third of the city's population suffering from respiratory diseases. Acid rain is taking its toll on nature from the Finnish border in the west to remote regions in northeastern Siberia. In Moscow, the pollution from 2,800 factories is blamed for birth defects and an infant death rate that is twice that of the United States. Several neighborhoods in the city most heavily contaminated with industrial pollutants have experienced a rash of children born with only one forearm.

Perhaps most dangerous of all, Russia is threatened by nuclear contamination. Its nuclear submarines and icebreakers have left tons of radioactive waste in its northern waters, especially in the Barents and Kara Seas. In an accident at a nuclear arms plant in the Urals in 1957, almost 9,000 square miles (23,310 sq km) of land were contaminated and 250,000 people exposed to high levels of radiation. Additional accidents and contamination have taken place since then. Most recently, an explosion at a nuclear arms plant contaminated about 50 square miles (130 sq km) in Siberia in 1993. Several Siberian rivers are tainted with nuclear waste, including the giant Ob, which rises near the site of the 1957 Urals nuclear accident. In addition, Russia has several nuclear power plants similar to the one that exploded at Chernobyl in Ukraine in 1986.

Russia's damaged environment is one of the heaviest burdens it carries into the post-Soviet era. It has left Russia with problems it will not be able to solve for generations, if it can solve them at all.

Russia and Its Regions

It has never been easy for the sprawling Russian state to control its outlying and non-Russian ethnic areas. Even during the Soviet era, the relationship between ethnic Russians and the minority non-Russians, who between themselves were almost 50 percent of the population, became an increasingly urgent question. When Russia emerged from the wreckage of the fallen Soviet Union, it was shorn of most of its former non-Russian population, and the ethnic Russian share of the population rose to about 82 percent. However, demands for autonomy by many of the ethnic republics that made up the Russian Federation, which were accompanied by vague declarations of "sovereignty," signaled a potential threat to the country's unity. The threat was compounded by demands for autonomy from some of Russia's 67 nonethnic territorial divisions.

The two major zones of instability were the Volga region and the North Caucasus. There are several ethnic republics in the Volga region, the most militant of which is Tatarstan. The Tatars, with 3.75 percent of the population, are the largest minority ethnic group in Russia. They make up just under half of Tatarstan's population, although only a quarter of all Russia's Tatars live in the republic. Located about 500 miles (805 km) from Moscow, Tatarstan is a vital territorial link holding Russia together. Major roads, railroads, and oil pipelines all cross its territory.

Ivan the Terrible conquered the Tatars and their capital of Kazan in 1552, and, over the next 440 years, they became the most Russified of the former Soviet Union's Muslim Turkic-speaking peoples. In fact, there was considerable intermarriage between Tatars and Russians. Yet in the early 1990s, a powerful national revival emerged in Tatarstan. Early in 1992 it refused, along with the republic of Chechnya, to sign Yeltsin's Federal Treaty that was designed to maintain Russian unity while permitting some local autonomy. In 1993, after adopting its own constitution, Tatarstan declared itself a "sovereign state." At the same time, it stopped short of declaring its independence. In 1994 Moscow and Kazan worked out a compromise that appears to be working. Tatarstan won broad authority, including some power over taxes and its natural resources; however, it made no claims to conduct its own foreign or security policy. Since the 1994 agreement, it increasingly has been drawn into the orbit of the overall Russian economy. Most of the republic's people seem to agree that Tatarstan's stability and prosperity are inseparable from remaining a part of the broader Russian economy. At the same time some developments in Tatarstan continue to worry the Kremlin. One decision taken by the Second World Congress of Tatars, which met in Kazan in August 1997, is especially disturbing. At that meeting Tatar leaders decided to change the alphabet used to write the Tatar language. They want to switch from the Cyrillic alphabet used to write Russian, which the Soviet regime imposed on the Tatars in 1939, to a Latin alphabet. It remains to be seen if this decision actually will be carried out and what effect it will have on the links between Tatarstan and the rest of Russia.

In the North Caucasus the secessionist movement in Chechnya and the war that resulted was a disaster for Moscow (see chapter 6). However, Chechen secessionism did not spread to the other six ethnic republics of the region, five of which have large non-Russian Muslim populations. Nonetheless, Russia's leaders were aware that the former Soviet identity of the region, long gone by 1997, was being replaced in part by a religious Islamic identity. The political and separatist implications of this development are likely to remain a major concern to Moscow for a long time.

Ethnic separatism was not Moscow's only problem with Russia's regions. The economic hardship of the 1990s fed regional dissatisfaction and a willingness to defy Moscow. The contrast between Moscow and regional cities and towns added to the anger. For example, in 1996, while Moscow prospered, the economy of Novosibirsk, Siberia's largest city, declined by a shocking 15 percent. The story was similar in other provincial cities, especially those, like Novosibirsk, whose factories once supplied the Soviet military machine but now stood idle. Making matters worse, as of 1997, none of Russia's 89 regions was receiving the federal money it needed to pay the pensions and the salaries of essential workers.

Unlike the Chechen leadership, regional leaders elsewhere in Russia did not talk of secession; however, anger and defiance could be seen both near Moscow and thousands of miles from the Kremlin's towers. Thus in March 1997 the governor of Tula, just 100 miles from Moscow, threatened not to send any tax revenues to Moscow unless his region received the federal funds due to it. The mood was the same in the republic of Udmurtia, about 650 miles east of Moscow at the edge of the Ural Mountains. Urdmurtia officially is one of Russia's 21 minority ethnic republics, but its population is about 60 percent Russian. A nurse there named Irina Ivanova spoke for many local people when she complained that "Moscow gets everything. They get our oil, our gas, the candy we make. We don't even get our wages."[12]

These sentiments were echoed by leaders in other regions. Adding to the difficulties was that even by the late 1990s there is no consensus over how power should be divided in the new post-Soviet Russia. In dispute was the relationship not only between Moscow and Russia's regions but

Arms control: According to an agreement reached by the United States, Russia, Ukraine, and Belarus, all short-range nuclear weapons in Ukraine and Belarus were transported to Russia. This nuclear warhead is being lowered onto a heavily guarded truck for shipment from Ukraine to Russia.

between the regional governments and local cities and towns. Almost all Russians understand that the centuries of autocratic rule from the center that existed under the czars and the Soviets is over. The problem is that few if any seem sure of how to operate under a democracy.

Foreign Policy

In 1992, Russia's main foreign policy challenge was to emerge from seven decades of Soviet hostility toward the West and establish a normal relationship with the international community. The Yeltsin government has tried to do this while assuring that Russia is recognized as a major player on the world scene. As Andrei Kozyrev, foreign minister in 1991, put it, Russia expects to play the international role of a "normal great power."

Russia certainly has a legitimate claim to great power status. When the Soviet Union collapsed, Russia inherited many of its positions on international bodies, including its permanent seat and veto on the United Nations Security Council. Russia also inherited most, though not all, of the Soviet Union's vast nuclear arsenal that had made it, along with the United States, one of the world's two superpowers. (Ukraine, Belarus, and Kazakhstan also ended up with a smaller number of nuclear arms that were stationed on what became their territory.) At the same time, Russia was in a position to build on the progress the Soviet Union had made under Gorbachev in improving relations with the United States and its allies. By 1991, the Cold War was over, significant treaties had been signed to reduce nuclear arms, and the United States and its allies were anxious to help Russia become a productive member of the international community.

However, Russia faced numerous difficulties in working out its new post-Soviet foreign policy. Not the least of them was the shock and humiliation of its reduced power, for the collapse of the Soviet Union also meant the breakup of the Russian Empire. Territory that Russia had controlled for centuries was lost. Russia was pushed back from most of the Baltic seacoast, losing warm-water ports Peter the Great had conquered in the early 18th century. Ukraine, parts of which fell under Russian control as early as the mid-17th century, also was lost. With it went rich farmland and other valuable resources, as well as much of the Black Sea coast. Belarus, the prize of victory after many battles with Poland, was gone as well. Losses in the Caucasus and in Central Asia further injured Russia's wounded pride.

The same divisions that plagued its internal, political, and economic life complicated the task of formulating a post-Soviet Russian foreign policy. While there were many opinions, two main camps existed. President Yeltsin and his supporters strongly favored continued cooperation and improved relations with the West. The other camp, while hardly unanimous, favored a harder line toward the West. It also openly hoped to reattach to Russia at least a part of the defunct Soviet/Russian Empire, particularly Ukraine and Belarus. While President Yeltsin officially set Russia's foreign policy, he was under constant pressure from his critics. By late 1992, that pressure forced him to take a tougher, more nationalistic line on a variety of issues.

In the welter of foreign policy issues facing Russia, several priorities stood out. One was nuclear arms control with the West and the related question of nuclear arms in Ukraine, Belarus, and Kazakhstan. During the Soviet era, the United States and the Soviet Union signed a historic arms reduction treaty called START I. In January 1993, the two countries went even further by signing START II, which cut nuclear arms even more deeply than START I. However, for START II to go into effect, Ukraine, Belarus, and Kazakhstan had to sign both START I and a second treaty designed to stop the spread of nuclear arms to nonnuclear countries (the Nuclear Non-Proliferation Treaty or NPT). Kazakhstan ratified START I in mid-1992, and became a party to the NPT in 1994, while Belarus accepted both treaties in 1993. The main holdout was Ukraine, which finally ratified START I in November 1993. It took another year, until December 1994, for Ukraine to ratify the NPT.

Russia had other problems with Ukraine, the most serious of which was the status of the Crimean Peninsula. The Crimea had been attached to Ukraine in 1954 by Soviet leader Nikita Khrushchev. However, its population was over 70 percent ethnic Russian. After Ukraine became independent in 1991, the Crimea threatened to secede. It wanted to reunite with Russia, a move supported by many nationalists in Russia. Although no secession occurred as of mid-1994, the issue was one of several that created chronic tension between Russia and Ukraine.

Elsewhere in the "near abroad," the Russian term for the 14 newly independent former Soviet republics, ethnic turmoil created a wedge for Russia to reassert its influence. As of early 1993, two of three in the

Caucasus region—Azerbaijan and Georgia—remained outside the CIS. Ajerbaijan had left in 1992, and Georgia had never joined. During 1993, Russia used regional ethnic conflicts to bring both into the fold. Moscow took advantage of Azerbaijan's military defeats in its war with Armenia over disputed territory to convince Azerbaijan to rejoin the CIS in September. A similar strategy brought Georgia into the CIS. Georgia's president, Eduard Shevardnadze, was desperate to end Russian support for two secessionist movements that were tearing his country apart. Russia's price was Georgia's membership in the CIS and the right to maintain military bases in Georgia. In Central Asia, thousands of Russian troops sent to defend the government of Tajikistan from a rebellion by Islamic fundamentalists turned that country into a Russian protectorate.

Another factor that led Russia to intrude into the affairs of the near abroad states was the presence in those countries of 25 million ethnic Russians. Moscow claimed that it was worried about discrimination against Russians in several countries. Disputes with Latvia and Estonia over treatment of their large Russian minority populations led Russia to delay the withdrawal of troops that had been stationed in those countries prior to 1991. Russia finally agreed to withdraw the troops in the summer of 1994.

The concentration of ethnic Russians along the Russian border in large parts of northern Kazakhstan and eastern Ukraine created additional tension. In both cases, there was concern that the established borders would not hold if strongly challenged by nationalists inside Russia and ethnic Russians just beyond its frontiers. The most immediate danger was in Kazakhstan, where Kazakhs make up barely 40 percent of the population and Russians about 38 percent. Many experts expected the border would indeed change because they doubted Kazakhstan would hold together in the long term.

Overall, by late 1994, Russia was reasserting its influence in several of the near abroad countries. Ukraine and Belarus were seeking closer ties with Russia to help solve their severe economic problems. In April, Belarus signed a treaty that tied its economy closely with Russia and gave Moscow a free lease on military bases for its troops in Belarus. Three months later, both Ukraine and Belarus elected new presidents who favored closer ties with their huge neighbor. Russia also tightened its grip on several countries in the Caucasus and Central Asia. It had a total of 16,000 troops stationed throughout the near abroad countries and announced plans to establish about 30 permanent bases there.

Over the next few years, Ukraine and Belarus moved in opposite directions. Leonid Kuchma (kuh-CHMAH), Ukraine's new president, distanced his country from Russia and turned it westward. Instead of facing Moscow, he stressed what he called "Ukraine's return to Europe."[13] Belarus, under its dictatorial and pro-Russian president Aleksandr Lukachenko, moved toward reunion with Russia. A series of agreements beginning in 1995 culminated in the so-called Russia-Belarus Union Charter in May 1997. That charter, however, was much less a reality than its name implied. The two countries have strengthened their economic and security ties, but for the immediate future remain separate states.

Russia was less able to impose its will on the former Communist states of Eastern Europe. Moscow was especially disturbed when several Eastern European countries asked to join NATO, the United States–led military alliance that had protected Western Europe from the Soviet Union during the Cold War. The Russians opposed this because it would bring Western power deep into a region they once controlled and considered important to their security. Russian opposition to NATO's eastward expansion slowed the process but could not stop it. NATO's first step was a compromise program called the Partnership for Peace. It allowed non-NATO countries to be associated with the alliance and cooperate with it militarily without becoming full-fledged members. Eastern European countries quickly signed up in the hope that the "partnership" eventually would turn into full membership. In June 1994 Russia itself joined Partnership for Peace, thereby taking a small step toward normal relations with the West.

The NATO powers did not consider the Partnership for Peace program a viable substitute for an expansion that would include at least a few of the former Soviet Eastern Europe satellites. Some Western arms control experts nonetheless opposed NATO expansion. They warned that it would harden Russian attitudes regarding further reduction of nuclear arms. In particular, these experts feared that the Russian Duma would not ratify the START II, which Russia and the United States had signed back in 1993. Tough antiexpansion statements by Yeltsin, Russia's new foreign minister Yevgeny Primakov, and other leading figures in the Yeltsin government and the Duma reinforced that concern.

These objections did not deter the NATO powers. Ultimately, Russia was forced to agree reluctantly to NATO expansion. Just before that happened, NATO and Russia in May 1996 signed a "NATO-Russia Founding Act." That agreement set up a NATO-Russian Council to discuss security issues and promote cooperation. In July 1997 NATO admitted Poland, Hungary, and the Czech Republic to full membership. Significantly, despite the United States Senate's ratification of START II, Russia's Duma persisted in its refusal to approve that treaty.

Between 1992 and 1996 the United States and Russia signed almost 100 formal agreements. Aside from START II, they included important measures such as the indefinite extension of the nuclear Non-Proliferation Treaty in 1995 and the Comprehensive Nuclear Test Ban in 1996. Russia also was developing ties with Western Europe. Yet there were new tensions as well. Many Russians continued to resent NATO's eastward expansion. In the West, and especially in Washington, there was concern about Russian support of aggressive Middle Eastern countries such as Iran and Iraq. Most disturbing was the growing evidence that Russia was helping Iran build long-range ballistic missiles that could be used to deliver nuclear weapons. By the second half of the 1990s Russia's relations with the West in general and the United States in particular were vastly different form the Soviet Union's decades-long Cold War confrontation with the West. Russia was becoming a "normal great power," but there was more to do before its relationship with the United States and the West would fulfill the hopes that were in the air in 1992.

Future Prospects

In the late 1990s Russia still faces what Boris Yeltsin called its main task:

> To emerge from the deep quagmire of crisis and to change to a life that will enable us and other peoples to live and work normally.[14]

Accomplishing that task requires three essential transitions. First, Russia must transform itself from a communist dictatorship into a democracy. Second, it must move from a centrally planned to a market economy. Third, it must transform itself from an empire into a nation-state. None of these transformations is close to completion, nor is there any guarantee that any will be successful.

To be sure, Russia is no longer a communist dictatorship; the Soviet planned economy is a thing of the past; and the old Soviet/Russian Empire

Aleksandr I. Lebed (1950 –)

Aleksandr Lebed was born in Novocherkassk (noh-voh-cheh-R'KASK), a Cossack town in the Rostov region of Russia on the lower Don River, close to where it runs into the Sea of Azov. He grew up in a working-class family. Like so many Russian families, Lebed's suffered under Stalin'e terror when his father spent time in one of Stalin's labor camps for the "crime" of twice coming late to work. In 1962, as a 12-year-old, Lebed was an eyewitness to the brutality of post-Stalin Soviet dictatorship when workers in Novocherkassk demonstrated against wage cuts and food price increases. Soviet troops fired on the crowd, killing more than 70 people, as young Aleksandr and his brother watched from atop a tree in front of their home. Despite this massacre, Lebed apparently grew up a firm believer in communism.

He also grew up tough. Not particulary interested in school, Lebed excelled at boxing and, like so many Russians, chess. He survived innumerable fights and accidents. Once a broken shoulder bone, one of many broken bones he suffered, had to be rebroken and reset after a botched operation. His deep gravelly voice, which has been described as resembling either the rumble of artillery or thunder, was the result of a brawl in which his neck was seriously injured. Lebed claims that as an army officer he once knocked out 11 soldiers who disobeyed an order.

Yet the men under his command deeply respected Lebed, as did his fellow military officers and enlisted men throughout the armed forces. Lebed became a paratrooper and hero in the Afghanistan war. During the Soviet Union's last years, he served in trouble spots in various parts of the country. In 1991, as commander of an elite paratroop division, he refused to storm Yeltsin's headquarters during the August coup against Gorbachev. Yeltsin in return publicly hailed Lebed as a hero. In 1992 Lebed took command of the former Soviet Fourteenth Army, which was stationed in Moldova. His support of ethnic Russians in Moldova's Trans-Dniestria region helped make him a hero among Russian nationalists. In 1993 Lebed stayed neutral when both sides appealed for his support during Yeltsin's struggle with his opponents in parliament.

Throughout his military career, Lebed criticized corruption in the army, unconcerned with how his stand might affect his career. He was a loner ready to fight bureaucratic battles unaided. As he put it in his autobiography, *I Pity the Great Power,* "I am a cat who hunts alone."[15]

Lebed opposed the war in Chechnya. In 1995 his criticism of a Russian defense minister led to his forced resignation from the army. That year Lebed won a seat in parliament, although the political party he joined did poorly. In the 1996 presidential election, his blunt straightforward manner made him popular with the voters and earned him a third place finish. Both Yeltsin and Zyuganov courted him after the first round. Lebed chose to support Yeltsin, who then appointed him as his national security adviser and head of Russia's Security Council. However, after Yeltsin's reelection Lebed feuded with insiders in the Yeltsin camp. In October, about six weeks after Lebed arranged the vital cease-fire in Chechnya, Yeltsin fired him from all his posts.

Despite his exile from the Kremlin, Lebed remains a leading candidate to succeed Yeltsin after he retires. In May 1998 he established a political base by winning election as governor of the Siberian region of Krasnoyarsk. Still, the former general's political program is unclear, as is his commitment to democracy. Lebed stands clearly for a war against crime and corruption and for military reform. He rejects communism, which he says "hasn't worked anywhere." He has expressed admiration for General Augusto Pinochet of Chile, who governed as a  military dictator, and General Charles de Gaulle of France, who governed as a constitutional president. Perhaps the best evaluation of Lebed came from a former member of parliament who said:

> He is no democrat, but he is also certainly not a dictator. He is actually something simpler: a genuine Russian officer trying to make chivalry a part of the political process. He is like a Tolstoy character, a man from a different age. He is honestly looking for truth, and doesn't know where to find it.[16]

It is in that search that Aleksandr Lebed most closely stands for and symbolizes Russia.

Soviet Science in Crisis

Just outside the Siberian city of Nobosibirsk is the city of Akademgorodok (ah-kah-DEHM-guh-rah-DOK). Its name means "academic town" in Russian, and for over three decades it was one of the jewels in the crown of Soviet science, which the Soviet regime had made a major priority and in which it took great pride. Akademgorodok was built beginning in 1957 as a center where the Soviet Union's best scientists could live and work. It became the home for the Siberian branch of the Soviet Academy of Sciences (which in 1991 changed its name to the Russian Academy of Sciences). As of mid-1994, the Siberian division of the Russian Academy of Sciences employed 34,000 people, including 11,000 scientists engaged in research. They worked in almost 100 institutes, the majority of them located in Akademgorodok.

For years the Soviet state generously financed these institutes, either through direct payments or military-industrial contracts the institutes made with state-owned companies. Now the struggling Russian government provides only 30 percent of the institutes' budgets, which already have been severely cut. For example, in only two years, between 1990 and 1992, the budget of the Russian Academy of Sciences was cut by 60 percent.

This means the institutes in Akademgorodok must struggle to find new means of support. The problem is summed up by Professor Fyodor A. Kuznetzov (kuh-znets-OFF), a distinguished chemist who is director of the Institute of Organic Chemistry in Akademgorodok:

> There isn't enough money. We're in a survival mode. We try to see what the future will be, but the model is unclear.[17]

has disintegrated. However, Russia's infant democratic institutions are weak, and they are threatened by a variety of hostile forces. There are extreme nationalists who openly reject democracy and favor a new dictatorship. Russia's horrendous crime wave and its severe economic chaos have created social conditions poisonous to democratic life. In addition, Russia's historical lack of a democratic tradition means that millions of ordinary people could easily give support to antidemocratic

What is clear is that the model will involve making products that can be sold commercially, something scientists never had to worry about in Akademgorodok. Professor Kuznetzov's institute, which designs and makes crystals for military lasers and new materials for superconductors, thus far has been unable to make the transition. That is not surprising, in light of the changes involved. As one scientist explained:

> Before everything was secret, and today they say, "Everything's for the Western market. It's too big a jump. But if we don't sell ourselves, there's no money for research."[18]

Meanwhile, the institutes of Akademgorodok, and Russia as a whole, are losing scientists. Some are moving into other areas. Igor Y. Paukov, the deputy director of the Institute of Organic Chemistry, mentions one colleague, a professor of theoretical physics, who abandoned science to become an officer in a bank. The man is doing well and can afford a new car, Paukov admits. But then Paukov adds, with a touch of both sadness and contempt, "What's he producing at the bank?"[19]

Some scientists are surviving and managing to stay in their fields. American companies like American Telephone and Telegraph have gone to Russia and hired the staffs of local institutes. Other American firms have sought out Russian scientists with potentially marketable inventions. One of the most important of these is a device for the early detection of cancer invented by Dr. Viktor Lazarev (LAH-zah-ryeff) of Moscow State University.

However, the success stories only involve a small minority of Russia's scientists. Many of the country's most talented scientists, especially those who are entering or are in the prime of their careers, are emigrating to the West. They are leaving behind a scientific community in crisis, like so much else in Russia.

forces if their lives do not improve—or if they worsen—in the near future. Recent surveys of popular opinion suggest that this could happen: for example, a poll taken in early 1993 showed that 45 percent of all Russians wanted to return to the way of life prior to 1985. By early 1996 the figure had risen to 58 percent. Other polls taken in 1996 revealed a widespread disillusionment with both political democracy and a market economy.

That is why the second transformation—to a market economy—is so important. It must be achieved in a way that combines economic freedom with a reasonable standard of living for the majority of the people and also provide a safety net to protect those in need. A Russia with a tiny, rich minority and a large, poor majority will be unstable and almost certainly undemocratic. While some progress has been made in promoting private businesses that actually provide goods and services that people need, much of what has taken place in Russia since 1991 has been painful and unproductive. Privatization has produced a concentration of wealth that is a tragic national scandal. The jury is still out on whether the new Russian economy will provide, within a reasonable period of time, a decent standard of living for the majority of its people.

Restoring St. Petersburg: Among the many buildings in St. Peterburg that are being restored after years of neglect is the Winter Palace, the beautiful 18th-century palace that is one of four buildings housing the world-renowned Hermitage Museum.

Russia's transition from an empire to a nation-state began when most of the non-Russians in the Soviet Union established their independence. Both the old Russian Empire before 1917 and the Soviet Union were only about half ethnically Russian. Russia today is over 80 percent ethnically Russian. However, Russia still must build a national identity that commands the loyalty of all of its people, both Russian and non-Russian alike.

In many ways, Russia, even seven years after the end of the Soviet era, still is back where it was in 1917. The old oppressive empire is gone. But its people are wounded and suffering, and there are many obstacles and pitfalls ahead. Hopefully, this time, Russia will find the strength and will to overcome its past and build a better future.

NOTES

1. The *New York Times,* June 10, 1994.
2. Quoted in Stephen Handleman, "The Russian Mafiya," *Foreign Affairs,* vol. 73, no. 2 (March/April 1994), p. 88.
3. The *New York Times,* May 10, 1994.
4. The *New York Times,* August 12, 1994.
5. The *New York Times,* August 14, 1994.
6. Ibid.
7. The *New York Times,* August 18, 1994.
8. Ibid., p. 91.
9. The *New York Times,* June 19, 1994.
10. Quoted in Mike Edwards, "A Broken Empire," *National Geographic,* March 1993, p. 9.
11. The *New York Times,* March 28, 1994.
12. The *New York Times,* March 25, 1997.
13. Quoted in Roman Solchanyk, "Ukraine," in *Problems of Communism,* November-December 1995, p. 49.
14. Quoted in Sakwa, p. 294.
15. Quoted in Michael Specter, "The Wars of Aleksandr Ivanovich Lebed," *New York Times Magazine,* October 13, 1996, p. 47.
16. Quoted in Ibid., p. 48.
17. The *New York Times,* November 21, 1993.
18. Ibid.
19. Ibid.

Chronology of Russian History

Old Russia

mid-9th century:	Kievian Rus organized
988:	Kievian Russia adopts Christianity
1240:	City of Kiev destroyed by the Mongols. Beginning of the "Mongol Yoke"
1380:	Prince Dmitri of Moscow defeats the Mongols in battle
1480:	Ivan III establishes Russia's independence from the Mongols
1613:	Romanov Dynasty begins
1670–71:	Serf rebellion led by Stenka Razin

Imperial Russia

1694–1725:	Reign of Peter the Great
1703:	St. Petersburg founded

1762–96:	Reign of Catherine the Great
1773–74:	Pugachev Rebellion
1812:	Alexander I leads Russia to victory over Napoleon. Russian soldiers reach Paris
1825:	Decembrist Revolt
1853–56:	Crimean War
1861:	Alexander II abolishes serfdom
1870:	Lenin born
1879:	Stalin born
1880s:	Marxism wins its first Russian converts
1881:	Alexander II assassinated
1891–92:	Serious famine in Russia
1892–1903:	Sergei Witte, as finance minister, promotes industrialization
1903:	Lenin organizes the Bolshevik Party
1904–05:	Russo-Japanese War
1905–06:	1905 Revolution
October 1905:	October Manifesto promises Russia a Duma, or parliament
1906–11:	Piotr Stolypin, as prime minister, introduces agricultural reforms
1914:	World War I begins
March 1917:	Popular revolution overthrows czarism. Provisional Government assumes power

Soviet Russia

November 7, 1917:	Bolsheviks overthrow the Provisional Government and seize power
November 1917:	Bolsheviks lose national election for a constitutional assembly, but disperse the assembly by force in January of 1918
1918–21:	Civil War in Russia; Era of "War Communism"
1921–29:	Era of the New Economic Policy (NEP)
1922:	Stalin appointed general secretary of the Communist Party

January 21, 1924:	Lenin dies
1924–29:	Stalin wins the struggle for power
1929:	Beginning of Stalin's industrialization drive, including forced collectivization of all farms that involved the arrest and deportation of millions of peasants
1932–33:	Famine in the Ukraine and other parts of the country kills at least 5 million peasants
1934–38:	Era of the Great Purge, which peaks between 1936 and 1938
August 23, 1939:	Nazi-Soviet Pact
September 1, 1939:	World War II begins
June 22, 1941:	Germany invades the Soviet Union
1945:	Allies defeat Germany, ending World War II. Cold War begins
March 5, 1953:	Stalin dies
February 1956:	20th Party Congress. Khrushchev gives his "Secret Speech"
October 1962:	Cuban Missile Crisis
October 1964:	Khrushchev removed from office. Brezhnev becomes Soviet leader
May 1972:	First Soviet-U.S. nuclear arms control agreement
December 1979:	Soviet Union invades Afghanistan
November 1982:	Brezhnev dies
1982–85:	Andropov and Chernenko serve briefly as Soviet leader, each dying after slightly over one year in office
March 11, 1985:	Gorbachev named general secretary of the Communist Party. Era of perestroika and glasnost begins
April 26, 1986:	Nuclear disaster at Chernobyl power plant
October 1987:	Boris Yeltsin demoted for criticizing slow pace of reform
December 1987:	Gorbachev and President Reagan sign nuclear arms control agreement banning all intermediate-range missiles in Europe

March 1989:	First free election in Soviet history. Voters cast ballots for deputies to newly created Congress of People's Deputies
March to December 1989:	Communism collapses in Eastern Europe
July 1990:	Yeltsin resigns from the Communist Party
November 1990:	Cold War declared over
June 1991:	Boris Yeltsin elected president of the Russian Republic within the USSR, thereby becoming the first freely elected leader in Russia's history
August 1991:	Coup against Gorbachev fails. Yeltsin plays crucial role in defeating the coup
December 8, 1991:	Commonwealth of Independent States founded by Boris Yeltsin and the leaders of Ukraine and Belarus
December 25, 1991:	Gorbachev resigns. Soviet Union is abolished and replaced by 15 independent states, one of which is the Russian Federation

The Russian Federation

1992

January 2:	Yeltsin frees most prices from government control. "Shock therapy" economic policy begins
March 31:	Russia and most of the ethnic republics sign Yeltsin's Federal Treaty, which is designed to preserve Russian unity while allowing local autonomy. However, Chechnya and Tatarstan refuse to sign
April:	Yeltsin's government narrowly beats back a vote of no confidence in the parliament. The struggle against Yelstin is led by Ruslan Khasbulatov and Alexandr Rutskoi
September:	Voucher system to privatize the Russian economy enacted into law
December:	Yeltsin beats back an attempt to limit his powers, but is forced to agree to Yegor Gaidar's

removal as prime minister. He is replaced by Victor Chernomyrdin on December 14

1993

January 3:	Russia and the United States sign the START II nuclear arms reduction treaty
April 25:	Nationwide referendum supports Yeltsin and his economic policies
September 20:	Azerbaijan joins the CIS
September 21:	Yeltsin dissolves parliament and calls for national elections in December
October 2:	Stone-throwing Yeltsin opponents battle police in Moscow. Anti-government violence intensifies the next day
October 3:	Yeltsin declares a state of emergency
October 4:	Government troops attack the White House, the parliament's headquarters and stronghold of Yeltsin's opponents. The building is taken by the afternoon
October 23:	Georgia joins the CIS
December 12:	Elections take place. Most observers are shocked when the ultranationalist Liberal Democratic Party led by Vladimir Zhirinovsky leads all parties with 23 percent of the vote. Voters also approve a new constitution giving the president greater powers

1994

January:	Yeltsin announces new cabinet led by moderate Victor Chernomyrdin
May 27:	Alexandr Solzhenitsyn returns to Russia
June 18:	Yeltsin announces strong anticrime decree
June:	Russia joins the NATO-sponsored "Partnership for Peace"
December 11:	Yeltsin orders thousands of troops into Chechnya to end independence movement there

1995

June 14:	Chechen guerrillas attack the Russian city of Budyonnovsk
July 11:	Yeltsin suffers his first heart attack. The second attack occurs on October 26
December 17:	Duma elections won by the Communist Party of the Russian Federation (CPRF)

1996

January 5:	Andrei Kozyrev resigns as foreign minister. He is replaced by Yevgeny Primakov
April 2:	Russia and Belarus agree to a "union" in which both states maintain their independence
June 16:	First round of the presidential elections. Yeltsin narrowly edges Zyuganov, while Lebed finishes a strong third
June 18:	Yeltsin appoints Lebed as national security adviser and head of the Russia's National Security Council
July 3:	Yeltsin is reelected by a decisive margin over Zyuganov
August 9:	Yeltsin inaugurated for a second term
August 31:	Lebed signs a peace accord with Chechen leaders
November 5:	Yeltsin undergoes bypass heart surgery
December 1:	Russian troops begin withdrawing from Chechnya according to the August 31 agreement

1997

January 27:	Chechnya holds presidential elections
March 8–18:	Yeltsin reorganizes his government. His new appointments include Anatoly Chubais and Boris Nemtsov as first deputy prime ministers
May 26:	Yeltsin and Belarus president Lukachenko sign the Russia-Belarus Union Charter
May 27:	NATO-Russia Founding Act signed

July 8:	Poland, Hungary, and the Czech Republic admitted to NATO
November 9:	Yeltsin arrives in China, beginning a visit designed to improve Russian-Chinese relations
December 4:	A new law permitting the sale of land, including agricultural land, comes into force in the Saratov region
December 6:	Dozens of people are killed when a military transport plane crashes into an apartment complex in southern Siberia

1998

January 1:	The government introduces a new ruble worth 1,000 old rubles
January 19:	Two Russian oil tycoons merge their companies, creating Russia's largest oil company and thus becoming the world's fourth biggest oil producer
March 5:	After months of bitter disagreement, the Duma approves Russia's 1998 budget
March 23–27:	On March 23, Yeltsin fires his entire cabinet. Four days later he appoints little-known Sergei Kiriyenko as Russia's new prime minister
April 24:	The Duma approves Kiriyenko as prime minister
May 13:	Russian stock market falls, beginning an economic crisis
May 17:	Aleksandr Lebed is elected governor of the Krasnoyarsk region
July 10:	International lenders agree to loan Russia $22.6 billion
August 17:	Russia devalues the ruble
August 23:	Yeltsin again dismisses entire cabinet, and he appoints Chernomyrdin as acting prime minister
September 10:	Yeltsin appoints Yevgeny Primakov as prime minister

Further Reading

Adelman, Deborah. *The "Children of Perestroika" Come of Age: Young People of Moscow Talk About Life in the New Russia.* Armonk, N.Y.: M.E. Sharpe, 1994. Fascinating interviews with young people who are trying to make their ways in the new and troubled Russia. This volume is a follow-up to the author's earlier and equally interesting book published in 1991: *Children of Perestroika: Moscow Teenagers Talk About Their Lives and Future.*

Daniels, Robert V., ed. *Soviet Communism from Reform to Collapse.* Lexington, Mass.: D.C. Heath, 1995. A collection of evaluations of the Gorbachev era by a variety of specialists with differing points of view from several countries, including Russia. Intended for use in college-level courses.

Edwards, Mike. "A Broken Empire." Photographs by Gerd Ludwig. *National Geographic* (March 1993), pp. 4–53. Actually three separate articles, one each on Russia, Kazakhstan, and Ukraine, all of which are accompanied by superb photographs. Covers both the terrible hardships and the new opportunities that have followed the collapse of the Soviet Union.

———. "Soviet Pollution." Photographs by Gerd Ludwig. *National Geographic* (August 1994), pp. 70–99. The text and photographs chronicle the terrible legacy of pollution that has poisoned the birth of post-Soviet Russia and the other post-Soviet successor states. An accompanying article in the same issue updates the situation at Chernobyl in Ukraine, site of the world's worst nuclear accident in 1986.

Hodgson, Bryan. "Kamchatka." Photographs by Sarah Leen. *National Geographic* (April 1994), pp. 36–67. A vividly written and pictorial overview of one of the most forbidding, and beautiful, regions of Russia, its peninsula of "fire and ice" on the shores of the Pacific Ocean.

193

Kaiser, Robert G. *Why Gorbachev Happened: His Triumphs, His Failure, and His Fall.* New York: Simon and Schuster, 1992. A comprehensive overview, by a leading American journalist, of the Gorbachev era.

Kort, Michael. *The Soviet Colossus: The Rise and Fall of the USSR,* 4th ed. Armonk, N.Y.: M.E. Sharpe, 1996. An overview of Soviet history that focuses on key turning points and also provides an overview of the pre-Soviet era. Written for college courses, but suitable for the general reader, including strong high school readers.

———. *Gorbachev.* New York: Franklin Watts, 1990. A biography for young adult readers about the the bold reformer whose policies ultimately led to the collapse of the Soviet Union. Covers the period up to early 1990.

McFaul, Michael, and Markov, Sergei. *The Troubled Birth of Russian Democracy: Parties, Personalities, and Programs.* Stanford, Calif.: Hoover Institution Press, 1993. An overview of the complex and volatile political situation in post-Soviet Russia, based on interviews with many of the leading players. Intended for a college-level audience.

Murray, Donald. *A Democracy of Despots.* Boulder, Colo.: Westview Press, 1995. A critical view of Gorbachev and Yeltsin as leaders by the Moscow correspondent for the Canadian Broacasting Company from 1988 to 1994.

Remnick, David. *Lenin's Tomb: The Last Days of the Soviet Empire.* New York: Random House, 1993. A highly acclaimed overview by an American journalist of events in the Soviet Union and Russia from the 1980s and through 1992.

———. *Resurrection: The Struggle for a New Russia.* New York: Random House, 1997. Remnick carries the story of the hardships that have plagued post-Soviet Russia through the mid-1990s.

Steele, Jonathan. *Eternal Russia: Yeltsin, Gorbachev, and the Mirage of Democracy.* Cambridge: Harvard University Press, 1994. A British journalist's overview of the collapse of the Soviet Union and the faltering struggle to build a new, democratic Russia. Steele has interviewed many of the key figures in this drama, including Mikhail Gorbachev and senior members of Yeltsin's inner circle.

Yeltsin, Boris. *Against the Grain.* Translated by Michael Glenny. New York: Summit Books, 1990. Yeltsin's autobiography, carrying his story up to 1990.

———. *The Struggle for Russia.* Translated by Catherine A. Fitzpatrick. New York: Times Books, 1994. Yeltsin's view of events in Russia from the August 1991 coup through his violent October 1993 showdown with parliament.

Index

Page numbers in *italics* indicate illustrations. Page numbers followed by *m* indicate maps; those followed by *c* indicate an item in the chronology.

A

abortion 152
acid rain 171
Agrarian Party 95, 97, 98, 111, 127
agriculture 69, 74
    collective farms 35–36, 119,
        121, 126, 129, 188*c*
    Khrushchev reforms 42, 43
    private farms 126–27, 129, 132
    production decline 132
    in Siberia 78
AIDS epidemic 153
Akademgorodok 75, 76–77,
    182–83
Akhmatova, Anna 56–57
alcohol abuse 45, 103, 124, 143,
    154
    Gorbachev campaign against
        120, 154
Aleksandr Nevsky 71
Alekseyev, Sergei 77
Alexander I (czar) 18, 187*c*
Alexander II (czar) 19, 21, 81, 187*c*
Alexander III (czar) 21, 81
Alexei II, Patriarch 157, 158
aluminum 68, 73
Amur River 66, 78
anarchy 80
Andropov, Yuri 45, 188*c*
Angara River 66
anti-Semitism 40, 95, 155, 158
Archangel 72
architecture 3–4, 61–62
Arctic Ocean 66, 68, 71–72
Armenia vi, 177
arms control 44, 50, *174*, 176,
    178, 179, 188*c*, 190*c*
army *See* military forces
arts *See* cultural heritage
Asia vi, vii, 10, 11*m*, 12, 68–69, 73
Astrakhan 72
atheism 154
August Coup (1991) 50–51, 82,
    84, 87, 101, 145, 148, 189*c*
autocracy 9, 18, 80, 81
Avtovaz 102
Azerbaijan 68, 177, 190*c*

B

Baikal, Lake 66
Baikal-Amur Mainline (BAM) 78,
    119
ballet 59, 142
Baptists 157
Barents Sea 71–72, 171
Barnaul 124–25
Baryshnikov, Mikhail 59
Bashkortostan 158
Belarus 49, 65, 177, 178, 191*c*
    in Commonwealth of Inde-
        pendent States 51, 85
    independence 175–76
    nuclear arms *174*, 175, 176
Belarusians vii, 1, 6
Bely, Andrei 56
Bezmyannaya (volcano) 77
birth defects 170, 171
black earth 69, 73–74
black market 45, 147, 166
Black Sea 2, 5, 65, 67, 68, 175
    pollution 170
    resorts and dachas 74, 148
Blok, Aleksandr 56
"Bloody Sunday" (January 1905)
    24
Bolotnikov, Ivan 10
Bolshevik coup (1917) 29, 60,
    80–81, 82, 187*c*
Bolshoi ballet 59
boyars (nobles) 2, 8
Brezhnev, Leonid 44–45, 49, 58,
    120, 188*c*
bribes *See* corruption
Bronze Horseman, The (Pushkin)
    16, 54
Buddhism 157
budget agreement (1998) 116,
    192*c*
Budyonnovsk 108
    crisis of June 1995 110, 191*c*
Bulgakov, Mikhail 60
Bulgaria 40
Bulgars 3
Buryats vii, 75
business *See* economy; entrepre-
    neurs; privatization

byliny (epics) 54
Byzantine Empire 3, 60, 61

C

Cancer Ward, The (Solzhenitsyn) 57
capitalism *See* free-market economy
Captive of the Caucasus (Pushkin) 67
Caspian Sea 2, 21, 65, 67, 68, 72, 74
    pollution 170
Catherine the Great 17, 80, 187*c*
Caucasus Mountains 66, 67, 74
caviar 72, 170
Central Asia 68, 175, 177
Central Siberian Plateau 65, 66
Chaliapin, Feodor 58
Chechens vii, 87, 105
Chechnya, war in (1994–96) 100,
    104, 105–9, 110, 158, 173, 180, 190*c*,
    191*c*
    cease-fire 114, 191*c*
Cheka (secret police) 31, 32
Chekhov, Anton 20–21, 53, 56, 59
chemical industry 70
Chernenko, Konstantin 45, 188*c*
Chernobyl disaster (1986) 49, 171,
    188*c*
Chernomyrdin, Viktor 88–89, 98,
    108, 111, *115*, 116, 117, 190*c*, 192*c*
chernozem *See* black earth
Chernyshevsky, Nikolai 22–23, 24
chess 153
children *See* youth
China 45, 192*c*
Chiquita Banana Company 142
Chkalov Aircraft Enterprise 130
Christianity 3, 54, 155, 186*c*
Christ Our Savior, Cathedral of (Mos-
    cow) 154–55
Chubais, Anatoly 112, 115–16, *115*,
    127, 137, 191*c*
Civic Union 87, 88
civil code (1995) 101–2
Civil War (1918–21) 31, 81, 187*c*
climate and weather 67–68, 71, 74,
    75, 78
coal vii, 68, 70, 71, 75
Cold War 40, 42–45, 48–49, 188*c*
    end of 49, 50, 175, 189*c*

collectivization 36–37, 40, 119, 121, 126, 127, 129, 188c
Commonwealth of Independent States (CIS) 51, 85, 177, 189c, 190c
Communist Party of the Russian Federation (CPRF) vii, 94–95, 97, 98
  1995 parliamentary election win 111, 112, 191c
  1996 presidential campaign 113, 114
Communist Party of Soviet Union 31, 32, 33, 96, 187c
  corruption within 45, 49
  cultural strictures 58, 61
  Gorbachev and 46, 48–51, 188c
  Khrushchev and 41–42, 43, 188c
  purges within 38–39
  Yeltsin and 83, 84–86, 87, 89–92, 94, 189c
  youth groups 159
Communist Youth League (Komsomol) 159
Comprehensive Nuclear Test Ban 179
Congress of People's Deputies 50, 82, 86, 88–93, 189c
Congress of Russian Communities (political party) 111
constitution (1978) 82–83, 86
constitution (1993) 93, 97, 98–105, 190c
  flaws 100–105
  provisions 99–100, 127
Constitutional Court 86, 92–93, 99, 100
consumer goods 37–38, 124, 135, 136
  free-market exchanges 140–41
  of Moscow's newly rich 161–62
contraceptives 152
cooperatives 121, 129
copper 68, 73
corruption 45, 49, 102–3, 120, 162
  criminal gang links 166, 169
  Soviet health-care system 146–47
court system 101–2
CPRF See Communist Party of the Russian Federation
crime 97, 104, 106, 110, 165–69, 182
  countermeasures 167, 169, 190c
  youth 145
Crimean Peninsula 176
Crimean War (1853–56) 18–19, 187c
Cuban Missile Crisis (1962) 43, 94, 188c
cultural freedom 43, 48, 49, 50
cultural heritage 53–62, 70, 142
currency 116, 122, 134
czars 8–26, 80, 186c, 187c

Czechoslovakia 40
Czech Republic 179, 192c

D

dacha (summer house) 148–49
daily life 139–62
dance 59, 142
death rates 147–48, 171
Decembrist Revolt (1825) 18, 187c
defectors 59
defense industry See military production
democracy 22, 23, 28, 29, 31
  current threats to 168–69, 182–83
Democratic Party of Russia 95
Democratic Reform Movement 94, 97
demokratizatsia (democratization) 48
dictatorship 23, 31, 37, 81
diet See food and diet
diphtheria epidemic 147
dissidents 44, 57–58
Dmitri, prince of Moscow 6, 186c
Dnieper River 2, 65
Don River 2, 65, 170
Dostoyevsky, Fyodor 53, 55, 56
drug use 143
Dudayev, Dzhokhar 105, 106, 108
Duma 25, 26, 28, 81, 187c See also parliament; State Duma
dumas (small assemblies) 93
Dyachenko, Tatiana 112

E

Eastern Europe 40, 44
  collapse of communism in 50, 189c
  NATO expansion into 178–79, 192c
East Slavs 1–2, 6
economy 118–38, 189c, 190c
  Bolshevik policy 32, 33, 35
  geographic regions 69–78
  Gorbachev's restructuring 48–50, 120–22
  growth slowdown (1970s) 45
  market See free-market economy, transition to
  Moscow's current growth 161–62
  problems in 1990s 127–38, 173
  Soviet 119–20, 128–29
  See also agriculture; industrialization; military production
education 25, 42–43, 158–60
Eisenstein, Sergei 60
elderly people 134, 135, 140, 162
elections
  first free (1989) 50, 189c
  for new parliament (1993–96) 93–98, 109–12, 190c, 191c
  presidential (1991) 86

  presidential (1996) 109, 112–14, 191c
  proportional representation 110–11
  referendum (1993) 89, 126, 190c
entrepreneurs 123, 124, 125, 127, 134, 140–42
environment and pollution 66, 72, 73, 129, 169–71
Estonia 39, 177
ethnic groups vii, 1, 6, 12, 16, 75, 86
  Brezhhnev policies 44
  See also secessionist movements; specific groups
Eugene Onegin (Pushkin) 54, 55
evangelicalism 157

F

factories See industrialization
famine 21, 32, 36–37, 40, 187c, 188c
fanaty (youth gangs) 143
Far East Region 78
fascism 95, 98
Federal Assembly (bicameral parliament) 93, 99, 100
Federal Security Service (FSB) 104–5, 106
Federation Council (upper house) 93, 98, 100
feminists 96
films 60, 152
Finland 64
five-year plans 35
food and diet 127, 153–54
forced labor 38
foreign debt 122
Foreign Intelligence Service (SVR) 104
foreign investments 161, 183
foreign policy 48, 50, 174–79, 191c
forests 68, 71–72, 75, 77, 171
freedom 139
freedom of religion 100, 155–56
free-market economy, transition to viii, 83, 85, 86, 88, 94, 98, 122–28, 140
  daily life adjustments 140–42, 151–52
  new wealth and 128, 135, 136–37, 161–62, 168, 184
  organized crime and 166
  shock therapy 124–27, 189c
  unresolved problems 184–85
  See also privatization
French Revolution 17, 18
FSB See Federal Security Service

G

Gaidar, Yegor 88, 89, 94, 97, 98, 111, 189–90c
gangs, criminal 166–68

Gazprom (company) 102, 137
geography v–vi, 63–78
Georgia 177, 190c
Germans (ethnic) vii, 44
Germany See Nazis; World War I;
  World War II
glasnost (openness) 48, 49, 50,
  152, 155, 188c
Glinka, Mikhail 58
Gogol, Nikolai 18, 55, 56, 59
Golden Horde 5, 6
Gorbachev, Mikhail 45–51, 47, 74,
  81, 85, 120–22, 188c
  antialcohol campaign 120, 154
  presidential candidacy (1996)
    112, 114
  resignation 189c
  unsuccesful coup against
    50–51, 82, 84, 87, 101, 145,
    148, 189c
  See also glasnost; perestroika
Gorky, Maxim 56, 59–60
government See politics and gov-
  ernment
Govorukhin, Stanislav 95
Grachev, Pavel 106, 114
Graham, Billy 157
grain harvest 129, 132
Great Purge 38–39, 188c
Great Reforms 19–21
Grozny 106–7, 108
GRU See Main Intelligence Direc-
  torate
Gulag See labor camps
Gulag Archipelago, The (Solzhenit-
  syn) 58

H

"Hajdi Murat" (Tolstoy) 67, 105
health 143, 146–49, 153, 154
  environmental hazards to 170,
    171
Hermitage Museum (St. Petersburg) 17, 70, 184
Hero of Our Time, A (Lermontov)
  67
Hitler, Adolf 39
homeless children 143, 144, 145,
  145
homosexuality 153
housing 149–52
  dachas 148–49
  Moscow luxury 162
Hungary 40, 179, 192c
hydroelectric plants 66, 72, 78

I

icons 4, 60–61, 156
incomes 161 See also poverty;
  wealth, new
industrialization vii–viii
  czarist programs 21, 81, 187c
  economic regions 70, 71, 72,
    73, 76, 78

Gorbachev reforms 121
  natural resources 68
  pollution 169–71
  privatization 85, 123, 125–29
  Stalin era 33, 35, 37–38, 40, 73,
    81, 119, 188c
  See also military production
inflation 122, 124, 134, 147
investment funds 128
Iran 179
Iraq 167
iron and steel 68, 71, 73, 75, 171
Irtysh River 66
Islamic Renaissance Party 158
Islam See Muslims
Ivan III (Ivan the Great) 6, 8, 9,
  62, 71, 186c
Ivan IV (Ivan the Terrible) 8–9,
  12, 62, 69, 80, 172
Ivanova, Irina 173
Ivanovo 70
Ivan the Terrible (film) 60
Izhevsk 131

J

Japan 24
Jehovah's Witnesses 157
Jews and Judaism vii, 44, 155,
  157–58 See also anti-Semitism
joint-stock companies 128, 129

K

Kamchatka Peninsula 76–77, 78
Kandinsky, Wassily 61
Karamzin, Nikolai 54
Kara Sea 171
Karelia 71–72
Kazakhstan vi, 68, 69, 74, 105
  ethnic Russians in 177
  nuclear arms 175, 176
Kazan 72, 148, 170, 172
KGB (secret police) 104, 105, 156
Khasbulatov, Ruslan 86, 87, 88,
  89, 90, 92, 189c
Khrushchev, Nikita 41–43, 48–49,
  57, 105, 120, 121, 148, 188c
Kiev 2, 3, 4, 5, 186c
Kievan Russia 2–4, 53, 54, 186c
kiosks 123, 124
Kiriyenko, Sergei 116, 192c
Kirov ballet 59
Klyuchevskaya (volcano) 76
kokoshnik (curved gable or head-
  dress) 62
Kola Peninsula 71–72, 170
Koloros factory (Moscow) 129
Komsomol 159
Korean War 42
Korovin, Constantin 61
Korzhakov, Aleksandr 104, 105,
  106, 112, 114
Kozyrev, Andrei 98, 112, 175, 191c
Kremlin 9, 69, 62
Krushchev, Nikita 41–43, 120

Kuchma, Leonid 178
kulaks (farmers) 36
Kulikov, Anatoly 116
Kulikovo, battle of (1380) 69
Kuznetsk Basin 76
Kuznetsov, Fyodor A. 182, 183
Kyrgyzstan vi

L

labor camps 36, 38, 40, 42, 43,
  56–58, 78
Ladoga, Lake 66
lakes 66, 72, 75
land ownership 126–27, 192c
Latvia 39, 177
Lawrence, D. H. 152
Lazarev, Viktor 183
Lebed, Aleksandr 108, 111, 112, 114,
  181, 191c, 192c
  profile of 180–81
Lena River 66, 171
Lenin, Vladimir 24, 29, 30, 31, 32,
  33, 48, 82, 187c, 188c
Leningrad See St. Petersburg
Leningrad, siege of (1941–44) 70–71
Lenin Mausoleum (Moscow) 93
Lermontov, Mikhail 18, 55–56, 67
Levitan, Isaac 61
Liberal Democratic Party (LPD) 95,
  97, 98, 111, 190c
life expectancy 148
Ligachev, Yegor 49
Listev, Vladimir 110
literacy 159
literature 43, 53–58
  on Caucasus 67
  free-market adjustments 142
  golden age of 18, 54–56
  popularity of reading 153
  Soviet censorship 57–58, 152
Lithuania 6, 39
Little Vera (film) 152
loggers See lumbering
Lolita (Nabokov) 152
Lomonosov, Mikhail 54
LPD See Liberal Democratic Party
Luch Experimental Works 131
Lukachenko, Aleksandr 178, 191c
lumbering 71, 76, 77, 171
Luzhkov, Yuri 152
Lyubimov, Yuri 60

M

Mafia See organized crime
Magnitogorsk 73, 171
Main Intelligence Directorate (GRU)
  104
Makarova, Natalia 59
Malevich, Casimir 61
Mandelstam, Osip 56
market economy See free-market
  economy
Marx, Karl 23, 154
Marxism 23–24, 29, 32, 159, 187c

Maskhadov, Aslan 108–9
Master and Margarita, The (Bulgakov) 60
McDonald's (fast-food chain) 161, *161*
Mensheviks 24, 25, 29
Meyerhold, Vsevolod 60
military forces
  in Chechyna 106–9, *107*, 110
  czarist 10, 14–15
  White House assault 91–92, *190c*
military production
  conversion to civilian goods 130–33
  Soviet buildup vii–viii, 37, 40, 44, 45, 81, 119
  See also nuclear weapons
Milkovo 76
Mineralnye Vody (resort) 74
mineral resources 68, 71, 73
minorities *See* ethnic groups
mirs (communal organizations) 20
Moldova vi
Mongols 5–6, 54, 62, *186c*
Moscow
  arts 59–60
  as capital city vii, 16, 69
  crime 165
  as economic region 69–70
  "fast" lifestyle 160–62, 173
  housing 151, 152
  pollution 171
  rise of 6–9, *7m*
  See also specific buildings
Moscow Art Theater 59–60
Moscow Choreographic School 142
Moscow River 129
Motozavod 131
mountain ranges 66–67, 75
Murmansk 72
music 58–59
Muslims 3, 105, 106, 155, 172, 173, 177
  religious revival 158

N

Nabokov, Vladimir 152
Napoleon Bonaparte 18, 56, 68, 69, *187c*
nationalist parties 95, 97, 157
National Security Council (Russia) 114, *191c*
NATO-Russia Founding Act (1997) 178–79, *191c*
natural gas vii, 68, 70, 71, 74, 75, 76, 78
natural resources 68–78
Nazis 39, 40, 61, 68
Nazi-Soviet Pact (1939) 39, *188c*
Nemtsov, Boris 115, *115*, 117, 137, 151–52, *191c*
Neva River 15, 16, 70

Nevsky, Aleksandr *See* Aleksandr Nevsky
New Economic Policy (NEP) 32, 33, *187c*
newly rich *See* wealth, new
"New Russians" 162
Nicholas I (czar) 18, 19
Nicholas II (czar) 25–26, 73, 81
nickel 68, 71, 72, 170
Nijinsky, Vaslav 59
Nizhnii Novgorod 70, 115
Nobosibirsk 182
nomads 4
North Atlantic Treaty Organization (NATO) 40, 178–79, *190c*, *191c*, *192c*
North Caucasus Region 67, 69, 73–74
  secessionists 158, 172, 173
  See also Chechnya, war in
Northern Dvina River 71–72
northern region 71–72
North European Plain 64
Novgorod 4, 8, 62, 71
Novikov, Nikolai 17–18
Novosibirsk vii, *75*, 76–77, 130, 131, 173
novoye myshlenie (new thinking) 48
nuclear accidents and fallout 49, 73, 171, *188c*
Nuclear Non-Proliferation Treaty 176, 179
nuclear weapons 175, 176, 179
  arms race 40, 44
  factory conversions 130
  materials theft 166–67
  See also arms control
Nureyev, Rudolf 59

O

Obninsk 130
Ob River 66, 171
October Manifesto (1905) 25, *187c*
October Revolt (1993) 89–92
oil vii, 21, 68, 70, 71, 72, 74, 76, 78
  merger of companies *192c*
  pollution from wells 170
  production decline 132
Okhotsk, Sea of 78
One Day in the Life of Ivan Denisovich (Solzhenitsyn) 43, 57
Onega, Lake 66
onion-shaped dome 3–4, 61–62, 65, 69
oprichnina (political police) 8
organized crime 97, 110, 165–68

P

Pacific Ring of Fire 76
painting 60–61
parliament
  budget agreement 116
  czarist 25, 26, 28, 81, *187c*

1993 composition 93–98, *198c*
Soviet 50, 83
two-house (1993) 93, 99
Yeltsin's conflicts with 82, 86, 88–93, 110, 126, *189c*, *190c*
See also elections; State Duma
Partnership for Peace 178, *190c*
Paukov, Igor Y. 183
Pavlova, Anna 59
peasants 4
  under czars 10, 15, 17, 18, 20–26, 80
  under Soviet rule 32, 36, 37, *188c*
  See also serfdom
Pechora River 71–72
Pentecostalists 157
People's Party of Free Russia 92
perestroika (restructuring) 48, 49, 50, 120–22, 134, *188c*
Peter I (Peter the Great) 13–17, 62, 80, 81, 175, *186c*
Peter and Paul Fortress (St. Petersburg) 70
petroleum *See* oil
Petropavlovsk 76
planned economy viii, 119–20
platinum 68, 73
plutonium 167, 168
Podolsk 131
Pogodin, Mikhail 63–64
Poland 6, 39, 40, 64, 121, 175, 179, *192c*
political parties and groups 92, 93–96, 110–12
politics and government 80–117, 181
pollution *See* environment and pollution
Polovtsians 4
populism 22–23
Potemkin (film) 60
poverty *134*, 135, 137, 140, 145, 147, 162
Preobrazhensky Prikaz (political police) 15
presidential elections 86, 109, 112–14, 181, *191c*
presidential powers 99
Presidential Security Service (SBP) 104
price controls 121, 123, 124
prices *See* inflation
Primakov, Yevgeny 112, 178, *191c*, *192c*
Primary Russian Chronicle, The 3, 54
prime minister 99, 116, 117
private schools 159–60
privatization 85, 123, 125–37, *189c*
  housing construction 150–51
  wealth concentration 137, 161–62, 184
  See also entrepreneurs
Prokofiev, Sergei 58
proletariat 24

Provisional Government (1917)
26, 28–29, 81–82, 99, 187c
Pskov 71
Pugachev Revolt 17, 187c
Pushkin, Aleksandr 16, 18, 53,
54–55, 67

R

Rachmaninoff, Sergei 58
radioactive waste 171
Radiozavod 131
Radishchev, Aleksandr 17–18
railroads 77–78, 119
rainfall 68
Razin, Stenka 10, 186c
Reagan, Ronald 50, 188c
recreation See sports and recreation
referendum (1993) 89, 126, 190c
reforms
    Alexander II 19–21
    Gorbachev 46 51, 81, 82,
    120–22, 152, 155
    Khrushchev 41, 42–43, 57, 120
    Nicholas II 25–26
    Peter the Great 13–17, 81
    Yeltsin 86, 122–27
religion 100, 140, 154–58
Repin, Ilya 61
republics vi–vii, 86–87, 172–73,
176–77, 189c
Requiem (Akhmatova) 57
restaurants 153–54, 161, 161
Revolution of 1905 24–25, 33, 187c
Revolution of 1917 26, 28–29, 81,
187c
revolutionaries 21–24
Riazan 5
rivers 2, 65–66, 75
    pollution 72, 169–70, 171
Roman Catholic Church 156, 157
Romania 40
Romanov Dynasty 12, 13–26, 186c
Rostropovich, Mstislav 58–59
ruble 116, 122, 134, 192c
Rublev, Andrei 60–61
Rus (people) 2
Russia-Belarus Union Charter
(1997) 178, 191c
Russia Is Our Home (political
party) 111
Russian Academy of Sciences 182
Russian Empire vi–vii, 11m, 67,
105, 186–87c
    collapse of (1917) vii, 26
    czars 8–26
    evolution of 1–12, 186c
Russian Federation ivm, 189–92c
    daily life 139–62
    economics 122–38
    foreign policy 174, 175–79
    land area and borders v–vi,
    64–78, 175
    outlying regions 171–75
    politics and government viii,
    85–117

population vi, 185
    problems and prospects 164–85
    religion 100, 155–58
    See also Commonwealth of
    Independent States
"Russian idea" 88
Russian Orthodox Church 3, 6,
60–62, 154–55, 156–57
Russians (ethnic) 1, 75, 86, 172,
173, 177, 185
Russian Unity and Accord Party
94, 98
Russian Women's Party 96, 98
Russia's Democratic Choice (politi-
cal party, formerly Russia's
Choice) 94, 97, 98, 111
Russo-Japanese War (1904–5) 24,
187c
Rutskoi, Aleksandr 83, 86, 87–88,
89, 90, 92, 189c

S

St. Basil's Cathedral (Moscow) 62,
69, 155, 156
St. George, Church of (Novgorod)
61–62
St. Petersburg vii, 25, 26
    architecture 62, 184
    as capital city 69
    cultural activity 59
    as economic region 70–71
    founding of 15–16, 17, 186c
    housing 151
    World War II siege of 70–71
St. Sofia Cathedral (Kiev) 3
Sakhalin Island 66, 78
Saratov region 116, 170, 192c
schools See education
scientific research 43, 182
seaports 71, 72, 78
secessionist movements 50, 158,
172–73, 176–77 See also Chechnya, war in
Second World Congress of Tatars
(1997) 172–73
secret police 8, 18, 31, 32, 103–5
"Secret Speech" (Khrushchev)
41–42, 188c
Seleznev, Gennady 112
serfdom 10, 15, 17, 18, 186c
    abolition of 19, 20, 81, 187c
Seventh-Day Adventists 157
sex and sexuality 152–53
Shevardnadze, Eduard 49, 177
shipbuilding 71, 78
shock therapy (economic)
124–27, 189c
Shostakovich, Dmitri 58
"shuttlers" 141
Siberia vii, 10, 65–67
    ecological problems 170–71
    economic problems 124–25,
    173
    as economic region 74–78
    natural resources 69

oil production 132, 133
    scientific center 75, 76–77, 182
Slavs 1
smelting 72, 170
Smolny Convent (St. Petersburg) 62
Sochi (resort) 74
Social Democrats 24
socialism 22, 28, 32
socialist realism 61
Solzhenitsyn, Aleksandr 43, 57–58,
57, 59, 190c
Solzhenitsyn, Ignat 59
Soviet Academy of Sciences 182
Soviets (regional councils) 93
Soviet Socialist Republics (SSRs)
See republics
Soviet Union 28–51, 34m, 187–89c
    art and architecture 61
    Brezhnev era 44–45, 49, 58, 188c
    collapse of (1991) vi–viii, 51, 64,
    82, 102, 122, 175, 189c
    dacha retreats 148–49
    economy 32, 33, 119–20, 128–29
    education 159
    environmental pollution 72, 73,
    77, 169
    Gorbachev era 45–51, 81, 82,
    102, 173
    health care 146–47
    housing shortage 150
    Khrushchev reforms 42–43
    Lenin policies 32–33
    organized crime 166
    religion 154–55, 156
    sexuality censorship 152
    Stalin era 33–40, 61, 81, 103
    youth unrest 143
space program 43, 119
sports and recreation 153–54
Stalin, Joseph 31, 33–40, 35, 44, 48,
81, 187c
    death and legacy of 40, 41, 188c
    Khrushchev's posthumous
    denunciation of 42
    See also industrialization; terror
Stalingrad, battle of (1942–43) 72
standard of living 41, 42, 44, 45, 81,
118, 140, 143
    Moscow's fast life 160–62
    See also consumer goods; poverty
Stanislavsky, Constantin 59–60
START I Treaty 176
START II Treaty 176, 178, 190c
State Duma (lower house) 93, 99,
100–101, 109–10
    1995 election results 111,
    112
Stavropol 74
steel See iron and steel
steppe 68, 73–74
Stolypin, Piotr 25–26, 187c
Stravinsky, Igor 58
sturgeon 72, 170
Supreme Soviet 83, 89
Sverdlovsk See Yekaterinburg
Svyazinvest (monopoly) 137

swamps 71–72
Sweden 14, 15

T

Taganka Theater (Moscow) 60
taiga (forest) 68, 74, 171
Tajikistan vi, 177
Tale of the Host of Igor, The 4, 54
Tatars vii, 172–73 *See also* Mongols
Tatarstan 158, 172–73, 189c
tax collection 102–3, 137
Tchaikovsky, Peter 53, 58, 59
Ten Days That Shook the World
(film) 60
terror
czarist era 8–9, 15
Mongol conquest 5
Stalin era 33, 38–42, 56–57, 60,
78, 105, 155, 188c
terrorism
Chechen 104, 107–8
organized crime 165–69
Texaco Oil 132
theater 59–60
Third Section (secret police) 18
timber *See* forests; lumbering
Tiumen 161
Tkachev, Peter 23, 24, 29
Tolstoy, Leo 18–19, 53, 56, 67, 105
totalitarianism 39, 81, 82
tourist industry 74
Trans-Siberian Railroad 77, 119
Travkin, Nikolai 95
Trotsky, Leon 31, 33
Tula 70, 173
tundra 68, 71–72, 75
Turkey vi
Turkmenistan vi

U

Udmurtia 173
Ukraine 65, 156, 177, 178
black earth 69, 74
Chernobyl disaster 49, 171
in Commonweatlh of Inde-
pendent States 51, 85, 189c
ethnic Russians in 177
independence 175
nuclear arms 174, 175, 176
Ukrainians vii, 1, 6

unemployment 133–34
Unification Church 157
Union of Soviet Socialist Republics
See Soviet Union
United Energy Systems 137
United Nations Security Council
175
United States
post-Soviet policy 167–68, 175,
179
See also arms control; Cold War
Ural Mountains 64, 66–67, 69, 74
Urals Region 73, 171
uranium 167, 168
Uzbekistan vi

V

vanadium 68
Varangians 2
veches (town assemblies) 2, 5
Vladimir, prince of Kiev 3
Vladivostok 77, 78, 78
vodka 154
volcanoes 76–77, 78
Volga Boatmen (Repin painting)
61
Volga Region 72, 158, 172
Volga River 2, 65, 65, 68, 72
dacha community 148–49
pollution 72, 170
Volgograd (formerly Stalingrad) 72
voucher system 125, 127–28, 189c

W

"War Communism" 32
Warsaw Pact 40
wealth, new 128, 135, 136–37,
161–62, 168, 184
weapons *See* nuclear weapons
weather *See* climate and weather
West Siberian Lowland 65
West Siberian Plain 66
White House (Moscow) 51,
89–92, 91, 190c
"White Night" 71
wildlife 75, 78
Winter Palace (St. Petersburg) 62,
184
winters 67–68, 71, 75
Witte, Sergei 21, 187c

Women of Russia Party 96, 98
World War I 26, 28–29, 31, 80,
187c
World War II 33, 39–40, 57, 68,
70–73, 155, 188c

Y

Yabloko (political party) 94, 98,
111
Yakuts vii, 75
Yaroslavl 65, 70
Yavlinsky, Gregory 94, 112
Yeats, William Butler 126
Yekaterinburg (Sverdlovsk) 73, 84
Yeltsin, Boris 49, 82–94, 83, 157,
179, 188–91c
as August coup hero 50–51,
84, 145, 189c
background and career 73,
84–85
cabinet dismissal 116–17, 192c
Chechen policy 106, 110, 114
conflicts with Parliament 82,
86, 88–93, 110, 126, 189c, 190c
on crime problem 165,
168–69, 190c
economic policies 122–37,
189c, 190c
health problems 85, 110, 112,
114, 191, 191c
popularity decline 97, 110, 112
presidential second term
114–17
secret police 104–5
Yenisey River 66, 171
youth 143–46, 147, 152–53 *See also*
education
Yugoslavia 40

Z

zemstvos (rural government) 19, 20
Zhirinovsky, Vladimir 95, 96, 96,
97, 98, 111, 112, 190c
zhuchki (bribers) 103
Zhukovka 148
Zorkin, Valery 86
Zyuganov, Gennady 94, 111–14,
113, 117, 181, 191c